# MIRROR OF THE INTELLECT

# Mirror
# of the Intellect

ESSAYS ON
TRADITIONAL SCIENCE & SACRED ART
BY
TITUS BURCKHARDT

*Translated and edited by*
*William Stoddart*

STATE UNIVERSITY
OF NEW YORK PRESS

First published in the USA
by State University of New York Press, Albany, 1987

For information address:
State University of New York Press,
State University Plaza
Albany, NY 12246

Library of Congress Cataloging in Publication Data
Burckhardt, Titus
Mirror of the intellect
(SUNY Series in Islam)
Posthumous collection of writings composed
mainly of articles originally published in a variety of
French and German periodicals.

Bibliography: p.
Includes index.
1. Cosmology. 2. Theology. 3. Symbolism.
4. Mythology. 5. Islam. I. Stoddart, William.
II. Title. III. Series
BD523.B87   1987   113      87-10103
ISBN 0-88706-683-6
ISBN 0-88706-684-4 (pbk.)

Printed in the United Kingdom

Now do I see that never can our Intellect be sated, unless that Truth do shine upon it.

*Dante*

Beauty is the splendour of the Truth.

*Plato*

# Contents

ILLUSTRATIONS

*Titlepage*: The design on the title-page is that of a rose-window from Lausanne Cathedral. Like the spider's web, the Hindu *chakra*, and the Red Indian feathered sun, the medieval rose-window symbolizes what the mirror that is the Intellect reflects, namely (at the cosmological level) the totality of the cosmos and (at the metaphysical level) the total Truth. The radii and concentric circles (whether explicitly represented, as in the spider's web, or merely implicit, as in the present rose-window) symbolize respectively the modes and degrees of Reality, (*Translator's Note*). From Villard de Honnecourt's sketch c. 1125–50.

*Page 103*: The Heavenly Jerusalem from the Apocalypse of Saint-Séver, eleventh century, (*courtesy of the Bibliothèque Nationale, Paris*).

*Page 105*: *Mandala* of the Paradise of Vaikuntha, the celestial abode of Vishnu, (anonymous drawing).

*Page 161*: Cretan double axe.

# INTRODUCTION

# Titus Burckhardt:
# An Outline of his Life and Works

TITUS BURCKHARDT, a German Swiss, was born in Florence in 1908 and died in Lausanne in 1984. He devoted all his life to the study and exposition of the different aspects of Wisdom and Tradition.

In the age of modern science and technocracy, Titus Burckhardt was one of the most remarkable of the exponents of universal truth, in the realm of metaphysics as well as in the realm of cosmology and of traditional art. In a world of existentialism, psychoanalysis, and sociology, he was a major voice of the *philosophia perennis*, that 'wisdom uncreate' that is expressed in Platonism, Vedanta, Sufism, Taoism, and other authentic esoteric or sapiential teachings. In literary and philosophic terms, he was an eminent member of the 'traditionalist school' of twentieth-century authors.

The great forerunner-cum-originator of the traditionalist school was René Guénon (1886–1951). Guénon traced the origin of what he called the modern deviation to the ending of the Middle Ages and the arrival of the Renaissance, that cataclysmic inrush of secularization, when nominalism vanquished realism, individualism (or humanism) replaced universalism, and empiricism banished scholasticism. An important part of Guénon's work was therefore his critique of the modern world from an implacably 'Platonic' or metaphysical point of view. This was fully expounded in his two masterly volumes *The Crisis of the Modern World* and *The Reign of Quantity*. The positive side of Guénon's work was his exposition of the immutable principles of universal metaphysics and traditional orthodoxy. His main source was the Shankaran doctrine of 'non-duality' (*advaita*), and his chief work in this respect is *Man and his becoming according to the Vedanta*. However, he also turned readily to other traditional sources, since he considered all traditional forms to be various expressions of the one supra-formal Truth. A final aspect of Guénon's work was his brilliant exposition of the intellectual content of traditional symbols, from whichever religion they might come. See in this connection his *Symboles fondamentaux de la Science sacrée.*

An illustrious scholar deeply influenced by Guénon was Ananda K. Coomaraswamy (1877–1947) who, while being distinguished and gifted in his own right, had the merit, relatively late in life, of making the acquaintance of, and being thoroughly convinced by, the traditional point of view as it had been expounded, so fully and so precisely, in Guénon's books.

It is important to note that Guénon's writings, decisively important though they were, were purely 'theoretical' in character, and made no pretence of dealing with the question of realization. In other words, they were generally concerned with intellectuality (or doctrine) and not directly with spirituality (or method).

The sun rose for the traditionalist school with the appearance of the work of Frithjof Schuon (born in Basle in 1907). Thirty years ago, an English Thomist wrote of him: 'His work has the intrinsic authority of a contemplative intelligence'.[1] More recently, a senior American academic declared: 'In depth and breadth, [he is] a paragon of our time. I know of no living thinker who begins to rival him'.[2] T. S. Eliot's perception was similar. Regarding Schuon's first book, he wrote in 1953: 'I have met with no more impressive work in the comparative study of Oriental and Occidental religion'.

Schuon's work began to appear during the latter part of Guénon's life. Until his dying day, Guénon used to refer to him (for example in the pages of *Etudes traditionnelles*) as 'notre éminent collaborateur'. Schuon continued, in even more notable fashion, the perspicacious and irrefutable critique of the modern world, and reached unsurpassable heights in his exposition of the essential truth—illuminating and saving—that lies at the heart of every revealed form. Schuon called this supra-formal truth the *religio perennis*. This term, which does not imply a rejection of the similar terms *philosophia perennis* and *sophia perennis*, nevertheless contains a hint of an additional dimension which is unfailingly present in Schuon's writings. This is that

[1] Bernard Kelly, in *Dominican Studies* (London), Vol. 7, 1954.
[2] Emeritus Professor Huston Smith, 1974.

intellectual understanding entails a spiritual responsibility, that intelligence requires to be complemented by sincerity and faith, and that 'seeing' (in height) implies 'believing' (in depth). In other words, the greater our perception of essential and saving truth, the greater our obligation towards an effort of inward or spiritual 'realization'.

Schuon's work began with a comprehensive general study, the very title of which serves to set the scene: *The Transcendent Unity of Religions*. His further works include: *Language of the Self* (on Hinduism), *In the Tracks of Buddhism*, *Understanding Islam*, *Castes and Races*, *Logic and Transcendence* and, more recently, a wide-ranging compendium of philosophic and spiritual enlightenment entitled *Esoterism as Principle and as Way*.

We can now return to Titus Burckhardt. Although he first saw the light of day in Florence, Burckhardt was the scion of a patrician family of Basle. He was the great-nephew of the famous art-historian Jacob Burckhardt and the son of the sculptor Carl Burckhardt. Titus Burckhardt was Frithjof Schuon's junior by one year, and they spent their early schooldays together in Basle around the time of the First World War. This was the beginning of an intimate friendship and a deeply harmonious intellectual and spiritual relationship that was to last a lifetime.

Burckhardt's chief metaphysical exposition, beautifully complementing the work of Schuon, is *An Introduction to Sufi Doctrine*. This is an intellectual masterpiece which analyzes comprehensively and with precision the nature of esoterism as such. It begins by making clear, by a series of lucid and economical definitions, what esoterism is and what it is not, goes on to examine the doctrinal foundations of Islamic esoterism or Sufism, and ends with an inspired description of 'spiritual alchemy', or the contemplative path that leads to spiritual realization. This work clearly established Burckhardt as the leading exponent, after Schuon, of intellectual doctrine and spiritual method.

Burckhardt devoted a large portion of his writings to traditional cosmology, which he saw in a sense as the 'handmaid of metaphysics'. He formally presented the principles at stake in a masterly and concise article 'The Cosmological Perspective', first published in French in 1948 and now constituting the first chapter in the present volume. Much later—in a series of articles published in both French and German in 1964—he covered the cosmological ground very fully indeed, and also made many detailed references to the main branches of modern science. These articles, under the title 'Traditional Cosmology and Modern Science' now form the second chapter in this collection. They were also included in *Sword of Gnosis* (an anthology of articles from the English journal *Studies in Comparative Religion*) edited by Jacob Needleman in 1974, and reprinted in 1986.

Not unconnected with his interest in cosmology, Burckhardt had a particular affinity with traditional art and craftsmanship and was skilled in the evaluation of traditional architecture, iconography, and other arts and crafts. In particular, he dwelt on how they had been—and could be—turned to account spiritually, both as meaningful activities which by virtue of their inherent symbolism harbour a doctrinal message, and above all as supports for spiritual realization and means of grace. *Ars sine scientia nihil.* Here of course it is a case of *scientia sacra* and *ars sacra*, these being the two sides of the same coin. This is the realm of the craft initiations of the various traditional civilizations, and specifically of such things, in the Middle Ages, as operative masonry and alchemy. Indeed Burckhardt's principal work in the field of cosmology was his full-length book *Alchemy: Science of the Cosmos, Science of the Soul*, a brilliant presentation of alchemy as the expression of a spiritual psychology and as an intellectual and symbolic support for contemplation and realization.

Burckhardt's main work in the field of art was his *Sacred Art in East and West*, which contains many wonderful chapters on the metaphysics and aesthetics of Hinduism, Buddhism, Taoism, Christianity, and Islam, and ends with a useful and practical insight into the contemporary situation entitled 'The Decadence and Renewal of Christian Art'. A comprehensive summary of the essential elements of this book is to be published for the first time in *The Unanimous Tradition*, a compendium of articles by traditionalist authors edited by Ranjit Fernando (Institute of Traditional Studies, Colombo, in preparation).

During the fifties and sixties Burckhardt was the artistic director of the Urs Graf Publishing House of Lausanne and Olten. His main activity during these years was the production and publication of a whole series of facsimiles of exquisite illuminated medieval manuscripts, especially early Celtic manuscripts of the Gospels, such as the Book of Kells and the Book of Durrow (from Trinity College, Dublin) and the Book of Lindisfarne (from the British Library, London). This was pioneer work of the highest quality and a publishing achievement which immediately received wide acclaim both from experts and the wider public.

His production of the magnificent facsimile of the Book of Kells brought him a remarkable encounter with Pope Pius XII. The Urs Graf Publishing House wished to present a copy of the edition to the saintly and princely Pope, and it was decided that there could be no better person to effect the presentation than the artistic director Burckhardt. In the eyes of the Pope, Burckhardt was ostensibly a Protestant gentleman from Basle. The Pope granted him a private audience at his summer residence at Castelgandolfo. When, in the audience chamber, the white-clad figure of the Pope suddenly appeared, he welcomingly approached his visitor and said to him in German: 'Sie sind also Herr Burckhardt?' ('So you are Herr Burckhardt?') Burckhardt bowed and, when the Pope offered him his hand bearing the Fisherman's Ring, he respectfully took it in his. As a non-Catholic, however, he kissed, not the ring (as is the custom amongst Catholics), but the Pope's fingers. 'Which the Pope smilingly permitted,' Burckhardt adds.

Together they talked about the Dark Ages and about the surpassingly beautiful manuscripts of the Gospels that had been so lovingly and so finely produced during them. At the end of the audience the Pope gave his blessing: 'From my heart I bless you, your family, your colleagues, and your friends.'

It was during these years with the Urs Graf Publishing House that Burckhardt presided over an interesting series of publications with the general title of *Stätten des Geistes* ('Homesteads of the Spirit'). These were historical-cum-spiritual studies of certain manifestations of sacred civilization, and covered such themes as Mount Athos, Celtic Ireland, Sinai, Constantinople, and other places. Burckhardt himself contributed the books *Siena, City of the Virgin*, *Chartres and the Genesis of the Gothic Cathedral*, and *Fez, City of Islam*. *Siena* is an enlightening account of the rise and fall of a Christian city which, architecturally speaking, remains to this day something of a Gothic jewel. Most interesting of all, however, is the story of its saints. Burckhardt devotes many of his pages to St. Catherine of Siena (who never hesitated to rebuke the Pope of her day, when she felt that it was necessary) and to St. Bernardino of Siena (who was one of the greatest Catholic practitioners—and teachers—of the saving power of the invocation of the Holy Name). *Chartres* is the story of the religious 'idealism' (in the best sense of the word) which lay behind the conception and practical realization of the medieval Cathedrals—the still extant monuments to an age of faith. In *Chartres*, Burckhardt expounds the intellectual and spiritual contents of the different architectural styles—not merely distinguishing between the Gothic and the Romanesque, but even between the different varieties of the Romanesque. It is a dazzling example of what is meant by intellectual discrimination.

One of Burckhardt's several masterpieces is undoubtedly his *Fez, City of Islam*. As a young man, in the 1930's, he spent a few years in Morocco, where he established intimate friendships with several remarkable representatives of the as yet intact spiritual heritage of the Maghrib. This was obviously a formative period in Burckhardt's life, and much of his subsequent message and style originates in these early years. Already, at the time concerned, he had committed much of his experience to writing (not immediately published), and it was only in the late 1950's that these writings and these experiences ripened into a definitive and masterly book. In *Fez, City of Islam*, Burckhardt relates the history of a people and its religion—a history that was often violent, often heroic, and sometimes holy. Throughout it all runs the thread of Islamic piety and civilization. These Burckhardt expounds with a sure and enlightening hand, relating many of the teachings, parables, and miracles of the saints of many centuries, and demonstrating not only the arts and crafts of Islamic civilization, but also its 'Aristotelian' sciences and its administrative skills. There is indeed much to be learnt about the governance of men and societies from Burckhardt's penetrating presentation of the principles behind dynastic and tribal vicissitudes—with their failures and their successes.

Close in spirit to *Fez* is another of Burckhardt's mature works, namely *Moorish Culture in Spain*. As always, this is a book of truth and beauty, of science and art, of piety and traditional culture. But in this book, perhaps more than in all others, it is a question of the romance, chivalry, and poetry of pre-modern life.

During his early years in Morocco, Burckhardt immersed himself in the Arabic language and assimilated the classics of Sufism in their original form. In later years, he was to share these treasures with a wider public through his translations of Ibn 'Arabî[3] and Jîlî[4]. One of his most important works of translation was of the spiritual letters of the renowned eighteenth-century Moroccan Shaikh Mulay al-'Arabî ad-Darqâwî[5]. These letters constitute a spiritual classic and are a precious document of practical spiritual counsel.

Burckhardt's last major work was his widely acclaimed and impressive monograph *Art of Islam*. Here the intellectual principles and the spiritual role of artistic creativity in its Islamic forms are richly and generously displayed before us. With this noble volume, the unique Burckhardtian literary corpus comes to its end.

This posthumous collection of writings is composed mainly of articles which were originally published in a variety of French and German periodicals, and have not previously appeared together in book form. One exception is the article entitled 'The Seven Liberal Arts and the West Door of Chartres Cathedral', which has been extracted from the book *Chartres und die Geburt der Kathedrale*. A full English translation of this book is in course of preparation. Attention is drawn to the bibliography (contained in the appendix to the present volume) in which details of all the original publications are given.

*William Stoddart*

---

[3] *La Sagesse des Prophètes* (Fusûs al-Hikam), Albin Michel, Paris, 1955.
[4] *De l'Homme Universel* (al-Insân al-Kâmil), Derain, Lyons, 1953.
[5] *Letters of a Sufi Master* (Rasâ'il), Perennial Books, Bedfont, England, 1969.

# I
# TRADITIONAL COSMOLOGY
# AND THE MODERN WORLD

# 1

# The Cosmological
# Perspective

THE SEVEN 'liberal arts' of the Middle Ages have as their
object disciplines which modern man would automatically
describe as 'sciences', such as mathematics, astronomy,
dialectic, and geometry. This medieval identification of
science with art, wholly in conformity with the contemplative
structure of the *Trivium* and *Quadrivium*, clearly indicates the
fundamental nature of the cosmological perspective.

When modern historians look at traditional cosmology—whether
this be the cosmological doctrines of ancient and oriental civilizations, or the cosmology of the medieval West—they generally see
in it merely childish and groping attempts to explain the causation of
phenomena. In so doing, they are guilty of an error in their way of
looking at things which is analogous to the error of those who, with a
'naturalistic' prejudice, judge medieval works of art according to the
criteria of the 'exact' observation of nature and of artistic 'ingenio-
sity'. Modern incomprehension of sacred art and contemplative
cosmology thus arises from one and the same error; and this is not
gainsaid by the fact that some scholars (often the very ones who look
on oriental or medieval cosmology with a combination of pity and
irony) pay homage to the arts in question and allow the artist the right
to 'exaggerate' some features of his natural models and to suppress
others with a view to suggesting realities of a more inward nature.
This tolerance only proves that, for modern man, artistic symbolism
has no more than an individual, psychological—or even merely
sentimental—bearing. Modern scholars are obviously unaware that
the artistic choice of forms, when it pertains to inspired and
regularly transmitted principles, is capable of tangibly conveying the
permanent and inexhaustible possibilities of the Spirit, and that
traditional art thus implies a 'logic' in the universal sense of this

term.[1] On the one hand, modern mentality is blinded by its attachment to the sentimental aspects of art forms (and only too often reacts as a result of a very particular psychic heredity); on the other, its starting-point is the prejudice that artistic intuition and science belong to two radically different domains. If this were not so, one would have in all fairness to grant to cosmology what one seems to grant to art, namely the license to express itself by means of allusions and to use sensible forms as parables.

For modern man, however, any science becomes suspect if it leaves the plane of physically verifiable facts, and it loses its plausibility if it detaches itself from the type of reasoning that is completely reliant on, as it were, a plastic continuity of the mental faculty. As if it could possibly be justifiable to suppose that the whole cosmos were made so as to reflect merely the 'material' or quantitative sides of the human imagination. Such an attitude moreover does not do justice to the full human reality. It represents more a mental limitation (resulting from an extremely unilateral and artificial activity) than a philosophical position, for all science, however relative or provisional it may be, presupposes a necessary correspondence between the order that is spontaneously inherent in the knowing mind and the compossibility of things, otherwise there would be no truth of any kind.[2] Now since the analogy between the macrocosm and the microcosm cannot be denied, and since it everywhere affirms principial unity—a unity that is like an axis in regard to which all things are ordered—it is impossible to see why the science (i.e. knowledge) of 'nature', in the vastest possible sense of this term, should not reject the crutches of a more or less quantitative experience, and why any intellectual vision (possessed as it were of a 'bird's eye view') should be immediately dismissed as a gratuitous hypothesis. But modern scientists have a veritable aversion to anything that goes beyond the allegedly down-to-earth nature of 'exact science'. In their eyes, to have recourse to the poetical quality

[1] See Frithjof Schuon: *The Transcendent Unity of Religions*, Chapter 4, 'Concerning Forms in Art' (Perennial Books, Bedfont, Middx, 1986).
[2] See René Guénon: *Introduction to the Study of the Hindu Doctrines* (Luzac, London, 1945), chapter on 'Nyaya': '. . . if the idea, to the extent that it is true and adequate, shares in the nature of the thing, it is because, conversely, the thing itself also shares in the nature of the idea.'

of a doctrine, is to discredit that doctrine as science. This heavy 'scientistic' distrust of the grandeur and beauty of a given conception shows a total incomprehension of the nature of primordial art and of the nature of things.

Traditional cosmology always comprises an aspect of 'art', in the primordial sense of this word: when science goes beyond the horizon of the corporeal world or when the traditional cosmologist gives his attention only to the manifestations, within this very world, of transcendent qualities, it becomes impossible to 'record' the object of knowledge as one records the contours and details of a sensory phenomenon. We are not saying that the intellection of realities higher than the corporeal world is imperfect; we are referring only to its mental and verbal 'fixation'. Whatever can be conveyed of these perceptions of reality is inevitably in the form of speculative keys, which are an aid to rediscovering the 'synthetic' vision in question. The proper application of these 'keys' to the endless multiplicity of the faces of the cosmos is dependent on what may indeed be called an art, in the sense that it presupposes a certain spiritual realization or at least a mastery of certain 'conceptual dimensions'.[3]

As for modern science, not only is it restricted, in its study of nature, to only one of its planes of existence (whence its 'horizontal' dispersion contrary to the contemplative spirit); it also dissects as far as possible the contents of nature, as if the more to emphasize the 'autonomous materiality' of things; and this fragmentation—both theoretical and technological—of reality is radically opposed to the nature of art; for art is nothing without fullness in unity, without rhythm, without proportion.

In other words, modern science is ugly, with an ugliness that has finished by taking possession of the very notion of 'reality'[4] and by arrogating to itself the prestige of the 'objective' judgement of things,[5] whence the irony of modern men with regard to whatever, in

---

[3] An example of such a speculative 'key' is the diagram of a horoscope. This symbolically summarizes all the relationships between a human microcosm and the macrocosm. The interpretation of a horoscope comprises innumerable applications, which, however, can only be properly divined by virtue of the unique 'form' of the being, a form which the horoscope both reveals and veils.

[4] Whence the use, in modern aesthetics, of the term 'realism'.

[5] For the overwhelming majority of moderns, the signs and characteristics of science are complex pieces of apparatus, endless reportings, a 'clinical' approach, etc.

the traditional sciences, may reveal an aspect of artless beauty. Conversely, the ugliness of modern science deprives it of any value from the point of view of the contemplative and inspired sciences, for the central object of these sciences is the unicity of everything that exists, a unicity that modern scientists cannot in fact deny—since everything implicitly affirms it—but which it nevertheless, by its dissecting approach, prevents one from 'tasting'.

# 2
# Traditional Cosmology and Modern Science

## (I) COSMOLOGIA PERENNIS

IN WHAT FOLLOWS attention will be drawn to certain fissures in modern science, and these will be judged by means of the criteria provided by cosmology in the traditional sense of this term. We know that the Greek word *cosmos* means 'order', implying the ideas of unity and totality. Cosmology is thus the science of the world inasmuch as this reflects its unique cause, Being. This reflection of the uncreated in the created necessarily presents itself under diverse aspects, and even under an indefinite variety of aspects, each of which has about it something whole and total, so that there are a multiplicity of visions of the cosmos, all equally possible and legitimate and springing from the same universal and immutable principles.

These principles, by reason of their very universality, are essentially inherent in human intelligence at its most profound; but this pure intellect only becomes 'disengaged', generally speaking and for the man who is predisposed thereto, with the aid of supernatural elements that an authentic and complete spiritual tradition alone can supply. This means that all genuine cosmology is attached to a divine revelation, even if the object it considers and the mode of its expression apparently lie outside the message that this revelation brings.

Such is the case, for instance, with Christian cosmology, whose origin at first sight appears somewhat heterogeneous, since on the one hand it refers to the Biblical account of creation, while on the other hand it bases itself on the heritage of the Greek cosmologists; if there seems to be a certain eclecticism here, it should be stressed that this is providential, since the two sources in question complement one another in a harmonious way, the first being presented in the form of a myth and the other under the form of a doctrine expressed in more or less rational terms, and thus neutral from the point of view of symbolism and of a spiritual perspective.

Moreover, there can only be a question of syncretism where there is a mixture, and hence a confusion, of planes and modes of expression. The Biblical myth of creation and Greek cosmology do not present any formally incompatible perspectives, nor do they duplicate one another, as would be the case, for example, if one attempted to mingle Buddhist cosmology with the figurative teaching of the Bible. The Biblical myth assumes the form of a drama, a divine action that seems to unfold in time, distinguishing the principial and the relative by a 'before' and an 'after'. Greek cosmology, for its part, corresponds to an essentially static vision of things; it depicts the structure of the world, such as it is 'now and always', as a hierarchy of degrees of existence, of which the lower are conditioned by time, space, and number, while the higher are situated beyond temporal succession and spatial or other limits. This doctrine thus presents itself quite naturally—and providentially—as a scientific commentary on the scriptural symbolism.

The Biblical myth is revealed, but Greek cosmology is likewise not of purely human origin; even with Aristotle, that distant founder of Western rationalism, certain basic ideas, like his distinction between form (*eidos*) and matter (*hyle*), for example, undoubtedly spring from a knowledge that is supra-rational, and therefore timeless and sacred. Aristotle translates this wisdom into a homogeneous dialectic, and his dialectic is valid because the law inherent in thought reflects in its own way the law of existence. At the same time, he demonstrates reality only to the extent that it can be logically defined. Plato and Plotinus go much further; they transcend the 'objectivized' cosmology of Aristotle, and restore to symbolism all its supra-rational significance. Christian cosmology borrowed the analytical thought of Aristotle, but it was from Plato that it derived the doctrine of archetypes that justifies symbolism and confirms the primacy of intellectual intuition over discursive thought.

The keystone of all Christian cosmology and the element that renders possible the linking of the Biblical myth with the Greek heritage is the evangelical doctrine of the Logos as source of both existence and knowledge. This doctrine, which in itself transcends

the plane of cosmology—the Gospels contain hardly any cosmological elements—constitutes nonetheless its spiritual axis; it is through
this doctrine that the science of the created is connected with the
knowledge of the uncreated. It is thus through its link with
metaphysics—comprised in this case in the Johannine doctrine of the
Word—that cosmology is in agreement with theology. It is first of all a
prolongation of gnosis; thereafter an *ancilla theologiae.*

The same can be said of all traditional cosmologies and in
particular of those belonging to Islam and Judaism; their immutable
axis is always a revealed doctrine of the Spirit or Intellect, whether
this be conceived as uncreated (as in the case of the Word) or as
created (as with the first Intellect) or as having two aspects, one
created and the other uncreated.[1]

We know that there were frequent exchanges between the
Christian, Moslem, and Jewish cosmologists, and the same certainly
occurred between the Hellenistic cosmologists and certain Asiatic
civilizations; but it goes without saying (as Guénon pointed out) that
the family resemblance between all the traditional cosmologies had
generally speaking nothing to do with historical borrowings, for in the
first place there is the nature of things and, after that, there is intuitive
knowledge. This knowledge, as we have said, must be vivified by a
sacred science, the written and oral repository of a divine revelation.
Be that as it may, everything is definitively contained within our own
soul, whose lower ramifications are identified with the domain of the
senses, but whose root reaches to pure Being and the supreme
Essence, so that man grasps within himself the axis of the cosmos. He
can 'measure' the whole of its 'vertical' dimension, and in this
connection his knowledge of the world can be adequate, in spite of
the fact that he will always be ignorant of much, or even nearly all, of
its 'horizontal' extension. It is thus perfectly possible for traditional
cosmology to possess, as it does, a knowledge that is real—and
incomparably more vast and profound than that offered by the
modern empirical sciences—while retaining childlike (or, more
precisely, 'human') opinions about realities of the physical order.

---

[1] Ibn 'Arabî says the same in speaking of *ar-Rûh*, the Universal Spirit, in accordance
with certain Koranic formulations. As for the first Intellect (*nous*) of Plotinus, it can
also be regarded under these two aspects; the Plotinian doctrine of divine emanations
does not introduce the distinction created-uncreated.

Western cosmology fell out of favour the moment the ancient geocentric system of the world was replaced by the heliocentric system of Copernicus. For that to be possible, cosmology had to be reduced to mere cosmography; thus the form was confused with the content, and the one was rejected with the other. In reality, the medieval conception of the physical world, of its ordonnance and of its extension, not only corresponded to a natural, and therefore realistic vision of things, it also expressed a spiritual order in which man had his organic place.

Let us pause for a moment at this vision of the world, known to us especially through the poetic works of Dante.[2] The planetary heavens and the heaven of fixed stars that surrounds them were presented as so many concentric spheres—'the vaster they are, the greater their virtue', as Dante explained—whose extreme limit, the invisible heaven of the Empyrean, is identified both with universal space and pure duration. Spatially, it represents a sphere of unlimited radius, and temporally, it is the background of all movement. Its continual rotation bears along with it all inferior movements, which are measured in relation to it, though it cannot itself be measured in any absolute way, since time cannot be divided except by reference to the marking out of a movement in space.

These spheres symbolize the higher states of consciousness and, more exactly, the modalities of the soul which, while still contained within the integral individuality, are more and more irradiated by the Divine Spirit. It is the Empyrean, the 'threshold' between time and non-time, that represents the extreme limit of the individual or formal world. It is in crossing this limit that Dante obtains a new vision, one that is to some extent inverse to the cosmic order. Up to that point the hierarchy of existence, which goes from corporeal to spiritual, expresses itself through a gradual expansion of space, the container being the cause and master of the contained. At this point the Divine Being reveals itself as the centre around which the angels revolve in closer and closer choirs. In reality there is no symmetry

---

[2] There has been much discussion as to whether the *Divine Comedy* was influenced by an Islamic model; though possible in itself, it is not necessarily so, given that the symbolism in question resulted on the one hand from the spiritual realities themselves and on the other from the Ptolemaic system that was common to both Christian and Moslem civilizations in the Middle Ages.

between the two orders, planetary and angelic, for God is at one and the same time the centre and container of all things. It is the physical order alone, that of the starry firmament, that represents the reflection of the superior order.

As for the circles of hell, which Dante[3] describes as a pit sunk into the earth as far as the 'point toward which all heaviness tends', they are not the inverse reflection but the opposite of the heavenly spheres. They are, as it were, these spheres overturned, whereas the mountain of purgatory, which the poet tells us was formed from the earth cast up by Lucifer in the course of his fall towards the centre of gravity, is properly speaking a compensation for hell. By this localization of hell and purgatory, Dante did not intend to establish a geography; he was not deluded concerning the provisional character of the symbolism, although he obviously believed in the geocentric system of Ptolemy.

The heliocentric system itself admits of an obvious symbolism, since it identifies the centre of the world with the source of light. Its rediscovery by Copernicus,[4] however, produced no new spiritual vision of the world; rather it was comparable to the popularization of an esoteric truth. The heliocentric system had no common measure with the subjective experiences of people; in it man had no organic place. Instead of helping the human mind to go beyond itself and to consider things in terms of the immensity of the cosmos, it only encouraged a materialistic Promethcanism which, far from being superhuman, ended by becoming inhuman.

Strictly speaking, a modern cosmology does not exist, in spite of the misuse of language whereby the modern science of the sensible universe is called cosmology. In fact, the modern science of nature expressly limits itself to the corporeal domain alone, which it isolates from the total cosmos while considering things in their purely spatial and temporal phenomenality, as if supra-sensible reality with its

---

[3] With regard to the symbolical localization of the hells, medieval authors differ and seem to contradict one another. For Dante, the hells are situated beneath the earth, which means that they correspond to inferior states; for others, and especially for certain Moslem cosmologists, they are to be found 'between heaven and earth', in other words, in the subtle world.

[4] For it is not a case of an unprecedented discovery. Copernicus himself refers to Nicetas of Syracuse as also to certain quotations in Plutarch.

differing levels were nothing at all and as if that reality were not knowable by means of the intellect, in which it is analogically inherent by virtue of the correspondence between the macrocosm and the microcosm. But the point we wish to stress here is the following: scientism is an objectivism which purports to be mathematical and exclusive. Because of this, it behaves as if the human subject did not exist, or as if this subject were not the subtle mirror indispensable for the phenomenal appearance of the world. It is deliberately ignored that the subject is the guarantor of the logical continuity of the world and, in its intellectual essence, the witness of all objective reality.

In fact, a knowledge that is 'objective', and thus independent of particular subjectivities presupposes immutable criteria, and these could not exist if there were not in the individual subject itself an impartial background, a witness transcending the individual, in other words the intellect. After all, knowledge of the world presupposes the underlying unity of the knowing subject, so that one might say of a voluntarily agnostic science what Meister Eckhart said about atheists: 'The more they blaspheme God, the more they praise Him'. The more science affirms an exclusively 'objective' order of things, the more it manifests the underlying unity of the intellect or spirit; it does this indirectly, unconsciously, and in spite of itself—in other words, contrarily to its own thesis—but when all is said and done, it proclaims in its own way what it purports to deny. In the perspective of scientism, the total human subject—composed of sensibility, reason, and intellect—is illusorily replaced by mathematical thought alone. According to a scientist of the present century,[5] 'All true progress in natural science consists in its disengaging itself more and more from subjectivity and in bringing out more and more clearly what exists independently of human conception, without troubling itself with the fact that the result has no longer anything but the most distant resemblance to what the original perception took for real.' According to this declaration, which is considered to be authoritative, the subjectivity from which one is to break loose is not reducible to the intrusion of sensorial accidents and emotional impulsions into the order of objective knowledge; it is the complete 'human conception' of things—in other words, both direct sensory

[5] Sir James Jeans, *The New Background of Science* (Cambridge, 1933).

perception and its spontaneous assimilation by the imagination—
which is called in question; only mathematical thought is allowed to
be objective or true. Mathematical thought in fact allows a maximum
of generalization while remaining bound to number, so that it can be
verified on the quantitative plane; but it in no wise includes the whole
of reality as it is communicated to us by our senses. It makes a
selection from out of this total reality, and the scientific prejudice of
which we have just been speaking regards as unreal everything that
this selection leaves out. Thus it is that those sensible qualities called
'secondary', such as colours, odours, savours, and the sensations of
hot and cold, are considered to be subjective impressions implying no
objective quality, and possessing no other reality than that belonging
to their indirect physical causes, as for example, in the case of
colours, the various frequencies of light waves: 'Once it be admitted
that in principle the sensible qualities cannot automatically be looked
on as being qualities of the things themselves, physics offers us an
entirely homogeneous and certain system, which answers every
question as to what really underlies those colours, sounds, temper-
atures, etc'.[6] What is this homogeneity but the result of a reduction of
the qualitative aspects of nature to quantitative modalities? Modern
science thus asks us to sacrifice a goodly part of what constitutes for
us the reality of the world, and offers us in exchange mathematical
formulae whose only advantage is to help us to manipulate matter on
its own plane, which is that of quantity.

This mathematical selection from out of total reality does not only
eliminate the 'secondary' qualities of perception, it also removes what
the Greek philosophers and the Scholastics called 'form', in other
words, the qualitative 'seal' imprinted on matter by the unique
essence of a being or a thing. For modern science, the essential form
does not exist: 'Some rare Aristotelians', writes a theoretician of
modern science,[7] 'still perhaps think they can intuitively attain,
through some illumination by the active intellect, the essential ideas
of the things of nature; but this is nothing but a beautiful dream. . .
The essences of things cannot be contemplated, they must be
discovered by experience, by means of a laborious work of investiga-

[6] B. Bavink, *Hauptfragen der heutigen Naturphilosophie* (Berlin, 1928).
[7] Josef Geiser, *Allgemeine Philosophie des Seins und der Natur* (Münster i. W., 1915).

tion'. To this a Plotinus, an Avicenna, or a St. Albert the Great would reply that in nature there is nothing more evident than the essences of things, since these manifest themselves in the 'forms' themselves. Only, they cannot be discovered by a 'laborious work of investigation' nor measured quantitatively; in fact the intuition that grasps them relies directly on sensory perception and imagination, inasmuch as the latter synthesizes the impressions received from outside.

In any case, what is this human reason that tries to grasp the essences of things by a 'laborious work of investigation'? Either this faculty of reason is truly capable of attaining its objects, or it is not. We know that reason is limited, but we also know that it is able to conceive truths that are independent of individuals, and that therefore a universal law is manifested in it. If human intelligence is not merely 'organized matter'—in which case it would not be intelligence—this means that it necessarily participates in a transcendent principle. Without entering into a philosophical discussion on the nature of reason, we can compare the relationship between it and its supra-individual source (which medieval cosmology calls the 'active intellect' and, in a more general sense, the 'first intellect') to the relationship between a reflection and its luminous source, and this image will be both more ample and more accurate than any philosophical definition. A reflection is always limited by the nature of its plane of reflection—in the case of reason, this plane is the mind and, in a more general sense, the human psyche—but the nature of light remains essentially the same, in its source as in its reflection. The same applies to the spirit, whatever be the formal limits a particular plane of reflection imposes on it. Now spirit is essentially and wholly knowledge; in itself it is subject to no external constraint, and in principle nothing can prevent it from knowing itself and at the same time knowing all the possibilities contained within itself. Therein lies the mode of access, not to the material structure of things in particular and in detail, but to their permanent essences.

All true cosmological knowledge is founded on the qualitative aspect of things, in other words, on 'forms' inasmuch as these are the mark of the essence. Because of this, cosmology is both direct and speculative, for it grasps the qualities of things in a direct way, and does not call them in question, and at the same time it disengages these qualities from their particular attachments so as to be able to consider them at their different levels of manifestation. In this way, the universe reveals its internal unity and at the same time shows the inexhaustible spectrum of its aspects and dimensions. That this vision should often have something poetic about it is obviously not to its detriment, since all genuine poetry comprises a presentiment of the essential harmony of the world; it was in this sense that Mohammed could say: 'Surely there is a part of wisdom in poetry'.

If one can reproach this vision of the world for being more contemplative than practical and for neglecting the material connections of things (which in reality is hardly a reproach), it can on the other hand be said about scientism that it empties the world of its qualitative sap. The traditional vision of things is above all 'static' and 'vertical'. It is static because it refers to constant and universal qualities, and it is vertical in the sense that it attaches the lower to the higher, the ephemeral to the imperishable. The modern vision, on the contrary, is fundamentally 'dynamic' and 'horizontal'; it is not the symbolism of things that interests it, but their material and historical connections.

The great argument in favour of the modern science of nature—an argument that counts for much in the eyes of the crowd (whatever may be the reservations of men of science themselves)—is its technical application; this, it is believed, proves the validity of the scientific principles,[8] as if a fragmentary and in some respects problematical efficacy could be a proof of their intrinsic and total value. In reality, modern science displays a certain number of fissures that are due to the fact that the world of phenomena is indefinite and that therefore no science can ever hope to exhaust it; these fissures derive above all from modern science's systematic exclusion of all the non-corporeal dimensions of reality. They manifest themselves right down to the foundations of modern science, and in domains as seemingly 'exact' as that of physics; they become gaping cracks when one turns to the disciplines connected with the study of life, not to mention psychology, where an empiricism that is relatively valid in the physical order encroaches in bizarre fashion on a foreign field. These fissures, which do not merely affect the theoretical domain,

---

[8] It is a fact, however, that most of the great technical inventions were effected on the basis of inadequate and even false theories.

are far from harmless; on the contrary, in their technical consequences, they constitute so many seeds of catastrophe.

Because the mathematical conception of things inevitably participates in the schematic and discontinuous character of number, it neglects, in the vast web of nature, everything that consists of pure continuity and of relations subtly kept in balance. Now, continuity and equilibrium exist before discontinuity and before crisis; they are more real than these latter, and incomparably more precious.

## (II) MODERN PHYSICS

In modern physics the space in which the heavenly bodies move, as also the space traversed by the trajectories of the minutest bodies such as electrons, is conceived as a void. The purely mathematical definition of the spatial and temporal relationships between various bodies great or small is thereby rendered easier. In reality, a corporeal 'point' 'suspended' in a total void would have no relationship whatever with any other corporeal 'points'; it would, so to speak, fall back into nothingness. One blithely speaks of 'fields of force', but by what are these fields supported? A totally empty space cannot exist; it is only an abstraction, an arbitrary idea that serves only to show where mathematical thinking can lead when arbitrarily detached from a concrete intuition of things.

According to traditional cosmology, ether fills all space without distinction. We know that modern physics denies the existence of ether, since it has been established that it offers no resistance to the rotatory movement of the earth; but it is forgotten that this quintessential element which is at the basis of all material differentiations, is not itself distinguished by any particular quality, so that it offers no opposition to anything whatsoever. It represents the continuous ground whence all material discontinuities detach themselves.

If modern science accepted the existence of ether, it might perhaps find an answer to the question whether light is propagated as a wave or as a corpuscular emanation; most probably its movement is neither one nor the other, and its apparently contradictory properties are explainable by the fact that it is most directly attached to ether and participates in the indistinctly continuous nature of the latter.

An indistinct continuum cannot be divided into a series of like units; if it does not necessarily escape from time or space, it nevertheless eludes graduated measurements. This is especially true of the speed of light, which always appears the same, independently of the movement of its observer, whether the latter moves in the same direction or in the opposite direction. The speed of light thus represents a limit value; it can neither be overtaken nor caught up with by any other movement, and this is like the physical expression of the simultaneity proper to the act of the intelligible light.

We know that the discovery of the fact that the speed of light, when measured both in the direction of the rotation of the earth and in the direction opposite to that rotation, is invariable, has confronted modern astronomers with the alternative either of accepting the immobility of the earth or else of rejecting the usual notions of time and space. Thus it was that Einstein was led into considering space and time as two relative dimensions, variable in function of the state of movement of the observer, the only constant dimension being the speed of light. The latter would everywhere and always be the same, whereas time and space vary in relation to one another: it is as if space could shrink in favour of time, and inversely.

If it be admitted that a movement is definable in terms of a certain relationship of time and space, it is contradictory to maintain that it is a movement, that of light, that measures space and time. It is true that on a quite different plane—when it is a question of the intelligible light—the image of light 'measuring' the cosmos and realizing it thereby is not devoid of deep meaning. But what we have in view here is the physical order, which alone is considered, and with good cause, by Einstein's theory; it is therefore in this context that we will put the following question: what is this famous 'constant number' that is supposed to express the speed of light? How can movement having a definite speed—and its definition will always be a relationship between space and time—itself be a quasi-'absolute' measure of these two conditions of the physical world? Is there not here a confusion between the principial and quantitative domains? That the movement of light is the fundamental 'measure' of the corporeal world we willingly believe, but why should this measure itself be a number, and even a definite number? Moreover, do the experiments which are supposed to prove the constant character of the speed of light really get beyond the earthly sphere, and do they not imply both space and time as usually imagined by us? Thus '300,000 km per second' is stated to be the speed of light, and it is held that here is a value which, if it be not necessarily everywhere expressed in this manner, does nonetheless remain constant throughout the physical universe. The astronomer who counts, by referring to the lines of the spectrum, the light-years separating us from the nebula of Andromeda, supposes without more ado that the universe is everywhere 'woven' in the same manner. Now, what would happen if the constant character of the speed of light ever came to be doubted—and there is every likelihood that it will be sooner or later—so that the only fixed pivot of Einstein's theory would fall down? The whole modern conception of the universe would immediately dissolve like a mirage.

We are told that reality does not necessarily correspond with our inborn conceptions of time and space; but at the same time it is never doubted for a moment that the physical universe conforms with certain mathematical formulas which necessarily proceed from axioms that are no less inborn.

In the same order of ideas mention must also be made of the theory according to which interstellar space is not the space of Euclid, but a space that does not admit the Euclidean axiom regarding parallel lines. Such a space, it is said, flows back on itself, without its being possible to assign to it a definite curve. One might see in this theory an expression of spatial indefinitude, since in fact space is neither finite nor infinite, something which the Ancients indicated by comparing space to a sphere whose radius exceeds every measure, and which itself is contained in the Universal Spirit. But this is not how modern theoreticians understand things, for they declare that our immediate conception of space is quite simply false and incomplete, and that we must therefore familiarize ourselves with non-Euclidean space, which, they say, is accessible to a disciplined imagination. Now this is simply not true, for non-Euclidean space is accessible only indirectly, namely, from the starting-point of Euclidean space, which thus remains the qualitative model for every conceivable kind of space. In this case, as in many others, modern science tries mathematically to go beyond the logic inherent in the imagination, and then to violate this by dint of mathematical principles, as if every intellectual faculty other than purely mathematical thought were suspect.

In conformity with this mathematical schematism, matter itself is conceived as being discontinuous, for atoms, and their constituent particles, are supposed to be even more isolated in space than are the stars. Whatever the current conception of the atomic order may be—and theories on this subject change at a disconcerting speed—it is always a case of groupings of corporeal 'points'.

Let us here recall the traditional doctrine of matter:[9] it is from the starting-point of 'first matter' that the world is constituted, by successive differentiation, under the 'non-acting' action of the form-bestowing Essence; but this *materia prima* is not tangible matter, it underlies all finite existence, and even its nearest modality, *materia signata quantitate*, which is the basis of the corporeal world, is not manifested as such. According to a most judicious expression of Boethius,[10] it is by its 'form'—in other words, its qualitative aspect—that a thing is known, 'form being like a light by means of which we know what a thing is'. Now *materia* as such is precisely that which is not yet formed and which by that very fact eludes all distinctive knowing. The world that is accessible to distinctive knowledge thus extends between two poles that are unmanifested as such (the form-bestowing Essence and undifferentiated *materia*) just as the range of colours in the spectrum unfolds through the refraction of white—and therefore colourless—light in a medium that is also colourless.

Modern science, which despite its pragmatism is not behindhand in claiming to offer a complete and comprehensive explanation of the sensible universe, strives to reduce the whole qualitative richness of this universe to a certain structure of matter, conceived as a variable grouping of minute bodies, whether these be defined as genuine bodies or as simple 'points' of energy. This means that all the 'bundles' of sensible qualities, everything that constitutes the world for us, except space and time, have to be reduced, scientifically speaking, to a series of atomic 'models' definable in terms of the

[9] René Guénon, *The Reign of Quantity and the Signs of the Times* (Penguin Books, Baltimore, Maryland, 1972), Chapter 2, *'Materia Signata Quantitate'*.
[10] *De Unitate et Uno*.

number, mass, trajectories, and speeds of the minute bodies concerned. It is obvious that this reduction is in vain, for although these 'models' still comprise certain qualitative elements—if only their imaginary spatial form—it is nonetheless a question of the reduction of quality to quantity—and quantity can never comprehend quality.

On the other hand, the elimination of the qualitative aspects in favour of a tighter and tighter mathematical definition of atomic structure must necessarily reach a limit, beyond which precision gives way to the indeterminate. This is exactly what is happening with modern atomist science, in which mathematical reflection is being more and more replaced by statistics and calculations of probability, and in which the very laws of causality seem to be facing bankruptcy. If the 'forms' of things are 'lights', as Boethius said, the reduction of the qualitative to the quantitative can be compared to the action of a man who puts out all the lights the better to scrutinize the nature of darkness.

Modern science can never reach that matter that is at the basis of this world. But between the qualitiatively differentiated world and undifferentiated matter lies something like an intermediate zone— and this is chaos. The sinister dangers of atomic fission are but one signpost indicating the frontier of chaos and dissolution.

## (III) TRADITIONAL SYMBOLISM & MODERN EMPIRICISM

If the ancient cosmogonies seem childish when one takes their symbolism literally—and this means not understanding them— modern theories about the origin of the world are frankly absurd. They are so, not so much in their mathematical formulations, but because of the total unawareness with which their authors set themselves up as sovereign witnesses of cosmic becoming, while at the same time claiming that the human mind itself is a product of this becoming. What connection is there between that primordial nebula —that vortex of matter whence they wish to derive earth, life, and man—and this little mental mirror that loses itself in conjectures (since for the scientists intelligence amounts to no more than this) and yet feels so sure of discovering the logic of things within itself?

How can the effect make judgements regarding its own cause? And if there exist constant laws of nature—those of causality, number, space, and time—and something which, within ourselves, has the right to say 'this is true and this is false', where is the guarantee of truth, either in the object or in the subject? Is the nature of our mind merely a little foam on the waves of the cosmic ocean, or is there to be found deep within it a timeless witness of reality?

Some protagonists of the theories in question will perhaps say that they are concerned only with the physical and objective domain, without seeking to prejudge the domain of the subjective. They can perhaps cite Descartes, who defined spirit and matter as two realities, coordinated by Providence, but separated in fact. In point of fact, this division of reality into watertight compartments served to prepare people's minds to leave aside everything that is not of the physical order, as if man were not himself proof of the complexity of the real.

The man of antiquity, who pictured the earth as an island surrounded by the primordial ocean and covered by the dome of heaven, and the medieval man, who saw the heavens as concentric spheres extending from the earth (viewed as the centre) to the limitless sphere of the Divine Spirit, were no doubt mistaken regarding the true disposition and proportions of the sensible universe. On the other hand, they were fully conscious of the fact—infinitely more important—that this corporeal world is not the whole of reality, and that it is as if surrounded and pervaded by a reality, both greater and more subtle, that in its turn is contained in the Spirit; and they knew, indirectly or directly, that the world in all its extension disappears in the face of the Infinite.

Modern man knows that the earth is only a ball suspended in a bottomless abyss and carried along in a dizzy and complex movement, and that this movement is governed by other celestial bodies incomparably larger than this earth and situated at immense distances from it. He knows that the earth on which he lives is but a grain in comparison with the sun, which itself is but a grain amidst other incandescent stars, and that all is in motion. An irregularity in this assemblage of sidereal movements, an interference from a star foreign to our planetary system, a deviation of the sun's trajectory, or any other cosmic accident, would suffice to make the earth unsteady in its rotation, to trouble the course of the seasons, to change the atmosphere, and to destroy mankind. Modern man also knows that the smallest atom contains forces which, if unleashed, could involve the earth in an almost instantaneous conflagration. All of this, from the 'infinitely small' to the 'infinitely great', presents itself, from the point of view of modern science, as a mechanism of unimaginable complexity, the functioning of which is only due to blind forces.

In spite of this, the man of our time lives and acts as if the normal and habitual operation of the rhythms of nature were something that was guaranteed to him. In actual practice, he thinks neither of the abysses of the stellar world nor of the terrible forces latent in every particle of matter. He sees the sky above him like any child sees it, with its sun and its stars, but the remembrance of the astronomical theories prevents him from recognizing divine signs in them. The sky for him is no longer the natural expression of the Spirit that enfolds and illuminates the world. Scientific knowledge has substituted itself for this 'naïve' and yet profound vision, not as a new consciousness of a vaster cosmic order, an order of which man forms part, but as an estrangement, as an irremediable disarray before abysses that no longer have any common measure with him. For nothing now reminds him that in reality this whole universe is contained within himself, not of course in his individual being, but in the spirit or intellect that is within him and that is both greater than himself and the whole phenomenal universe.

## (IV) EVOLUTIONISM

The least phenomenon participates in several continuities or cosmic dimensions incommensurable in relation to each other; thus, ice is water as regards its substance—and in this respect it is indistinguishable from liquid water or water vapour—but as regards its state it belongs to the class of solid bodies. Similarly, when a thing is constituted by diverse elements, it participates in their natures while being different from them. Cinnabar, for example, is a synthesis of sulphur and mercury; it is thus in one sense the sum of these two elements, but at the same time it possesses qualities that are not to be found in either of these two substances. Quantities can be added to one another, but a quality is never merely the sum of other qualities.

By mixing the colours blue and yellow, green is obtained; this third colour is thus a synthesis of the other two, but it is not the product of a simple addition, for it represents at the same time a chromatic quality that is new and unique in itself.

There is here something like a 'discontinuous continuity', which is even more marked in the biological order, where the qualitative unity of an organism is plainly distinguishable from its material composition. The bird that is born from the egg is made from the same elements as the egg, but it is not the egg. Likewise, the butterfly that emerges from a chrysalis is neither that chrysalis nor the caterpillar that produced it. A kinship exists between these various organisms, a genetic continuity, but they also display a qualitative discontinuity, since between the caterpillar and the butterfly there is something like a rupture of level.

At every point in the cosmic web there is thus a warp and a woof that intersect one another, and this is indicated by the traditional symbolism of weaving, according to which the threads of the warp, which hang vertically on the primitive loom, represent the permanent essences of things—and thus also the essential qualities and forms—while the woof, which binds horizontally the threads of the warp, and at the same time covers them with its alternating waves, corresponds to the substantial or 'material' continuity of the world.[11]

The same law is expressed by classical hylomorphism, which distinguishes the 'form' of a thing or being—the seal of its essential unity—from its 'matter', namely the plastic substance which receives this seal and furnishes it with a concrete and limited existence. No modern theory has ever been able to replace this ancient theory, for the fact of reducing the whole plenitude of the real to one or other of its 'dimensions' hardly amounts to an explanation of it. Modern science is ignorant above all of what the Ancients designated by the term 'form', precisely because it is here a question of a non-quantitative aspect of things, and this ignorance is not unconnected with the fact that modern science sees no criterion in the beauty or ugliness of a phenomenon: the beauty of a thing is the sign of its internal unity, its conformity with an indivisible essence, and thus with a reality that will not let itself be counted or measured.

[11] René Guénon, *The Symbolism of the Cross*, chapter on the symbolism of weaving.

It is necessary to point out here that the notion of 'form' necessarily includes a twofold meaning: on the one hand it means the delimitation of a thing, and this is its most usual meaning; in this connection, form is situated on the side of matter or, in a more general sense, on the side of plastic substance, which limits and separates realities.[12] On the other hand, 'form' understood in the sense given to it by the Greek philosophers and following them the Scholastics, is the aggregate of qualities pertaining to a being or a thing, and thus the expression or the trace of its immutable essence.

The individual world is the 'formal' world because it is the domain of those realities that are constituted by the conjunction of a 'form' and a 'matter', whether subtle or corporeal. It is only in connection with a 'matter', a plastic substance, that 'form' plays the role of a principle of individuation; in itself, in its ontological basis, it is not an individual reality but an archetype, and as such beyond limitations and change. Thus a species is an archetype, and if it is only manifested by the individuals that belong to it, it is nevertheless just as real, and even incomparably more real, than they. As for the rationalist objection that tries to prove the absurdity of the doctrine of archetypes by arguing that a multiplication of mental notions would imply a corresponding multiplication of archetypes—leading to the idea of the idea of the idea, and so on—it quite misses the point, since multiplicity can in no wise be transposed onto the level of the archetypal roots. The latter are distinguished in a principial way, within Being and by virtue of Being; in this connection, Being can be envisaged as a unique and homogeneous crystal potentially containing all possible crystalline forms.[13] Multiplicity and quantity thus only exist at the level of the 'material' reflections of the archetypes.

From what has just been said, it follows that a species is in itself an immutable 'form'; it cannot evolve and be transformed into another species, although it may include variants, which are diverse 'projections' of a unique essential form, from which they can never be

[12] In Hindu parlance, the distinction nâma-rupa, 'name and form', is related to this aspect of the notion under study, 'name' here standing for the essence of a being or thing, and 'form' for its limited and outward existence.

[13] It is self-evident that all the images that one can offer of the non-separative distinction of the possibilities contained in Being must remain imperfect and paradoxical.

detached, any more than the branches of a tree can be detached from the trunk.

It has been justly said[14] that the whole thesis of the evolution of species, inaugurated by Darwin, is founded on a confusion between species and simple variation. Its advocates put forward as the 'bud' or the beginning of a new species what in reality is no more than a variant within the framework of a determinate specific type. This false assimilation is, however, not enough to fill the numberless gaps that occur in the paleontological succession of species; not only are related species separated by profound gaps, but there do not even exist any forms that would indicate any possible connection between different orders such as fish, reptiles, birds, and mammals. One can doubtless find some fishes that use their fins to crawl onto a bank, but one will seek in vain in these fins for the slightest beginning of that articulation which would render possible the formation of an arm or a paw. Likewise, if there are certain resemblances between reptiles and birds, their respective skeletons are nonetheless of a fundamentally different structure. Thus, for example, the very complex articulation in the jaws of a bird, and the related organization of its hearing apparatus, pertain to an entirely different plan from the one found in reptiles; it is difficult to conceive how one might have developed from the other.[15] As for the famous fossil bird *Archaeopteryx*, it is fairly and squarely a bird, despite the claws at the end of its wings, its teeth, and its long tail.[16]

In order to explain the absence of intermediate forms, the partisans of transformism have sometimes argued that these forms must have disappeared because of their very imperfection and precariousness; but this argument is plainly in contradiction with the principle of selection that is supposed to be the operative factor in the evolution of species: the trial forms should be incomparably more numerous than the ancestors having already acquired a definitive form. Besides, if the evolution of species represents, as is declared, a

---

[14] Douglas Dewar, *The Transformist Illusion* (Dehoff Publications, Murfreesboro, Tennessee, 1957). See also Louis Bounoure, *Déterminisme et Finalité* (Collection Philosophie, Flammarion, Paris).

[15] Dewar, *The Transformist Illusion*.

[16] *Ibid.*

gradual and continual process, all the real links in the chain—therefore all those that are destined to be followed—will be both endpoints and intermediaries, in which case it is difficult to see why the ones would be much more precarious than the others.[17]

The more conscientious among modern biologists either reject the transformist theory, or else maintain it as a 'working hypothesis', being unable to conceive any genesis of species that would not be situated on the 'horizontal line' of a purely physical and temporal becoming. For Jean Rostand,

> the world postulated by transformism is a fairly-like world, phantasmagoric, surrealistic. The chief point, to which one always returns, is that we have never been present, even in a small way, at *one* authentic phenomenon of evolution . . . we keep the impression that nature today has nothing to offer that might be capable of reducing our embarrassment before the veritably organic metamorphoses implied in the transformist thesis. We keep the impression that, in the matter of the genesis of species as in that of the genesis of life, the forces that constructed nature are now absent from nature. . .[18]

Even so, this biologist sticks to the transformist theory:

> I firmly believe—because I see no means of doing otherwise —that mammals have come from lizards, and lizards from fish; but when I declare and when I think such a thing, I try not to avoid seeing its indigestible enormity and I prefer to leave vague the origin of these scandalous metamorphoses rather than add to their improbability that of a ludicrous interpretation.[19]

---

[17] Teilhard de Chardin (*The Human Phenomenon*, p. 129) writes on this subject: 'Nothing is by nature so delicate and fugitive as a beginning. As long as a zoological group is young, its characteristics remain undecided. Its dimensions are weak. Relatively few individuals compose it, and these are rapidly changing. Both in space and duration, the peduncle (or the bud, which comes to the same thing) of a living branch corresponds to a minimum of differentiation, expansion, and resistance. How then is time going to act on this weak zone? Inevitably by destroying it in its vestiges.' This reasoning, which abusively exploits the purely external and conventional analogy between a genealogical 'tree' and a real plant, is an example of the 'imaginative abstraction' that characterizes this author's thought.

[18] *Le Figaro Littéraire*, April 20, 1957.     [19] *Ibid.*

All that paleontology proves to us is that the various animal forms, such as are shown by fossils preserved in successive earthly layers, made their appearance in a vaguely ascending order, going from relatively undifferentiated organisms—but not simple ones[20]—to ever more complex forms, without this ascension representing, however, an unequivocal and continuous line. It seems to move in jumps; in other words, whole categories of animals appear all at once, without real predecessors. What does this order mean? Simply that, on the material plane, the simple or relatively undifferentiated always precedes the complex and differentiated. All 'matter' is like a mirror that reflects the activity of the essences, while also inverting it; this is why the seed comes before the tree and the bud before the flower, whereas in the principial order the perfect 'forms' pre-exist. The successive appearance of animal forms according to an ascending hierarchy therefore in no wise proves their continual and cumulative genesis.[21]

On the contrary, what links the various animal forms to one another is something like a common model, which reveals itself more or less through their structures and which is more apparent in the case of animals endowed with superior consciousness such as birds and mammals. This model is expressed especially in the symmetrical disposition of the body, in the number of extremities and sensory organs, and also in the general form of the chief internal organs. It might be suggested that the design and number of certain organs, and especially those of sensation, simply correspond to the terrestrial surroundings; but this argument is reversible, because those surroundings are precisely what the sensory organs grasp and delimit. In

---

[20] The electron microscope has revealed the surprising complexity of the functions at work within a unicellular being.

[21] The most commonly mentioned example in favour of the transformist thesis is the hypothetical genealogy of the *Equidae*. Charles Depéret criticizes it as follows: 'Geological observation establishes in a formal manner that no gradual passage took place between these genera; the last *Palaeotherium* had for long been extinct, without having transformed itself, when the first *Architherium* made its appearance, and the latter disappeared in its turn, without modification, before being suddenly replaced by the invasion of the *Hipparion*.' (*Les Transformations du Monde animal*, p. 107) To this it can be added that the supposed primitive forms of the horse are hardly to be observed in equine embryology, though the development of the embryo is commonly looked on as a recapitulation of the genesis of the species.

fact, the model underlying all animal forms establishes the analogy between the microcosm and the macrocosm. Against the background of this common cosmic pattern the differences between species and the gaps that separate them are all the more marked.

Instead of 'missing links', which the partisans of transformism seek in vain, nature offers us, as if in irony, a large variety of animal forms which, without transgressing the pre-established framework of a species, imitate the appearance and habits of a species or order foreign to them. Thus, for example, whales are mammals, but they assume the appearance and behaviour of fishes; hummingbirds have the appearance, iridescent colours, flight, and mode of feeding of butterflies; the armadillo is covered with scales like a reptile, although it is a mammal; and so on. Most of these animals with imitative forms are higher species that have taken on the forms of relatively lower species, a fact which *a priori* excludes an interpretation of them as intermediary links in an evolution. As for their interpretation as forms of adaptation to a given set of surroundings, this seems more than dubious, for what could be, for example, the intermediate forms between some land mammal or other and the dolphin?[22] Among these 'imitative' forms, which constitute so many extreme cases, we must also include the fossil bird *Archaeopteryx* mentioned above.

Since each animal order represents an archetype that includes the archetypes of the corresponding species, one might well ask oneself whether the existence of 'imitative' animal forms does not contradict the immutability of the essential forms; but this is not the case, for the existence of these forms demonstrates, on the contrary, that very immutability by a logical exhausting of all the possibilities inherent in a given type or essential form. It is as if nature, after bringing forth fishes, reptiles, birds, and mammals, with their distinctive characteristics, wished still to show that she was able to produce an animal like the dolphin which, while being a true mammal, at the same time possesses almost all the faculties of a fish, or a creature like the tortoise, which possesses a skeleton covered by flesh, yet at the same

---

[22] On the subject of the hypothetical transformation of a land animal into the whale, Douglas Dewar writes: 'I have often challenged transformists to describe plausible ancestors situated in the intermediate phases of this supposed transformation': (*What the Animal Fossils tell us*, Trans. Vict. Instit, vol. LXXIV)

time is enclosed in an exterior carapace after the fashion of certain molluscs.[23] Thus does nature manifest her protean power, her inexhaustible capacity for generation, while remaining faithful to the essential forms, which in fact are never blurred.

Each essential form—or each archetype—includes after its fashion all the others, but without confusion; it is like a mirror reflecting other mirrors, which reflect it in their turn.[24] In its deepest meaning the mutual reflection of types is an expression of the metaphysical homogeneity of Existence, or of the unity of Being.

Some biologists, when confronted with the discontinuity in the paleontological succession of species, postulate an evolution by leaps and, in order to make this theory plausible, refer to the sudden mutations observed in some living species. But these mutations never exceed the limits of an anomaly or a decadence, as for example the sudden appearance of albinos, or of dwarfs or giants; even when these characteristics become hereditary, they remain as anomalies and never constitute new specific forms.[25] For this to happen, it would be necessary for the vital substance of an existing species to serve as the 'plastic material' for a newly manifested specific form; in practice, this means that one or several females of this existing species would suddenly bear offspring of a new species. Now, as the hermetist Richard the Englishman writes:

> Nothing can be produced from a thing that is not contained in it; for this reason, every species, every genus, and every natural order develops within the limits proper to it and bears fruits according to its own kind and not according to an essentially different order; everything that receives a seed must be of the same seed.[26]

Fundamentally, the evolutionist thesis is an attempt to replace, not simply the 'miracle of creation', but the cosmogonic process—largely

[23] It is significant that the tortoise, whose skeleton seems to indicate an extravagant adaptation to an animal 'armoured' state, appears all at once among the fossils, without evolution. Similarly, the spider appears simultaneously with its prey and with its faculty of weaving already developed.

[24] This is the image used by the Sufi 'Abd al-Karîm al-Jîlî in his book *al-Insân al-Kamil*, chapter on 'Divine Unicity'.

[25] Bounoure, *Déterminisme et Finalité*.

[26] Quoted in the *Golden Treatise, Museum Hermeticum* (Frankfurt, 1678).

suprasensory—of which the Biblical narrative is a Scriptural symbol; evolutionism, by absurdly making the greater derive from the lesser, is the opposite of this process, or this 'emanation'. (This term has nothing to do with the emanationist heresy, since the transcendence and immutability of the ontological principle are here in no wise called in question.) In a word, evolutionism results from an incapacity—peculiar to modern science—to conceive 'dimensions' of reality other than purely physical ones; to understand the 'vertical' genesis of species, it is worth recalling what Guénon said about the progressive solidification of the corporeal state through the various terrestrial ages.[27] This solidification must obviously not be taken to imply that the stones of the earliest ages were soft, for this would be tantamount to saying that certain physical qualities—and in particular hardness and density—were then wanting; what has hardened and become fixed with time is the corporeal state taken as a whole, with the result that it no longer receives directly the imprint of subtle forms. Assuredly, it cannot become detached from the subtle state, which is its ontological root and which dominates it entirely, but the relationship between the two states of existence no longer has the creative character that it possessed at the origin; it is as when a fruit, having reached maturity, becomes surrounded by an ever harder husk and ceases to absorb the sap of the tree. In a cyclic phase in which corporeal existence had not yet reached this degree of solidification, a new specific form could manifest itself directly from the starting-point of its first 'condensation' in the subtle or animic state;[28] this means that the different types of animals pre-existed at the level immediately superior to the corporeal world as non-spatial forms, but nevertheless clothed in a certain 'matter', namely that of the subtle world. From there these forms 'descended' into the corporeal state each time the latter was ready to receive them; this 'descent' had the nature of a sudden coagulation and hence also the

[27] Guénon, *The Reign of Quantity and the Signs of the Times.*
[28] Concerning the creation of species in a subtle 'proto-matter'—in which they still preserve an androgynous form, comparable to a sphere—and their subsequent exteriorization by 'crystallization' in sensible matter (which is heavy, opaque, and mortal), see Frithjof Schuon, *Light on the Ancient Worlds* (World Wisdom Books, Bloomington, Indiana, 1984), ch. 2, 'In the Wake of the Fall', and *Dimensions of Islam* (Fernhill House, New York, 1970), chap. 2, 'The Five Divine Presences'.

nature of a limitation and fragmentation of the original animic form.

Indo-Tibetan cosmology describes this descent—which is also a fall—in the case of human beings under the form of the mythological combat of the *devas* and *asûras:* the *devas* having created man with a body that was fluid, protean, and diaphanous—in other words, in a subtle form—the *asûras* try to destroy it by a progressive petrification; it becomes opaque, gets fixed, and its skeleton, affected by the petrification, is immobilized. Thereupon the *devas*, turning evil into good, create joints, after having fractured the bones, and they also open the pathways of the senses, by piercing the skull, which threatens to imprison the seat of the mind. In this way the process of solidification stops before it reaches its extreme limit, and certain organs in man, such as the eye, still retain something of the nature of the non-corporeal states.[29]

In this story, the pictorial description of the subtle world must not be misunderstood. However, it is certain that the process of materialization, from the supra-sensory to the sensory, had to be reflected within the material or corporeal state itself, so that one can say without risk of error, that the first generations of a new species did not leave a mark in the great book of earthly layers; it is therefore vain to seek in sensible matter the ancestors of a species, and especially that of man.

Since the transformist theory is not founded on any real proof, its corollary and conclusion, namely the theory of the infra-human origin of man, remains suspended in the void. The facts adduced in favour of this thesis are restricted to a few groups of skeletons of disparate chronology: it happens that some skeletal types deemed to be more 'evolved', such as 'Steinheim man', precede others, of a seemingly more primitive character, such as 'Neanderthal man', even though the latter was doubtless not so apelike as tendentious reconstructions would have us believe.[30]

If, instead of always putting the questions: at what point does humankind begin, and what is the degree of evolution of such and

[29] See Krasinsky, *Tibetische Medizin-Philosophie.*

[30] In general, this domain of science has been almost smothered by tendentious theories, hoaxes, and imprudently popularized discoveries. See Dewar, *The Transformist Illusion.*

such a type regarded as being pre-human, we were to ask ourselves: how far does the monkey go, things might well appear in a very different light, for a fragment from a skeleton, even one related to that of man, is hardly enough to establish the presence of that which constitutes man, namely reason, whereas it is possible to conceive of a great variety of anthropoid apes whose anatomies are more or less close to that of man.

However paradoxical this may seem, the anatomical resemblance between man and the anthropoid apes is explainable precisely by the difference—not gradual, but essential—that separates man from all other animals. Since the anthropoid form is able to exist without that 'central' element that characterizes man—this 'central' element manifesting itself anatomically by his vertical position, amongst other things—the anthropoid form must exist; in other words, there cannot but be found, at the purely animal level, a form that realizes in its own way—that is to say, according to the laws of its own level—the very plan of the human anatomy; the ape is a prefiguration of man, not in the sense of an evolutive phase, but by virtue of the law that decrees that at every level of existence analogous possibilities will be found.

A further question arises in the case of the fossils attributed to primitive men: did some of these skeletons belong to men we can look upon as being ancestors of men presently alive, or do they bear witness to a few groups that survived the cataclysm at the end of a terrestrial age, only to disappear in their turn before the beginning of our present humanity? Instead of primitive men, it might well be a case of degenerate men, who may or may not have existed alongside our real ancestors. We know that the folklore of most peoples speaks of giants or dwarfs who lived long ago, in remote countries; now, among these skeletons, several cases of gigantism are to be found.[31]

Finally, let it be recalled once more that the bodies of the most ancient men did not necessarily leave solid traces, either because their bodies were not yet at that point materialized or 'solidified', or because the spiritual state of these men, along with the cosmic conditions of their time, rendered possible a resorption of the physical body into the subtle 'body' at the moment of death.[32]

[31] Like the Meganthrope of Java and the *Gigantopithecus* of China.
[32] In some very exceptional cases—such as Enoch, Elijah, and the Virgin Mary—such a resorption took place even in the present terrestrial age.

We must now say a few words about a thesis, much in vogue today, which claims to be something like a spiritual integration of paleontology, but which in reality is nothing but a purely mental sublimation of the crudest materialism, with all the prejudices this includes, from belief in the indefinite progress of humanity to a levelling and totalitarian collectivism, without forgetting the cult of the machine that is at the centre of all this; it will be apparent that we are here referring to Teilhardian evolutionism.[33] According to Teilhard de Chardin, who is not given to worrying over the gaps inherent in the evolutionist system and largely relies on the climate created by the premature popularization of the transformist thesis, man himself represents only an intermediate state in an evolution that starts with unicellular organisms and ends in a sort of global cosmic entity, united to God. The craze for trying to bring everything back to a single unequivocal and uninterrupted genetic line here exceeds the material plane and launches out wildly into an irresponsible and avid 'mentalization' characterized by an abstraction clothed in artificial images which their author ends up by taking literally, as if he were dealing with concrete realities. We have already mentioned the imaginary genealogical tree of species, whose supposed unity is no more than a snare, being composed of the hypothetical conjunction of many disjointed elements. Teilhard amplifies this notion to his heart's content, in a manner that is purely graphic, by completing its branches—or 'scales', as he likes to call them—and by constructing a pinnacle in the direction of which humankind is supposed to be situated. By a similar sliding of thought from the abstract to the

[33] Teilhard's materialism is revealed in all its crudity, and all its perversity, when this philosopher advocates the use of surgical means to accelerate 'collective cerebralization' *Man's Place in Nature*, (Harper & Row, New York, 1966). Let us also quote the further highly revealing words of the same author: 'It is finally on the dazzling notion of Progress and on faith in Progress that today's divided humanity can be reformed . . . Act I is over! We have access to the heart of the atom! Now come the next steps, such as the vitalization of matter by the building of supermolecules, the modelling of the human organism by hormones, the control of heredity and of the sexes by the play of genes and chromosomes, the readjustment and liberation by direct action of the springs laid bare by psychoanalysis, the awakening and taking hold of the still dormant intellectual and emotional forces in the human mass!' (*Planète* III, 1944), p. 30. Quite naturally, Teilhard proposes the fashioning of mankind by a universal scientific government—in short, all that is needed for the reign of the Antichrist.

concrete, from the metaphorical to the supposedly real, he aggluti-
nates, in one and the same pseudo-scientific outburst, the most
diverse realities, such as mechanical laws, vital forces, psychic
elements, and spiritual entities. Let us quote a characteristic passage:

> What explains the biological revolution caused by the appearance
> of Man, is an explosion of consciousness; and what, in its turn,
> explains this explosion of consciousness, is simply the passage of
> a privileged radius of 'corpusculization', in other words, of a
> zoological phylum, across the surface, hitherto impermeable,
> separating the zone of direct Psychism from that of reflective
> Psychism. Having reached, following this particular radius, a
> critical point of arrangement (or, as we say here, of enrolment),
> Life became hypercentred on itself, to the point of becoming
> capable of foresight and invention . . .[34]

Thus, 'corpusculization' (which is a physical process) would have as
its effect that a 'zoological phylum' (which is no more than a figure)
should pass across the surface (purely hypothetical) separating two
psychic zones . . . But we must not be surprised at the absence of
*distinguos* in Teilhard's thinking since, according to his own theory,
the mind is but a metamorphosis of matter!

Without stopping to discuss the strange theology of this author, for
whom God himself evolves along with matter, and without daring to
define what he thinks of the prophets and sages of antiquity and other
'underdeveloped' beings of this kind, we will say the following: if
man, in respect of both his physical nature and his spiritual nature,
were really nothing but a phase of an evolution going from the
amoeba to the superman, how could he know objectively where he
stands in all this? Let us suppose that this alleged evolution forms a
curve, or a spiral. The man who is but a fragment thereof—and let it
not be forgotten that a 'fragment' of a movement is no more than a
phase of that movement—can that man step out of it and say to
himself: I am a fragment of a spiral which is developing in such and
such a way? Now it is certain—and moreover Teilhard de Chardin
himself recognizes this—that man is able to judge of his own state.
Indeed he knows his own rank amongst the other earthly creatures,

[34] *Man's Place in Nature*, pp. 62–63.

and he is even the only one to know objectively both himself and the world. Far from being a mere phase in an indefinite evolution, man essentially represents a central possibility, and one that is thus unique, irreplaceable, and definitive. If the human species had to evolve towards another more perfect and more 'spiritual' form, man would not already now be the 'point of intersection' of the Divine Spirit with the earthly plane; he would neither be capable of salvation, nor able intellectually to surmount the flux of becoming. To express these thoughts according to the perspective of the Gospels: would God have become man if the form of man were not virtually 'god on earth', in other words, qualitatively central as well as definitive with regard to his own cosmic level?

As a symptom of our time, Teilhardism is comparable to one of those cracks that are due to the very solidification of the mental carapace,[35] and that do not open upward, toward the heaven of real and transcendent unity, but downward toward the realm of lower psychism. Weary of its own discontinuous vision of the world, the materialist mind lets itself slide toward a false continuity or unity, toward a pseudo-spiritual intoxication, of which this falsified and materialized faith—or this sublimated materialism—that we have just described marks a phase of particular significance.

## (V) MODERN PSYCHOLOGY

'The object of psychology is the psychic; unfortunately it is also its subject.' Thus wrote a famous psychologist of our time.[36] According to this opinion, every psychological judgement inevitably participates in the essentially subjective, not to say passionate and tendentious, nature of its object; for, according to this logic, no one understands the soul except by means of his own soul, and the latter, for the psychologist, is, precisely, purely psychic, and nothing else. Thus no psychologist, whatever be his claim to objectivity, escapes this dilemma, and the more categorical and general his affirmations in

[35] Guénon, *The Reign of Quantity and the Signs of the Times*, Chap. 15 'The Illusion of "Ordinary Life"'.

[36] C. G. Jung, *Psychology and Religion* (New Haven, Yale, 1938) p. 62

this realm are, the more they are suspect; such is the verdict that modern psychology pronounces in its own cause, when it is being sincere towards itself. But whether it be sincere or not, the relativism expressed in the words just quoted is always inherent in it. This relativism is also a kind of Prometheanism that would make of the psychic element the ultimate reality of man. It is the root of the numerous divergences within this discipline, and it dominates it to the point of contaminating everything that it touches: history, philosophy, art, and religion; all of them become psychological at its touch, and thereby also subjective, and thus devoid of objective and immutable certainties.[37]

But all *a priori* relativism is inconsequential towards itself. Despite the admitted precariousness of its point of view, modern psychology behaves like every other science: it passes judgements and believes in their validity, and in this connection it leans unwittingly, and without admitting it, on an innate certainty: indeed, if we can observe that the psychic is 'subjective', in the sense of being dominated by a certain egocentric bias that imposes on it certain limits, or by a particular 'colouring', this is because there is something in us which is not subject to these limits and tendencies, but which transcends them and in principle dominates them. This something is the intellect, and it is the intellect that normally provides us with the criteria which alone can shed light on the fluctuating and uncertain world of the *psyché;* this is obvious, but it nevertheless remains totally outside modern scientific and philosophical thinking.

It is important above all not to confuse intellect and reason: the latter is indeed the mental reflection of the transcendent intellect, but

---

[37] 'I can find no reason to be surprised at seeing psychology exchange visits with philosophy, for is not the act of thinking, the foundation of all philosophy, a psychic activity which, as such, directly concerns psychology? Must not psychology embrace the soul in its total extension, which includes philosophy, theology, and countless other things? In the face of all the richly diversified religions, there rise up, as the supreme instance perhaps of truth or error, the immutable data of the human soul.' (C. C. Jung, *L'Homme à la Découverte de son Ame* [Paris, 1962], p. 238) This amounts to replacing truth by psychology; it is totally forgotten that there are no 'immutable data' outside of that which is immutable by its own nature, namely, the intellect. In any case, if the 'act of thinking' is no more than a 'psychic activity', by what right does psychology set itself up as the 'supreme instance', since it too is but one 'psychic activity' amongst others?

in practice it is only what one makes of it, by which we mean that, in the case of the modern sciences, its functioning is limited by the empirical method itself; at the level of the latter, reason is not so much a source of truth as a principle of coherence. For modern psychology it is even less than that, for if scientific rationalism lends a relatively stable framework to one's observation of the physical world, it reveals itself as entirely insufficient when it comes to describing the world of the soul; for surface psychic movements, those whose causes and aims are situated on the plane of current experience, can hardly be translated into rational terms. The whole chaos of lower—and mostly unconscious—psychic possibilities escapes both rationality and what transcends rationality, and this means that both the major part of the psychic world and the metaphysical realm will appear 'irrational' according to this way of thinking. Hence a certain tendency, inherent in modern psychology, to relativize reason itself, a tendency that is self-contradictory, since psychology cannot dispense with rational methods. Psychology finds itself confronted with a domain which on all sides overflows the horizon of a science founded on empiricism and Cartesianism.

For this reason, the majority of modern psychologists ensconce themselves in a sort of pragmatism; it is in 'committed' experience, together with a coldly clinical attitude, that they see some guarantee of 'objectivity'. In point of fact, the movements of the soul cannot be studied from the outside, as in the case of corporeal phenomena; to know what they mean, they have in a sense to be lived, and this involves the subject of the observer, as was justly pointed out by the psychologist at the outset. As for the mental faculty that 'controls' the experiment, what is this but a more or less arbitrary 'common sense', one inevitably coloured by preconceived ideas? Thus the would-be objectivity of the psychic attitude changes nothing in regard to the uncertain nature of the experiment, and so, in the absence of a principle that is both inward and immutable, one returns to the dilemma of the psychic striving to grasp the psychic.

The soul, like every other domain of reality, can only be truly known by what transcends it. Moreover, this is spontaneously and implicitly admitted in people's recognition of the moral principle of justice, which demands that men should overcome their individual subjectivity. Now we could not overcome it, if the intelligence, which guides our will, were itself nothing but a psychic reality; and intelligence would not transcend the *psyché* if, in its essence, it did not transcend the plane of phenomena, both inward and outward. This observation suffices to prove the necessity and the existence of a psychology deriving in a sense from above and not claiming *a priori* an empirical character. But although this order of things is inscribed in our very nature, it will never be recognized by modern psychology; despite its own reactions against the rationalism of yesterday, it is no closer to metaphysics than any other empirical science—indeed quite the contrary, since its perspective, which assimilates the suprarational to the irrational, predisposes it to the worst of errors.

What modern psychology lacks entirely is criteria enabling it to situate the aspects or tendencies of the soul in their cosmic context. In traditional psychology, these criteria are provided according to two principal 'dimensions': on the one hand, according to a cosmology that 'situates' the soul and its modalities in the hierarchy of states of existence, and, on the other hand, according to a morality directed toward a spiritual end. The latter may provisionally espouse the individual horizon; it nonetheless keeps in view the universal principles attaching the soul to an order more vast than itself. Cosmology in a sense circumscribes the soul; spiritual morality sounds its depths. For just as a current of water reveals its force and direction only when it breaks against an object that resists it, so the soul can show its tendencies and fluctuations only in relation to an immutable principle; whoever wishes to know the nature of the *psyché* must resist it, and one truly resists it only when one places oneself at a point which corresponds, if not effectively then at least virtually or symbolically, to the Divine Self, or to the intellect which is like a ray that emanates from the latter.

Thus traditional psychology possesses both an impersonal and 'static' dimension (namely, cosmology), and a personal and 'operative' dimension (namely, morality or the science of the virtues), and it is necessarily so, because genuine knowledge of the soul results from knowledge of oneself. He who, by the eye of his essence, is able to 'objectivize' his own psychic form, by that very fact knows all the possibilities of the psychic or subtle world; and this intellectual 'vision' is both the outcome and, if need be, the guarantor of every sacred science of the soul.

For the majority of modern psychologists, traditional morality—which they readily confuse with a purely social or conventional morality—is nothing but a kind of psychic dam, useful on occasion but more often a hindrance or even harmful for the 'normal' development of the individual. This opinion is propagated especially by Freudian psychoanalysis, which became widely applied in some countries, where it has practically usurped the function that elsewhere belongs to the sacrament of confession: the psychiatrist replaces the priest, and the bursting of complexes that had previously been repressed takes the place of absolution. In ritual confession the priest is but the impersonal representative—necessarily discreet—of the Truth that judges and pardons; the penitent, by admitting his sins, in a sense 'objectivizes' the psychic tendencies that these sins manifest. By repenting, he detaches himself from them, and by receiving sacramental absolution, his soul is virtually reintegrated in its primitive equilibrium and centred on its divine essence. In the case of Freudian psychoanalysis,[38] on the other hand, man lays bare his psychic entrails, not before God, but to his fellow. He does not distance himself from the chaotic and obscure depths of his soul, which the analyst unveils or stirs up, but on the contrary, he accepts them as his own, for he must say to himself: 'This is what I am like in reality.' And if he does not overcome, with the help of some salutary instinct, this kind of disillusionment from below, he will retain from it something like an intimate sullying; in most cases it will be his self-abandonment to collective mediocrity that for him will play the part of absolution, for it is easier to endure one's own degradation when it is shared with others. Whatever may be the occasional or partial usefulness of such an analysis in certain cases, the state described above is its more usual result, its premises being what they are.[39]

If the medicine of the traditional civilizations knows nothing

[38] The use of the adjective is to make it clear that it is indeed the method of Freud that we are discussing here, for in our own day some forms of psychoanalysis are more neutral and less pernicious, a fact which, from our point of view, is in no wise a justification.

[39] René Guénon has observed that the principle whereby every psychoanalyst requires to be psychoanalyzed himself before being empowered to analyze others, raises the troublesome question as to who occupied the first place in the queue.

analogous to modern psychotherapy, this is because the psychic cannot be treated by the psychic. The *psyché* is the realm of indefinite actions and reactions. By its own specific nature, it is essentially unstable and deceptive, so that it can be cured only by resorting to something situated 'outside' or 'above' it. In some cases one will act favourably upon it by re-establishing the humoral balance of the body, commonly upset by psychic affections;[40] in other cases it is only by the use of spiritual means, such as exorcism,[41] prayer, or a sojourn in holy places, that the soul can be restored to health.

Everyone is aware of the fact that modern psychology tries to explain psychologically the spiritual means just mentioned. In its eyes, the effect of a rite is one thing, and its theological or mystical interpretation is another. The effect of a rite, arbitrarily limited to the psychic and subjective domain alone, is attributed to psychic dispositions of ancestral origin, which the form of the rite is supposed to actualize. There is no hint of the timeless and superhuman meaning inherent in the rite or symbol—as if the soul could cure itself through believing in the illusory projection of its own preoccupations, whether individual or collective. There is nothing, however, in this supposition that would trouble modern psychology, since it is ready to go much further than this, when it asserts, for example, that the fundamental forms of thought, the laws of logic, merely represent a residue of ancestral habits.[42] This path is one that leads to the outright denial of intelligence and to its replacement by biological fatalities, if indeed psychology can go that far without encompassing its own ruin.

In order to be able to 'situate' the soul in relation to other cosmic realities or realms, one must refer to the cosmological scheme that represents the degrees of existence in the form of concentric circles

[40] Usually a vicious circle ensues, with the psychic imbalance engendering a physical intoxication, which in its turn causes the psychic imbalance to worsen.

[41] Cases of diabolical possession, such as manifestly call for the application of the rites of exorcism, seem to have become rarer nowadays, doubtless because demonic influences are no longer 'compressed' by the dam of tradition, but are able to spread more or less everywhere in forms that are in a fashion 'diluted'.

[42] They will say, for example, that logic is merely an expression of the physiological structure of our brain, and forget that, were it so, this statement would also be an expression of this same physiological fatality.

or spheres. This scheme, which makes symbolical use of the geocentric conception of the visible universe, symbolically identifies the corporeal world with our terrestrial surroundings; around this centre extends the sphere—or spheres—of the subtle or psychic world, surrounded in turn by the sphere of the world of pure Spirit. This representation is naturally limited by its own spatial character, but it nevertheless expresses very well the relationship that exists between these various states. Each of the spheres, considered in itself, presents itself as a complete and perfectly homogeneous whole, whereas from the 'point of view' of the sphere immediately above, it is but a content thereof. Thus the corporeal world, envisaged at its own level, does not know the subtle world, just as the latter does not know the supra-formal world, precisely because it encloses only that which has a form. Furthermore, each of these worlds is known and dominated by that which exceeds and surrounds it. It is from the immutable and formless background of the Spirit that the subtle realities become detached as forms, and it is the soul which, through its sensory faculties, knows the corporeal.

This double relationship of things, which *a priori* is hidden from our individual vision, can be grasped in all its reality when one considers the very nature of sensible perception. On the one hand, this truly reaches the corporeal world, and no philosophical artifice will be able to convince us of the contrary; on the other hand, there is no doubt that all we perceive of the world are but those 'images' of it that our mental faculty is able to keep hold of, and in this respect the whole fabric of impressions, memories, and anticipations—in short, everything that for us constitutes the sensible continuity and logical coherence of the world—is of a psychic or subtle nature. It is in vain that one will try to know what the world is 'outside' this subtle continuity, since this 'outside' does not exist: surrounded as it is by the subtle state, the corporeal world is but a content thereof, even though it appears, in the mirror of this state itself, as a materially autonomous order.[43]

It is obviously not the individual soul, but the entire subtle state that contains the physical world. The logical coherence of the latter

---

[43] Nothing is more absurd than attempts to explain the perception of the material world in material terms.

presupposes the unity of the former, and this is manifested indirectly by the fact that the multiple individual visions of the sensible world, fragmentary though they be, substantially coincide and are integrated in one continuous whole. The individual soul participates in this unity both by the structure of its cognitive faculties, which is in conformity with the cosmic order, and also by its nature as subject, containing the physical world in its own way; in other words, the physical world is a 'world' only in relation to the individual subject, by virtue of the cleaving of consciousness into object and subject, a cleaving that results precisely from the 'egoic' polarization of the soul. By this same polarization, the soul is distinguished from the totality of the subtle state—the 'total' or 'universal soul' of Plotinus—without, however, being separated from it substantially. For if it were separated from it, our vision of the world would not be adequate to reality; but in fact it is so, in spite of the limitations and the relativity of all perception.

It is true that we ordinarily perceive only a fragment of the subtle world—the fragment that we 'are', and that constitutes our 'myself'—whereas the sensible world reveals itself to us in its macrocosmic continuity, as a whole that seems to include us. This is because the subtle world is the very field of individuation; in reality, we are plunged in the ocean of the subtle world as fishes are in water, and like them, we do not see that which constitutes our own element.

As for the opposition between the 'inward' psychic world and the 'outward' corporeal world, this is actualized only in relation to, and in function of, the latter. In itself, the subtle world is neither 'inward' nor 'outward'; it is at most 'non-outward', whereas the corporeal world is outward as such, which furthermore proves that it does not enjoy an autonomous existence.

The corporeal state and the psychic state together constitute formal existence; in its total extension, the subtle state is none other than formal existence, but one calls it 'subtle' inasmuch as it escapes the laws of corporeity. According to one of the most ancient and most natural symbolisms, the subtle state may be compared to the atmosphere surrounding the earth which pervades all porous bodies and is the vehicle of life.

A phenomenon can only be truly understood through its relations, both 'horizontal' and 'vertical', with total Reality. This truth applies particularly, and in a certain sense practically, to psychic phenomena. The same psychic 'event' can simultaneously be the response to a sensory impulsion, the manifestation of a wish, the consequence of a previous action, the trace of the typical and ancestral form of the individual, the expression of his genius, and the reflection of a supra-individual reality. It is legitimate to consider the psychic phenomenon in question under one or other of these aspects, but it would be unwarranted to seek to explain the movements and purposes of the soul by one—or even by several—of these aspects exclusively. In this connection let us quote the words of a therapist who is aware of the limitations of contemporary psychology:

There is an ancient Hindu maxim whose truth is incontestable: 'What a man thinks, that he becomes'. If one steadfastly thinks of good deeds, one will end by becoming a good man; if one always thinks of weakness, one will become weak; if one thinks of how to develop one's strength (bodily or mental), one will become strong. Similarly, if for years one is engaged almost daily in stirring up Hades,[44] in explaining systematically the higher in terms of the lower, and at the same time ignoring everything in man's cultural history which, despite lamentable errors and misdeeds, has been regarded as worthwhile, one can scarcely avoid the risk of losing all discernment, of levelling down the imagination (a source of our life), and of severely reducing one's mental horizon.'[45]

Ordinary consciousness illuminates only a restricted portion of the individual soul, and the latter represents only a tiny part of the psychic world. Nevertheless, the soul is not cut off from the rest of this world; its situation is not that of a body rigorously limited by its own extension and separated from other bodies. What distinguishes the soul from the rest of the vast subtle world is uniquely its own particular tendencies, which define it—if one may employ a simpli-

---

[44] An allusion to the words of Virgil *Flectere si nequeo superos, Acheronta movebo* ('If I cannot bend the Heavens, I shall stir up hell'), which Freud quoted at the beginning of his *Interpretation of Dreams*.

[45] Hans Jacob, *Western Psychology and Hindu Sâdhana* (London, Allen & Unwin, 1961). The author of this work is a former disciple of Jung, who later discovered the doctrine and method—immeasurably greater—of the Hindu *sâdhana*, which enabled him to subject Western psychology to a just criticism.

fied image—as a spatial direction defines the ray of light that follows it. By these very tendencies, the soul is in communion with all the cosmic possibilities of analogous tendencies or qualities; it assimilates them and is assimilated by them. For this reason, the science of cosmic tendencies—the *gunas* of Hindu cosmology—is fundamental for the knowledge of the soul. In this connection, it is not the outward context of a psychic phenomenon—the accidental occasion for its manifestation—that matters essentially, but its connection with *sattva, rajas,* or *tamas*—the 'upward', 'expansive', and 'downward' tendencies—which confers on it its rank in the hierarchy of inward values.

Since the motives of the soul are perceptible only through the forms that manifest them, it is on these forms or manifestations that a psychological assessment must needs be founded. Now, the part played by the *gunas* in any form whatsoever can be measured only in a purely qualitative manner, by means of precise and decisive—but in no wise quantitative—criteria, such as are entirely lacking in the wholly profane psychology of our time.

There are some psychic 'events' whose repercussions traverse all the degrees of the subtle world 'vertically', since they touch on the essences; others—these are ordinary psychic movements—only obey the 'horizontal' coming and going of the *psyché;* and finally, there are those that come from the subhuman depths. The first mentioned are not capable of being expressed entirely—they comprise an element of mystery—and yet the forms which they may from time to time evoke in the imagination are clear and precise, like those that characterize authentic sacred arts. The last mentioned, namely demonic 'inspirations', are unintelligible in their very forms; they 'ape' the genuinely mysterious by the nebulous, obscure, and equivocal character of their formal manifestations; examples of this are readily to be found in contemporary art.

When studying the formal manifestation of the soul, one must, however, not forget that man's psycho-physical organism can display strange caesuras or discontinuities. Thus, for instance, in the case of the somewhat 'anarchical' category of contemplatives known as 'fools of God', the spiritual states do not manifest themselves harmoniously and normally and do not make use of the reason; inversely, an intrinsically pathological state—and as such dominated by infra-human and chaotic tendencies—may incidentally and by accident comprise openings onto supra-terrestrial realities; this is but saying that the human soul is of an inexhaustible complexity.

Viewed as a whole, the subtle world is incomparably vaster and more varied than the corporeal world. Dante expresses this by making the entire hierarchy of planetary spheres correspond to the subtle world, whereas he makes only the terrestrial domain correspond to the corporeal world. The subterranean position of the hells, in his system, merely indicates that the states in question are situated below the normal human state; in reality, they are also part of the subtle state, and this is why some medieval cosmologists place the hells symbolically between heaven and earth.[46]

Experience of the subtle world is subjective—except in the case of certain sciences quite unknown to the moderns—because consciousness, in identifying itself with subtle forms, is affected by their tendencies, just as a ray of light is turned from its course by the form of a wave that it happens to traverse. The subtle world is made up of forms; in other words, it comprises diversity and contrast; but these forms do not possess, in themselves or outside of their projection in the sensible imagination,[47]spatial and defined contours as in the case of corporeal forms. They are entirely active or, to be more exact, dynamic, pure activity belonging only to the essential 'forms' or archetypes that are to be found in the pure Spirit. Now the ego or individual soul is itself one of the forms of the subtle world, and the consciousness that espouses this form is necessarily dynamic and exclusive; it realizes other subtle forms only insofar as these become modalities of its own egoic form.

Thus it is that in the dream state individual consciousness, even though reabsorbed into the subtle world, nonetheless remains turned back on itself; all the forms that it experiences in this state present themselves as simple prolongations of the individual subject, or at least they appear so in retrospect and inasmuch as they verge on the

---

[46] In Islam, it is said that the throne of the devil is located between earth and heaven, a doctrine which also makes clear the temptations to which those who follow the 'vertical' path are exposed.

[47] If some masters have compared the subtle world to the imagination, it is the imaginative activity, and not the images produced by the imagination, that they had in view.

waking state. For in itself, and despite this subjectivism, the consciousness of the dreamer is obviously not impermeable to influences coming from the most diverse 'regions' of the subtle world, as is proved, for example, by premonitory or telepathic dreams, which many people have experienced.[48] Indeed, while the imagery of a dream is woven from the very 'substance' of the subject—a 'substance' that is none other than the progressive actualization of his own psychic form—it nonetheless manifests, incidentally and to different degrees, realities of a cosmic order.

The content of a dream can be considered in many different ways. If one analyzes the *materia* of which it is composed one will find that it is constituted by all sorts of memories, and in this respect the current psychological explanation, which makes the dream the expression of subconscious residues, is largely right. It is not, however, excluded that a dream may also comprise 'matters' that in no wise proceed from the personal experience of the dreamer and that are like traces of a psychic transfusion from one individual to another. There is also the economy of the dream, and in this connection we can quote the following description by C. G. Jung, which is exact despite the radically false theses of the author:

> The dream, deriving from the activity of the unconscious, gives a representation of the contents that slumber there; not of all the contents that figure in it, but only of certain of them which, by way of association, are actualized, crystallized, and selected, in correlation with the momentary state of consciousness.[49]

As for the hermeneutics of dreams, this eludes modern psychology in spite of the latter's efforts in this direction, because one cannot validly interpret images reflected by the soul without knowing to which level of reality they refer.

The images one retains on waking from a dream generally represent only a shadow of the psychic forms experienced in the dream state itself. On passing into the waking state, a sort of decantation occurs—one can be aware of this—and something of the reality inherent in the dream evaporates more or less rapidly. There

[48] Empirical psychology no longer dares to deny this phenomenon.
[49] *L'Homme à la Découverte de son Ame*, p. 205.

exists, nevertheless, a certain category of dreams, well-known to traditional oneirocrisy, the memory of which persists with an incisive clarity, and this can happen even if the profound content of these dreams appears to conceal itself. Such dreams, which mostly occur at dawn and continue until waking, are accompanied by an irrefutable feeling of objectivity; otherwise put, they comprise a more than merely mental certainty. But what characterizes them above all, and independently of their moral influence on the dreamer, is the high quality of their forms, disengaged from every turbid or chaotic residue. These are the dreams that come from the Angel; in other words, from the Essence that connects the soul to the supra-formal states of the being.

Since there are dreams of divine or angelic inspiration, their opposite must also exist, and these are dreams of satanic impulsion, containing palpable caricatures of sacred forms. The sensation accompanying them is not one of cool and serene lucidity, but of obsession and vertigo; it is the attraction of an abyss. The infernal influences sometimes ride the wave of a natural passion, which opens the way for them, so to speak. They are, however, distinguishable from the elementary character of passion by their prideful and negative tendency, accompanied either by bitterness or else by sadness. As Pascal said: 'He who tries to play the angel will play the beast', and indeed nothing is so apt to provoke caricatures, both in dreams and out of them, as the unconsciously pretentious attitude of the man who mixes God with his own highly particularized ego—the classical cause of many of the psychoses studied by post-Freudian psychologism.[50]

It was starting from the analysis of dreams that C. G. Jung developed his famous theory about the 'collective unconscious'. His observation of the fact that a certain category of dream images could not be explained simply on the basis of their being residues of individual experiences led Jung to distinguish, within the unconscious domain whence dreams are fed, between a 'personal' zone whose contents represent basically the other face of individual psychic life, and a 'collective' zone made up of latent psychic

---

[50] In a general way, contemporary psychology delves into the observation of pathological cases, and views the soul only through this clinical perspective.

dispositions of an impersonal character, such as never offer themselves to direct observation, but manifest themselves indirectly
through 'symbolic' dreams and 'irrational' impulsions. At first sight,
this theory has nothing extravagant about it, except its use of the term
'irrational' in connection with symbolism. It is easy to understand
that the individual consciousness centred on the empirical ego leaves
on the margin or even outside itself everything which, in the psychic
order, is not effectively attached to that centre, just as a light
projected in a given direction decreases towards the surrounding
darkness. But this is not how Jung understands the matter. For him,
the non-personal zone of the soul is unconscious as such; in other
words, its contents can never become the direct object of the
intelligence, whatever be its modality or however great its extension.

> Just as the human body displays a common anatomy, independen-
> tly of racial differences, so also the psyché possesses, beyond all
> cultural and mental differences, a common *substratum*, which I
> have named the collective unconscious. This unconscious psyché,
> which is common to all men, is not made up of contents capable of
> becoming conscious, but solely of latent dispositions giving rise to
> certain reactions that are always identical.[51]

And the author goes on to insinuate that it is here a question of
ancestral structures that have their origin in the physical order:

> The fact that this collective unconscious exists is simply the
> psychic expression of the identity of cerebral structures beyond all
> racial differences . . . the different lines of psychic evolution start
> out from one and the same trunk, whose roots plunge through all
> the ages. It is here that the psychic parallel with the animal is
> situated.[52]

One notices the plainly Darwinian turn of this thesis, the disastrous
consequences of which show themselves in the following passage: 'It
is this that explains the analogy, indeed the identity, of mythological
motives and of symbols as means of human communication in
general.'[53] Myths and symbols would thus be the expression of an

---

[51] C. G. Jung, *The Secret of the Golden Flower* (New York, 1931), Introduction
[52] *Ibid.*        [53] *Ibid.*

ancestral psychic fund that brings man near to the animal! They have no intellectual or spiritual foundation, since

> from the purely psychological point of view, it is a question of common instincts of imagining and acting. All conscious imagination and action have evolved on the basis of these unconscious prototypes and remain permanently attached to them, and this is especially so when consciousness has not yet attained a very high degree of lucidity, in other words, as long as it is still, in all its functions, more dependent on instinct than on conscious will, or more affective than rational . . .'[54]

This quotation clearly indicates that, for Jung, the 'collective unconscious' is situated 'below', at the level of physiological instincts. It is important to bear this in mind, since the term 'collective unconscious' in itself could carry a wider and in a fashion more spiritual meaning, as certain assimilations made by Jung seem to suggest, especially his use—or rather his usurpation—of the term 'archetype' to signify the latent, and as such inaccesible, contents of the 'collective unconscious'. For though the archetypes do not belong to the psychic realm, but to the world of pure Spirit, they are nevertheless reflected at the psychic level—as virtualities of images in the first place—before becoming crystallized, according to the circumstances, in images properly so-called, so that a certain psychological application of the term 'archetype' could at a pinch be justified. But Jung defines the 'archetype' as an 'innate complex'[55] and describes its action on the soul thus: 'Possession by an archetype makes of a man a purely collective personage, a kind of mask, under which human nature can no longer develop, but degenerates progressively.'[56] As if an archetype, which is an immediate and supra-formal determination of Being—and non-limitative by this very fact—could in some way cast a spell on and vampirize the soul! What is really in question in the more or less pathological case envisaged by Jung? Simply a dissociation of the possibilities inherent in the subtle form of a man, a form that includes multiple aspects,

[54] *Ibid.*    [55] See *L'Homme à la Découverte de son Ame*, p. 311.
[56] See *Two Essays on Analytical Psychology* (Pantheon, New York, 1966), p. 234.

each of which has something unique and irreplaceable about it. In every non-degenerate human individual there is to be found in potency a man and a woman, a father and a mother, a child and an old man, as well as various qualities or 'dignities' inseparable from the original and ontological position of man, such as priestly and royal qualities, those of a creative craftsman, of a servant, and so forth. Normally all these possibilities complete one another; here there is no irrational fund of the soul, for the coexistence of these diverse possibilities or aspects of the human form is perfectly intelligible in itself and can be hidden only from the eyes of a mentality or civilization that has become one-sided and false. Any genius-like development of one of these multiple possibilities or dispositions inherent in the human soul requires, moreover, the integration of the complementary possibilities; the true man of genius is a balanced being, for where there is no balance there is no greatness either. The opposite of such a development is a barren and pathological exaggeration of one of the soul's possibilities at the expense of the others, leading to that kind of moral caricature compared by Jung to a mask; and let it be added that it is the carnivalesque mask one must think of here, and not the sacred mask which, for its part, does indeed express a true archetype and therefore a possibility that does not bewitch the soul but on the contrary liberates it.[57]

Psychic dissociation always produces a fixation as well as a tearing apart between opposing poles, and this is rendered possible only by the clouding over of that which, in the soul, corresponds to the archetype. At the antipodes of this imbalance productive of hypertrophies, perfect virility, for example, in no wise excludes femininity, but on the contrary includes and adapts it, and the inverse is also true. Similarly, the genuine archetypes, which are not situated at the psychic level, do not mutually exclude but comprise and imply one another. According to the Platonic and hallowed meaning of the term, the archetypes are the source of being and knowledge and not, as Jung conceives them, unconscious dispositions to act and imagine. The fact that the archetypes cannot be grasped by discursive thought has no connection with the irrational and obscure character of the supposed 'collective unconscious', whose contents are said to be

[57] See the chapter 'The Sacred Mask' in the present book.

known only indirectly through their 'eruptions' on the surface. There is not only discursive thought, there is also intellectual intuition, and this attains to the archetypes from the starting-point of their symbols.

No doubt the theory according to which ancestral structures constitute the 'collective unconscious' imposes itself on modern thought all the more easily in that it seems to be in agreement with the evolutionist explanation of the instinct of animals. According to this view, instinct is the expression of the heredity of a species, of an accumulation of analogous experiences down the ages. This is how they explain, for example, the fact that a flock of sheep hastily gathers together around the lambs the moment it perceives the shadow of a bird of prey, or that a kitten while playing already employs all the tricks of a hunter, or that birds know how to build their nests. In fact, it is enough to watch animals to see that their instinct has nothing of an automatism about it. The formation of such a mechanism by a purely cumulative—and consequently vague and problematical—process is highly improbable, to say the least. Instinct is a non-reflective modality of the intelligence; it is determined, not by a series of automatic reflexes, but by the 'form'—the qualitative determination—of the species. This form is like a filter through which the universal intelligence is manifested. Nor must it be forgotten that the subtle form of a being is incomparably more complex than its bodily form. The same is also true for man: his intelligence too is determined by the subtle form of his species. This form, however, includes the reflective faculty, which allows of a singularization of the individual such as does not exist among the animals. Man alone is able to objectivize himself. He can say: 'I am this or that.' He alone possesses this two-edged faculty. Man, by virtue of his own central position in the cosmos, is able to transcend his specific norm; he can also betray it, and sink lower; *corruptio optimi pessima*. A normal animal remains true to the form and genius of its species; if its intelligence is not reflective and objectifying, but in some sort existential, it is nonetheless spontaneous; it is assuredly a form of the universal intelligence even if it is not recognized as such by men who, from prejudice or ignorance, identify intelligence with discursive thought exclusively.

As for Jung's thesis that certain dreams, which cannot be explained by personal reminiscences and which seem to arise from an unconscious fund common to all men, contain motives and forms that are also to be found in myths and in traditional symbolism, the thing is possible in principle; not that there is in the soul a repertory of types inherited from distant ancestors and bearing witness to a primitive vision of the world, but because true symbols are always 'actual' inasmuch as they express non-temporal realities. In fact, under certain conditions, the soul is able to take on the function of a mirror that reflects, in a purely passive and imaginative manner, universal truths contained in the intellect. Nevertheless, 'inspirations' of this nature remain fairly rare; they depend on circumstances that are, so to speak, providential, as in the case of dreams communicating truths or announcing future events, to which allusion has previously been made. Moreover, symbolic dreams are not clothed in just any traditional 'style'; their formal language is normally determined by the tradition or religion to which the individual is effectively or virtually attached, for there is nothing arbitrary in this domain.

Now, if one examines examples of supposedly symbolical dreams quoted by Jung and other psychologists of his school, one notices that in most cases it is a matter of false symbolism, of the kind commonly met with in pseudo-spiritual circles. The soul is not only a sacred mirror; more often it is a magic mirror that deceives the one who views himself in it. Jung should have known this, since he himself speaks of the tricks of the *anima*, indicating by this term the feminine aspect of the soul; and some of his own experiences, as described in his memoirs,[58] should have told him that an investigator of the unconscious depths of the *psyché* exposes himself, not merely to the wiles of the egocentric soul, but also to psychic influences coming from elsewhere, from unknown beings and entities, especially when the methods of analysis used derive from hypnosis or mediumship. In this context must be placed certain designs executed by sick patients of Jung and which the latter tries to palm off as genuine *mandalas*.[59]

---

[58] The kind of introspection practised by Jung by way of psychological investigation and of which he speaks in his memoirs, as well as certain parapsychological phenomena that he provoked by this method, takes one into a frankly spiritualistic ambience. The fact that the author proposed to study these phenomena 'scientifically' changes nothing in regard to the influence they in fact had on his theory of 'archetypes'.

[59] See the Introduction to *The Secret of the Golden Flower*.

Over and above all this, there exists a symbolism, very general in nature and inherent in language itself, as for instance when one compares truth to light and error to darkness, or progress to an ascent or moral danger to an abyss, or when one represents fidelity by a dog or craftiness by a fox. Now, to explain the occurrence of a similar symbolism in dreams, of which the language is naturally figurative and not discursive, there is no need to refer to a 'collective unconscious'; it is enough to note that rational thought is not the whole of thought and that consciousness in the waking state does not cover the whole domain of mental activity. If the figurative language of dreams is not discursive, this does not necessarily make it irrational, and it is possible, as indeed Jung has properly observed, that a dreamer may be more intelligent in his dreams than in the waking state. It would even seem that this difference of level between the two states is fairly frequent among men of our own time, doubtless because the frameworks imposed by modern life are particularly unintelligent and incapable of vehicling in any normal manner the essential contents of human life.

This has obviously nothing to do with the role of purely symbolic or sacred dreams, whether these be spontaneous or evoked through rites; we are thinking here of the example of the Indians of North America, whose whole tradition, as well as their vital ambience, favours a kind of oneiric prophetism.

So as to neglect no aspect of this question, the following should also be said: In every collectivity that has become unfaithful to its own traditional form, to the sacred framework of its life, there occurs a collapse or a sort of mummification of the symbols it had received, and this process will be reflected in the psychic life of every individual belonging to that collectivity and participating in that infidelity. To every truth there corresponds a formal trace, and every spiritual form projects a psychic shadow; when these shadows are all that remains, they do in fact take on the character of ancestral phantoms that haunt the subconscious. The most pernicious of psychological errors is to reduce the meaning of symbolism to such phantoms.

As for the definition of 'unconscious', it must never be forgotten that this is eminently relative and provisional. Consciousness is capable of gradation like light and is similarly refracted in contact with the media it meets. The ego is the form of individual consciousness, not its luminous source. The latter coincides with the source of the intelligence itself. In its universal nature, consciousness is in a sense an existential aspect of the intellect, and this amounts to saying that basically nothing is situated outside it.[60] Whence it follows that the 'unconscious' of the psychologists is quite simply everything which, in the soul, lies outside ordinary consciousness—that of the empirical 'I' oriented towards the corporeal world—in other words, this 'unconscious' is made to include both lower chaos and the higher states. The latter (which the Hindus compare to the bliss of deep sleep, the state of *prajna*) radiate from the luminous source of the Universal Spirit; the definition of the 'unconscious' thus in no wise corresponds to a particular concrete modality of the soul. Many of the errors of 'depth psychology', of which Jung is one of the chief protagonists, result from the fact that it operates with the 'unconscious' as if it were a definite entity. One often hears it said that Jung's psychology has 're-established the autonomous reality of the soul'. In truth, according to the perspective inherent in this psychology, the soul is neither independent of the body nor immortal; it is merely a sort of irrational fatality situated outside any intelligible cosmic order. If the moral and mental behaviour of man were determined behind the scenes by some collection of ancestral 'types' issuing from a fund that is completely unconscious and completely inaccessible to the intelligence, man would be as if suspended between two irreconcilable and divergent realities, namely that of things and that of the soul.

For all modern psychology, the luminous point of the soul, or its existential summit, is the consciousness of the 'I', which only exists to the extent that it can disengage itself from the darkness of the 'unconscious'. Now, according to Jung, this darkness contains the vital roots of the individuality: the 'collective unconscious' would then be endowed with a regulatory instinct, a kind of somnambulant wisdom, no doubt of a biological nature; from this fact, the conscious emancipation of the ego would comprise the danger of a vital uprooting. According to Jung, the ideal is a balance between the two poles—the conscious and the unconscious—a balance that can be

---

[60] Let us here recall the Vedantic ternary *Sat-chit-ananda* (Being, Consciousness, Bliss).

realized only by the help of a third term, a sort of centre of crystallization, which he calls the 'self', a term borrowed from the doctrines of Hinduism. Here is what he has written on the subject:

> With the sensation of the self as an irrational and indefinable entity, to which the 'I' is neither opposed nor subordinated, but to which it adheres and round which it moves in some sort, like the earth around the sun, the aim of individuation is attained. I use this term 'sensation' to express the empirical character of the relationship between the 'I' and the self. In this relationship there is nothing intelligible, for one can say nothing about the contents of the self. The 'I' is the only content of the self that we know. The individualized 'I' feels itself to be the object of a subject unknown and superior to itself. It seems to me that psychological observation here touches its extreme limit, for the idea of a self is in itself a transcendent postulate, which one can admittedly justify psychologically, but cannot prove scientifically. The step beyond science is an absolute requirement for the psychological evolution described here, for without the postulate in question I could not sufficiently formulate the psychic processes observed from experience. Because of this, the idea of a self at least possesses the value of a hypothesis like the theories about the structure of the atom. And if it be true that here too we are prisoners of an image, it is in any case a very living image, the interpretation of which exceeds my capacities. I scarcely doubt that it is a question of an image, but it is an image that contains us.[61]

Despite a terminology too much bound up with current scientism, one might be tempted to grant full credit to the presentiments expressed in this passage and to find in it an approach to traditional metaphysical doctrines, if Jung, in a further passage, did not relativize the notion of the self by treating it this time, not as a transcendent principle, but as the outcome of a psychological process:

> One could define the self as a sort of compensation in reference to the contrast between inward and outward. Such a definition could well be applied to the self in so far as the latter possesses the

[61] See *Two Essays on Analytical Psychology*, p. 240.

character of a result, of an aim to reach, of a thing that has only been produced little by little and of which the experience has cost much travail. Thus, the self is also the aim of life, for it is the most complete expression of that combination of destiny we call an 'individual', and not only of man in the singular but also of a whole group, where the one is the complement of the others with a view to a perfect image.[62]

There are some realms where dilettantism is unforgivable.

It is the balance to be realized between the unconscious and the conscious, or the integration, in the empirical 'personality', of certain forces or impulsions emanating from the unconscious, that Jung paradoxically labels as 'individuation', using a term by which was traditionally designated, not some psychological process or other, but the differentiation of individuals from the starting point of the species. But what Jung understands by this term is a kind of definitive pronunciation of the individuality which is taken as an end in itself. In such a perspective, the notion of 'self' plainly loses all metaphysical meaning, but this is not the only traditional notion that Jung appropriates in order to debase it to a purely psychological and even clinical level; thus he compares psycho-analysis, which he uses precisely to promote this 'individuation', to an initiation in the proper and sacred meaning of the term, and he even declares that psycho-analysis represents 'the only form of initiation still valid in the modern age!'[63] Whence proceed a whole series of false assimilations, and intrusions into a realm where psychology is devoid of competence.[64]

---

[62] *Ibid.*     [63] See psychological commentary of the *Tibetan Book of the Dead.*

[64] Jung's psychological interpretation of alchemy has been expressly refuted in my book *Alchemy: Science of the Cosmos, Science of the Soul* (Element Books Shaftesbury, England, 1986. Frithjof Schuon, after reading the present chapter, sent me the following reflections in writing: 'People generally see in Jungism, as compared with Freudism, a step towards reconciliation with the traditional spiritualities, but this is in no wise the case. From this point of view, the only difference is that, whereas Freud boasted of being an irreconcilable enemy of religion, Jung sympathizes with it while emptying it of its contents, which he replaces by collective psychism, that is to say by something infra-intellectual and therefore anti-spiritual. In this there is an immense danger for the ancient spiritualities, whose representatives, especially in the East, are

Here it is not a case of the involuntary ignorance of some isolated seeker, for Jung carefully avoided all contact with the representatives of living tradition. During his visit to India, for example, he did not wish to see Sri Râmana Mahârishi—alleging a motive of insolent frivolity[65]—doubtless because he feared instinctively and 'unconsciously' (it is a case for saying it) a contact with a reality that would give the lie to his theories. For him, metaphysics was but a speculation in the void or, to be more exact, an illusory attempt by the psychic to reach beyond itself, comparable to the senseless gesture of a man who would pull himself out of a mudhole by his own hair. This conception is typical of modern psychologism, and this is why we mention it. To the absurd argument that metaphysics is only a production of the *psyché* one can immediately object that this judgement itself is but a similar production. Man lives by truth; to accept any truth, however relative it may be, is to accept that *intellectus adequatio rei*. Merely to say 'this is that' is automatically to affirm the very principle of adequation, and therefore the presence of the absolute in the relative.

Jung breached certain strictly materialistic frameworks of modern science, but this fact is of no use to anyone, to say the least—one wishes one could have rejoiced over it—because the influences that filter through this breach come from lower psychism and not from the Spirit, which alone is true and alone can save us.

too often lacking in critical sense with regard to the modern spirit, and this by reason of a complex of "rehabilitation"; also it is not with much surprise, though with grave disquiet, that one has come across echoes of this kind from Japan, where the psychoanalyst's "equilibrium" has been compared to the *satori* of Zen; and there is little doubt that it would be easy to meet with similar confusions in India and elsewhere. Be that as it may, the confusions in question are greatly favoured by the almost universal refusal of people to see the devil and to call him by his name, in other words, by a kind of tacit convention compounded of optimism to order, tolerance that in reality hates truth, and compulsory alignment with scientism and official taste, without forgetting "culture", which swallows everything and commits one to nothing, except complicity in its neutralism; to which must be added a no less universal and quasi-official contempt for whatever is, we will not say intellectualist, but truly intellectual, and therefore tainted, in people's minds, with dogmatism, scholasticism, fanaticism, and prejudice. All this goes hand in hand with the psychologism of our time and is in large measure its result.'

[65] See the preface to Heinrich Zimmer's book on Shri Râmana Mahârshi.

# 3
# 'Riding the Tiger'

IN HIS BOOK entitled *Calvacare la Tigre*,[1] Julius Evola seeks to show how the 'naturally traditional' man, the man who is aware of an inner reality transcending the plane of individual experiences, may not only survive in the anti-traditional ambience of the modern world, but may even use it for his own spiritual ends, according to the well-known Chinese metaphor of the man riding a tiger: if he does not let himself be unseated, he will end by gaining the advantage over it.

The tiger, in the sense envisaged by Evola, is the dissolving and destructive force that comes into play towards the end of every cosmic cycle. In the face of this, the author says, it would be vain to maintain the forms and structure of a civilization that is already played out; the only thing to be done is to carry the negation beyond its dead point, so that, by a conscious transposition, it may end up, not in nothingness, but in a 'new empty space, which may perhaps be the premiss of a new formative activity'.

The world that is to be negated because it is doomed to destruction, is above all the 'materialistic and bourgeois civilization' which in itself already represents the negation of an earlier and superior world. On this point, we are in agreement with the author, but we note immediately that he does not distinguish between the forms pertaining to this 'bourgeois' civilization and the sacred heritage which survives within it and despite it. Likewise, he seems to include in the fate of this civilization everything that remains of the Oriental civilizations, and here too he makes no distinction between their social structures and their spiritual kernel. We shall return to this later.

Let us first refer to another aspect of this book, with which we can agree almost without reservation. This is the author's critique, often masterly, of the various currents of modern thought. Evola does not

[1]Milan, Scheiwiller, 1961.

place himself on the ground of philosophical discussion, for the modern philosophy in question is no longer a 'science of the true'—it does not even claim to be so. He considers it as a symptom, as the mental reflection of a vital and existential situation, essentially dominated by despair: since the dimension of transcendence has been denied, there can henceforth only be impasses; there is no longer any exit from the vicious circle of the mental element left to its own devices; all that remains is a description of one's own defeat. As starting-point of this analysis, the author chooses the 'philosophy' of Nietzsche, in which he detects a presentiment of transcendent realities and as it were an attempt to go beyond the purely mental order, an attempt foredoomed to failure by the absence of a spiritual doctrine and discipline.

With the same acuity, the author analyzes the foundations of modern science. From this chapter, we will quote the following passage, which replies pertinently to the pseudo-spiritual illusions of certain scientific circles:

From this latter point of view, the most recent science offers no advantage over the materialistic science of yesterday. With the help of atoms and the mechanical conception of the universe, one could still imagine something (albeit in a very crude way); the entities of the latest physico-mathematical science, on the contrary, are absolutely unimaginable; they amount to nothing more than the holes in a network constructed and perfected not in order to know in the concrete, intuitive, and living sense of the term—in other words, according to the only mode that has any value for a still undegenerate humanity—but solely in order to exert a control, ever greater but always exterior, over nature which, in its essence, remains closed to man and more mysterious than ever. For its mysteries have in fact merely been 'covered over'; our gaze has been diverted from them by the spectacular achievements of technology and industry onto a plane where it is no longer a question of knowing the world, but only of transforming it for the ends of a humanity that has become exclusively worldly . . .

Let us repeat that it is a hoax to speak of the spiritual value of recent science because in it one now speaks of energy instead of matter, because it peers inside the mass of coagulated irradiations,

or because it envisages a space of more than three dimensions . . .
These are notions which, when they have been substituted for
those of earlier physics, can in no wise alter the experience which
the man of today can have of the world . . . When people say that
there is no matter, only energy, that we do not live in a Euclidean
space of three dimensions, but in a 'curved' space of four or more
dimensions, and so on, things remain as they were before, my real
experience changes in nothing, the ultimate meaning of what I
see—light, sun, fire, sea, sky, plants that flower and beings that
die—the ultimate meaning of every process and phenomenon has
in no way become more transparent for me. There is no
justification for speaking of a knowledge that goes beyond
appearances, or that knows in depth, in the spiritual and truly
intellectual meaning of the term . . . .

No less pertinent are the author's remarks on the social structures
and the arts of the contemporary world. We must nevertheless
express a reservation regarding the thesis of the 'enslavement of the
negative force', as he applies it to certain aspects of modern life. Let
us quote a typical passage:

The positive possibilities (of the reign of the machine) can only
concern a tiny minority, namely those beings in whom the
dimension of transcendence pre-exists or in whom it can be
awakened . . . They alone can give a completely different value to
the 'soulless world' of machines, technologies, modern cities, in
short, of everything that is pure reality and objectivity, which
appears cold, inhuman, menacing, devoid of intimacy, depersona-
lizing, 'barbarous'. It is precisely by entirely accepting this reality
and these processes that the differentiated man will be able to
realize his essence and form himself according to a valid personal
equation . . .

In this connection the machine itself and everything, in certain
sectors of modern life, that has been formed in terms of pure
functionality (especially architecture) can become symbol. As
symbol, the machine represents a form born of an exact and
objective adequation of means to an end, excluding everything
that is superfluous, arbitrary, dispersive, and subjective; it is a
form that realizes with precision an idea (that of the end to which it

is destined). On its level, it thus reflects in a certain way the value which, in the classical world, pure geometric form (the number as essence) possessed, just like the Doric principle of nothing too much . . .

Here the author forgets that the symbol is not a form that is 'objectively' adequate to just any kind of end, but a form that is adequate to a spiritual end or to an intellectual essence; if there is a coincidence, in some traditional arts, between conformity to a practical end and conformity to a spiritual end, this is because the first does not contradict the second, something that cannot be said of the machine, which is inconceivable outside the context of a desacralized world. In fact, the form of the machine expresses exactly what it is, namely a sort of challenge offered to the cosmic and divine order; it may well be composed of 'objective' geometric elements such as circles and squares, but in its relationship—or rather non-relationship—with the cosmic ambience, it translates, not a 'Platonic idea', but a 'mental coagulation', or indeed an agitation or a trick. There are certainly some border-line cases, like that of a machine that is still close to a tool, or like that of a modern ship whose shape espouses to a certain degree the movements of water and wind, but this is no more than a fragmentary conformity and does not contradict what we have just said. As for 'functional' architecture, including modern urbanism, it can only be called 'objective' if one accepts that its purpose is objective, which is obviously not the case: all architecture is co-ordinated to a certain conception of life and of man; now Evola himself condemns the social programme underlying modern architecture. In reality, the apparent 'objectivity' of modern architecture is merely a mysticism in reverse, a congealed sentimentality disguised as objectivity; moreover one has seen often enough just how quickly this attitude is converted, in its protagonists, into the most changeable and arbitrary of subjectivisms.

It is true that there is no form that is totally cut off from its eternal archetype; but this entirely general law cannot be invoked here, for the following reason: for a form to be a symbol, it is necessary that it be situated in a certain hierarchical order in relation to man. In order to be as precise as possible, let us distinguish three aspects of the symbolism inherent in things: the first is simply the very existence of the form concerned, and in this sense, each thing manifests its celestial origin; the second aspect is the meaning of a form, its intellectual interpretation, either within a given system or in itself, by virtue of its more or less essential or prototypical nature; the third aspect is the spiritual efficacy of the symbol, which presupposes, in the man who uses it, both a psychic and a ritual conformity to a given tradition.

We have emphasized this point, because Julius Evola fails to recognize the crucial importance of a traditional attachment, while admitting the possibility of a spontaneous or irregular spiritual development, guided by a sort of inborn instinct that may be actualized by accepting the crisis of the present world as a liberating *catharsis*. For Evola, this is almost the only perspective remaining open for the 'differentiated man' of our time, for adherence to a religion, in Evola's view, amounts to integration in a more or less decadent collective milieu, and the possibility of a regular initiation is dismissed.

We conclude that in our day this possibility must be practically excluded, as a result of the almost complete non-existence of the respective organizations. If organizations of this kind have always had a more or less underground character in the West—because of the nature of the religion which succeeded in gaining dominance there and its repressive and persecuting activities—they have completely disappeared in latter times. As regards other parts of the globe, especially the Orient, these organizations have become more and more rare and inaccessible, even if the forces of which they were the vehicles had not withdrawn from them, in parallel with the general process of degeneration and modernization, which has finished by invading even these regions. In our day, even the Orient is no longer capable of supplying anything but offshoots or a 'régime of residues'; one is already forced to admit this when one considers the spiritual level of those Asiatics who have begun to export Eastern wisdom and to divulge it amongst us.

The last argument is absolutely inconclusive: if the Asiatics in question were true representatives of Eastern traditions, would they divulge them? But, even if Evola were right in his judgement of the traditional organizations as human groups, his way of seeing things nonetheless involves a serious error, for as long as a tradition preserves its essential forms intact, it continues to be the guarantor of a spiritual influence—or of a divine grace—whose action, if not always apparent, immeasurably transcends anything that is in the the power of man. We know full well that there exist methods or ways, such as *Zen*, which are founded on the 'power of one's self' and which thereby distinguish themselves from other ways founded on the 'power of the other', that is to say making an appeal to Grace; but neither the ones nor the others are situated outside the formal framework of a given tradition. For example *Zen*, which perhaps offers us the most striking example of a non-formal spirituality, is completely, and even especially, aware of the value of sacred forms. One transcends forms, not by rejecting them in advance, but by integrating them in their supra-formal essences.

Moreover, Evola himself defines the mediating function of form when he speaks of the role of the spiritual 'type', which he opposes to the individual or the 'personality' in the profane and modern sense of the term: 'The type (*la tipicità*) represents the point of contact between the individual and the supra-individual, the demarcation line between the two corresponding to a perfect form. The type de-individualizes, in the sense that the person then essentially incarnates an idea, a law, a function . . .' The author says rightly that the spiritual type is normally situated within the framework of a tradition, but apparently this does not lead him to believe in the 'typical'—or supra-individual—nature of all sacred forms, doubtless because he does not take into account what the monotheistic religions call revelation. Now it is illogical to accept the 'transcendent dimension' of the being—in other words the effective participation of the human intellect in the Universal Intellect—without also accepting revelation, that is to say the manifestation of this Intellect or Spirit in objective forms. There is a rigorous relationship between the supra-formal, free, and undetermined nature of the Spirit and its spontaneous—and thus 'Heaven-inspired'—expression, in forms necessarily determined and immutable. In their origin, which is unlimited and inexhaustible, the sacred forms (although limited and 'arrested') are the vehicles of spiritual influences, and thus of virtualities of the infinite, and in this regard it is completely improper to speak of a tradition of which only the form remains—the spirit having withdrawn from it like the soul from a dead body: the death of a tradition always starts with the corruption of its essential forms.

According to all the prophecies, the sacred deposit of the integral Tradition will remain until the end of the cycle; this means that there will always be somewhere an open door. For men capable of transcending outward shells, and animated by a sincere will, neither the decadence of the surrounding world, nor belonging to a given people or milieu, constitute absolute obstacles.

*Quaerite et invenietis.*

Let us return for a moment to the title of Evola's book: the adage that one must 'ride the tiger' if one does not want to be torn to pieces by it, obviously contains a tantric meaning. The tiger is then the image of the passional force which one must tame. One may well wonder whether this metaphor really corresponds to the spiritual man's attitude regarding the destructive tendencies of the modern world: let us note first of all that not just anything is a 'tiger'; behind the tendencies and forms that Julius Evola envisages, we shall find no natural and organic force, no *shakti* dispensing power and beauty; now, the spiritual man can use *rajas*, but he must reject *tamas;* finally, there are forms and attitudes that are incompatible with the intimate nature of the spiritual man and with the rhythms of every form of spirituality. In reality, it is not the particular, artificial, and hybrid characteristics of the modern world that can serve as spiritual supports, but that which, within this world, is of all time.

# II
# CHRISTIAN THEMES

# 4

# The Seven Liberal Arts
# and the West Door
# of Chartres Cathedral

CCORDING to the Medieval theologians the Virgin Mary, by
virtue of the innate perfection of her soul, possessed all the
wisdom of which man is capable. A direct reference to this
wisdom is to be found in the allegories of the seven liberal
arts which, just outside an inner circle of adoring angels, decorate the
tympanum of the Door of the Virgin.[1] In the Medieval context the
seven sciences—which were classified as the *trivium* of grammar,
logic and rhetoric and the *quadrivium* of arithmetic, music, geometry
and astronomy—were not exclusively empirical sciences, as are those
we know today. They were the expression of so many faculties of the
soul, faculties demanding harmonious development. This is why
they were also called arts.

Following ancient tradition, Dante, in his 'Convivio', compares
the seven liberal arts to the seven planets, grammar corresponding to
the Moon, logic to Mercury, rhetoric to Venus, arithmetic to the Sun,
music to Mars, geometry to Jupiter, and astronomy to Saturn. The
creators of the Royal Door of Chartres were certainly aware of this
correspondence. It is thus doubly significant that on the tympanum of
the left of the three doors the signs of the zodiac are portrayed. These
belong to the unchanging heaven of fixed stars and thus represent the
kingdom of the Divine Spirit, to Whom this door, with its representation of the ascension of Christ, is dedicated. The seven planets, on
the other hand, govern, according to the ancient viewpoint, the world
of the soul. And Mary is the human soul in all its perfection.

[1] The Door of the Virgin is the right-hand of the three constituent doors of the
Royal Door of the West Façade. On the tympanum of the central door is a portrayal of
Christ in Majesty.

By means of the signs of the zodiac—not all of which, incidentally, appear on the same door, *Pisces* and *Gemini* having had to be transposed, for want of room, to the Door of the Virgin—the arches surrounding the representation of Christ's ascension (on the left-hand door) can be seen to represent the firmament. Beside each of the twelve signs of the zodiac the corresponding month is represented pictorially in the form of its natural activity.

These natural activities—one for each month—are the terrestrial reflections of the twelve signs of the zodiac. From them one learns to what extent the course of human existence depends upon the heavens: in seedtime and harvest, in work and leisure; for the heavens, in their cycle, bring heat after cold, dry after wet, and thus keep life in being.

This is significant for medieval art: in the two tympanums and in the arches surrounding them, the whole cosmos is represented, in its three great divisions: spiritual, psychic, and corporeal. Medieval man always kept the profound order of things in mind.

The order in which the seven liberal arts are listed, when properly understood, testifies to a Pythagorean view of things, and this was not without influence on medieval art. The division of these sciences—and all their elements—into *trivium* and *quadrivium* came into Christian culture from Greek antiquity in a late and simplified form. The medieval spirit, however, was able to reanimate the integral vision originally inherent in it.

'Philosophy has two main instruments,' writes Thierry of Chartres, 'namely intellect *(intellectus)* and its expression. Intellect is illumined by the *quadrivium* (arithmetic, music, geometry and astronomy). Its expression is the concern of the *trivium* (grammar, logic and rhetoric).'

In fact the *trivium* was a schooling both in language and in thought. It is language which makes man man; and this is why grammar comes at the beginning. Not without humour, the sculptor of the Door of the Virgin has portrayed this art as a woman threatening with a rod two young children who are writing. The figures of the famous grammarians Donat and Priscian stand beside her. Dialectic, whose feminine representation in Chartres carries a scorpion and has Aristotle as a companion, is none other than logic. Rhetoric is the art of speaking, or rather, speaking in so far as it is an art; Cicero accompanies its allegorical figure.

The four members of the *quadrivium* are likewise represented in a feminine form in Chartres. They are: arithmetic with a reckoning board, music with a glockenspiel, geometry with a drawing-board, and astronomy, contemplating the heavens and accompanied by Boethius, Pythagoras, Euclid and Ptolemy. These four arts or sciences refer to the four conditions of corporeal existence: number, time, space and motion. Music, of course, is not only concerned with time, but also with sound; but it is in the realm of sound that time manifests itself most immediately and characteristically; otherwise we can only grasp it in movement, in which it is united with space.

'Everything proceeding from the profound nature of things,' writes Boethius, the great transmitter of the *quadrivium*, 'shows the influence of the law of number; for this is the highest prototype contained in the mind of the Founder. From this are derived the four elements, the succession of the seasons, the movements of the stars, and the course of the heavens.'

It is a qualitative, and not a quantitative, conception of number that lies at the basis of medieval arithmetic. It is thus less a method of reckoning than a way of understanding the nature of number, its properties, and the uniqueness of numerical series obtained by certain constant relationships.

That each individual number does not merely represent a sum of elements, but in itself is an expression of an essential unity, appears most clearly when one transposes each number into its corresponding geometrical form: three into an equilateral triangle, four into a square, five into a regular pentagon, etc. In each of these figures, innumerable relationships appear, which multifariously throw light on the inner law proper to the figure in question.

The connection between arithmetic, geometry and music can be seen in that the relationship of musical notes to one another is made visible in the mutual relationship of the variously long strings which produce them. This can easily be demonstrated on a monochord, which has a single string and a movable bridge.

Following Greek tradition, Boethius distinguishes three kinds of proportions: the arithmetic, in which the same interval obtains between all members of the series, as, for example: 1, 2, 3, 4, 5,

## THE SEVEN LIBERAL ARTS

| | | | |
|---|---|---|---|
| *Trivium*<br>'the expression<br>of intellect' | Grammar<br>*language* | — | Moon |
| | Logic<br>*logic* | — | Mercury |
| | Rhetoric<br>*speech as an art* | — | Venus |
| *Quadrivium*<br>'intellect' | Arithmetic<br>*number* | — | Sun |
| | Music<br>*time (harmony)* | — | Mars |
| | Geometry<br>*space (proportion)* | — | Jupiter |
| | Astronomy<br>*motion (rhythm)* | — | Saturn |

6 . . . ; the geometric, which progresses by means of a constant multiplication (a:c = c:b); and the harmonic, which unites the preceding two, according to the formula a:c = a−b:b−c. This is the most perfect proportion: in music it is made manifest as harmony, and in geometry as the 'golden section'.

The regular relationship of different movements to one another is rhythm. The day, the year, the cycle of the moon—these are the great rhythms which measure all change, and in this regard astronomy, the last member of the *quadrivium*, is the science of cosmic rhythms.

Number, proportion, harmony and rhythm are clear manifestations of unity in diversity and also clear indications of how to find the way back from diversity to unity. According to Boethius, the essence of things is intimately connected with unity: the more unity a thing possesses in itself, the more profoundly it participates in being.

In medieval science, it is less a question of knowing many things, than of having a 'whole' view of existence. Its method was anything but designed for the investigation of the material world and the furthering of technology. On the contrary: it possessed the means to open the spiritual eye to the beauty of mathematical proportions, and the spiritual ear to the music of the spheres.

# 5

# Because Dante is Right

THE INCOMPARABLE greatness of the *Divine Comedy* shows itself not least in the fact that, in spite of the exceptionally wide range and variety of its influence—it even shaped the language of a nation—it has been but seldom understood in the fullness of its meaning. Already in Dante's own lifetime those who ventured out upon the ocean of the spirit in the wake of his ship (*Paradiso,* II, 1 ff) were to remain a relatively small company. They more or less disappeared with the Renaissance; the individualistic mode of thought of this period, tossed to and fro between passion and calculating reason, was already far removed from Dante's inward-looking spirit. Even Michelangelo, though he revered his fellow-Florentine to the highest degree, could no longer understand him.[1] At the time of the Renaissance, however, people did at least still debate as to whether Dante had actually seen Heaven and hell or not. At a later date concern with the *Divine Comedy* dropped to the level of a purely scientific interest that busied itself with historical connections, or of an aesthetic appreciation that no longer bothered about the spiritual sense of the work at all. Admittedly, it was known that the verses of the *Divine Comedy* contained more than just the superficial meaning of the narrative; Dante himself pointed this out in several places in his work and also in his *Convivio* (II, 1), where he talks about the multiple meanings of holy scripture, and quite undisguisedly makes the same remarks apply to his own poem; the symbolical nature of the work therefore could not be overlooked. However, excuses were made for the poet, and his artistic mastery was even credited with enabling him to bridge

---

[1] How greatly Michelangelo revered Dante can be seen from certain of his own sonnets. That he was not really capable of understanding him is apparent from the titanism of his sculpture: if Michelangelo had known the law of symbolism according to which higher realities are reflected in lower ones, his creations, in all their corporeality, would not have attempted to take heaven by storm.

over poetically 'this scholastic sophistry' about multiple meanings. Thus people fundamentally misunderstood the source upon which the poet drew for his work of creation, since the multiplicity of meaning in it is not the result of a preconceived mental construction grafted onto the actual poem; it arises directly and spontaneously out of a supra-mental inspiration, which at one and the same time penetrates and shines through every level of the soul—the reason, as well as the imagination and the inward ear. It is not 'in spite of his philosophy' that Dante is a great poet; he is so thanks to his spiritual vision, and because through his art, however caught up in time it may be as regards its details, there shines forth a timeless truth, at once blissful and terrifying—in short, it is because Dante is right.

The most profound passages of the *Divine Comedy* are not simply those where a theological or philosophical explanation is placed in the mouth of one of the characters, nor those which possess an obviously allegorical nature; it is above all the most highly imaged and in a sense concrete expressions that are most highly charged with meaning.

How a spiritual truth, without the slightest degree of mental involvement, can congeal into an image, can be seen most easily in the metaphors that Dante uses in his description of hell, as, for example, the metaphor of the wood composed of dried-up, barren thorn bushes, in which the souls of those who took their own lives are shut up (*Inferno*, XIII): it depicts a situation devoid of all freedom and all pleasure, an existence bordering on the nothingness that corresponds to the inner contradiction implied by suicide, namely a will that denies the very existence that is its own basis and substance. As the ego itself cannot cast itself into nothingness, it falls as a consequence of its destructive act into the seeming nothingness that the desolate thorn bush represents, but even there it still remains 'I', riveted to itself more than ever in its impotent suffering.

Everything that Dante says about the infernal wood serves to emphasize this truth: how the tree from which he unsuspectingly breaks off a branch, cries out at the wound and scolds him mercilessly; how, pursued by dogs, the souls of the dissolute—they, too, despisers of their God-given existence—break through the thorn wood, making it bleed; and how the tree, bereft of its branches, implores the poet to gather the broken pieces together at the foot of the trunk, as if the powerless ego imprisoned within still felt itself united with these dead and severed fragments. Here, as in other places in the description of hell, everything in the representation possesses an uncanny sharpness, never in the slightest degree arbitrary.

Dante's images of hell are so veridical precisely because they are fashioned from the same 'stuff' as that out of which the passional human soul is made. In the description of the mount of Purgatory a different and less immediately graspable dimension is introduced: the soul's reality now opens out on a cosmic scale, embracing the starry heavens, day and night, and all the fragrance of things: at the sight of the earthly paradise on the summit of the mount of Purgatory Dante conjures up in a few verses the whole miracle of spring; the earthly spring turns directly into the spring of the soul, it becomes the symbol of the original and holy state of the human soul.

In representing the purely spiritual states belonging to the celestial spheres, Dante is often obliged to make use of circumlocutions, as for example when he explains how the human spirit, by penetrating more and more deeply into the Divine Wisdom, becomes gradually transformed into it: Dante looks at Beatrice, who herself keeps her eyes fixed on the 'eternal wheels', and as he becomes more deeply absorbed in his vision of her, he experiences something like what befell Glaucus, who was turned into one of the sea-gods through consuming a miraculous herb:

> Trasumanar significar per verba
> Non si porìa; però l'esempio basti
> A cui esperienza grazia serba.

*To pass beyond the human state is not to be described in words; wherefore let the example satisfy him for whom grace has reserved the experience.* (*Paradiso*, I, 70–1)

If in this way the language of the cantos of the *Paradiso* sometimes becomes more abstract, in their turn the images that Dante uses here are even richer in meaning: they possess an inscrutable magic, which shows that Dante has seen in spirit what he seeks to express in words, and that he is to an equal degree poet and spiritual visionary, as for example when he compares the uninterrupted ascension of blessed souls, moving in response to the power of the Divine attraction, to snowflakes that are floating upwards instead of downwards. (*Paradiso*, XXVII, 67–72).

The simpler an image, the less unrestricted its content; for it is the symbol's prerogative, thanks to its concrete and yet open character, to be capable of expressing truths that cannot be enclosed in rationalized concepts; which, however, in no way implies that symbols have an irrational and permanently 'unconscious' background. A symbol's meaning is completely knowable, even though it does transcend reason as such; it comes from the Spirit, and opens itself to the spirit or intellect, which Dante speaks of as the highest and innermost faculty of knowledge, a faculty that is fundamentally independent of any form, either sensory or mental, and is capable of penetrating to the imperishable essence of things:

> Nel ciel che più della sua luce prende,
> Fu' io; e vidi cose che ridire
> Nè sa nè può qual di lassù discende:
> Perchè, appressando sè al suo disire,
> Nostro intelletto si profonda tanto
> Che retro la memoria non può ire.

*In that heaven which most receiveth of His light, have I been; and have seen things which whoso descendeth from up there, hath neither faculty nor power to re-tell; because, as it draweth nigh to its desire, our intellect sinketh so deep, that memory cannot go back upon the track.* (*Paradiso*, I, 4–9)[2]

True symbolism lies in the things themselves, in their essential qualities, which belong more to being than to becoming. This explains how Dante, in his description of the hierarchical degrees of the spiritual world, was able to relate it to the structure of the visible universe, as it appears from the earthly standpoint. This cosmic comparison was just as convincing to the medieval reader as it is

---

[2] See Dante's own commentary on these verses in his letter to Can Grande della Scala: '*Intellectus humanus in hac vita propter connaturalitatem et affinitatem quam habet ad substantiam separatam, quando elevatur, in tantum elevatur, ut memoriam post reditum deficiat propter transcendisse humanum modum.*'

unconvincing to the reader of today. How is it possible, the latter asks, to base a genuine vision of the spiritual worlds on a scientifically incorrect view of things? In answer to this it must be said that every picture of the universe that man makes for himself can only possess a conditional and provisional accuracy; it always remains in one way or another attached to sensory experience and imagination, and hence will never be entirely free from 'naïve' prejudice; it is, however, scientific to the extent that it is able to provide logically satisfying answers to the questions that man has always asked. The Ptolemaic representation of the world, which Dante used as the scaffolding for his work, was in this sense completely scientific. But at the same time it was perceptible to the eye and not so remote from sensory experience as the modern, purely mathematical explanation of the universe, and it is precisely in this clarity—a clarity that still corresponds to 'naïve' perceptions—that its capacity to be a symbol resides. Because it comprehends the world order in relationship to man, it demonstrates the inner unity joining man to the universe and the universe to God:

> . . . Le cose tutte quante
> Hann' ordine tra loro: e questo è forma
> Che l'universo a Dio fa simigliante.

*. . . All things whatsoever observe a mutual order; and this is the form that maketh the universe like unto God. (Paradiso, I, 103)*

Dante interpreted the quantitative difference between the planetary heavens that surround one another concentrically, as a qualitative gradation in accordance with the basic notion that the higher is reflected in the lower:

> Li cerchi corporai sono ampii ed arti
> Secondo il più e il men della virtute
> Che si distende per tutte lor parti . . .
> Dunque costui che tutto quanto rape
> L'alto universo seco, corrisponde
> Al cerchio che più ama e che più sape.

*The corporeal circles are wider or narrower according to the greater or lesser amount of virtue that spreads through all their parts . . . Therefore the one* [the highest heaven], *that sweepeth with it all the rest of the universe, corresponds to the circle that most loveth and most knoweth.* (Paradiso, XXVIII, 64–66; 70–72)

The geocentric—and therefore homocentric—arrangement of the planetary spheres is seen as the inverse image of the theocentric hierarchy of the angels, while hell's pit, with its circles, is its negative reflection, to which the mount of Purgatory, thrown up in the centre of the earth through Lucifer's fall, provides the compensating counter-balance.[3]

Even more than by the 'antiquated' world-picture that forms the framework of the *Divine Comedy*, most present-day readers—and not only 'freethinkers' among them—find themselves repelled by Dante's sharp and apparently presumptuously drawn distinction between the damned, those undergoing purgation, and the blessed. To this one can reply that Dante, as a man living in the thirteenth century, could not have watered down psychologically the traditional teaching about salvation and damnation, nor could he have regarded the historical examples he mentions as anything but typical. But that is not the decisive factor: Dante is completely imbued with and overwhelmed by his perception of man's original dignity, measured against which the traces of hell in this world appear as they really are. He perceives the ray of Divine Light in man, and hence is bound also to recognize as such the darkness of soul that is refractory to that light.

For Dante, man's original dignity consists essentially in the gift of the 'Intellect', by which is meant not merely reason or the thinking faculty, but rather that ray of light that connects the reason and indeed the whole soul with the Divine source of all knowledge. This is why Dante says of the damned that they have lost the gift of the intellect (*Inferno*, III, 18), which is not to imply that they cannot think,

---

[3] The significance of Dante's cosmography is fully discussed in the earlier chapter 'Traditional Cosmology and Modern Science' and also in the author's book *Alchemy: Science of the Cosmos, Science of the Soul*, (Element Books, Shaftesbury, England, 1986).

since he allows of their arguing among themselves: what they lack, and what for them has been forever cast out, is the capacity to recognize God and to understand themselves and the world in relation to Him. This capacity has its seat, as it were, in the heart, in the being's centre, where love and knowledge coincide, for which reason Dante describes true love as a kind of knowledge[4], and the spirit or intellect as loving: both have fundamentally one goal, which is infinite.

In the true man, all other faculties of the soul are referred to the being's centre: 'I am like the centre of the circle upon which every part of the circumference depends equally', Dante makes Amor-Intellectus say in his *Vita Nuova*, 'but thou art not so'. (*Ego tanquam centrum circuli, cui simili modo se habent circumferentie partes, tu autem non sic.* XII, 4) To the extent that desire and will tend away from this centre, even so is the soul prevented from opening spiritually onto the Eternal: *L'affetto l'intelletto lega*—'passion fetters the spirit' (*Paradiso*, XIII, 20). When Dante says of the damned that they have lost the gift of the Intellect, this means that in their case the will has become completely alienated from the centre of their being. With them, the God-denying of the will has become the ruling impulse: they go to hell because basically hell is what they want: 'Those who die in the wrath of God cross over Acheron quickly, since Divine justice spurs them on, so that fear is turned into desire' (*Inferno*, III, 121–126). It is different for the souls who have to endure the punishments of Purgatory: their will has not repudiated the Divine in man, but has simply looked for it in the wrong place; in their longing for the Infinite, they have allowed themselves to be deceived: 'I clearly see', says Beatrice to Dante, in one place in the *Paradiso*, 'how in thy spirit already is reflected the Eternal Light, which, no sooner seen, ever enkindles love; and if aught else seduce thy love, it is naught but some vestige of that light, ill understood, that shineth through therein'. (V, 7–12) When at death the object of passion, and its illusion regarding the Divine good, fall away, these souls experience their passion as it really is, namely as a burning up of oneself on an appearance that only causes pain. By coming up against the limits of the enjoyment they

---

[4] See 'Intelletto d'Amore' by Pierre Ponsoye (*Etudes Traditionnelles*, Paris, May–June 1962).

sought, they learn to know, negatively and indirectly, what Divine Reality is, and this knowledge is their contrition. Thanks to this, their falsely-directed impulse is gradually exhausted; it continues to work within them—but now without the consent of their hearts—until the denial of their denial turns into the affirmation of the original, Godward-directed freedom:

> Della mondizia il sol voler far prova,
> Che, tutto libero a mutar convento,
> L'alma sorprende, ed il voler le giova.
> Prima vuol ben, ma non lascia il talento
> Che divina giustizia contra voglia
> Come fu al peccar, pone al tormento.

*The will alone proves the state of cleansing that has been reached; the will, now fully free, invades the soul, which now is capable of what she will. She wills well before, but that urge permits it not, which, just as it once inclined towards sin, is now directed by divine justice towards punishment, against her own will.* (Purgatorio, xxi, 61–66)

Here we are touching upon one of the main themes of the *Divine Comedy*, which we must investigate more closely, even if to do so should divert us somewhat from our opening subjects; it is the question of the reciprocal relationship between knowledge and will, on which Dante, throughout his work, throws light from all sides. Knowledge of the eternal truths is potentially present in the human spirit or intellect, but its unfolding is directly conditioned by the will, negatively when the soul falls into sin, and positively when this fall is overcome. The different punishments in Purgatory that Dante describes can be regarded, not only as posthumous states, but also as stages in ascesis, that lead to the integral and primordial condition, in which knowledge and will—or, more precisely, knowledge of man's eternal goal and his striving after pleasure—are no longer separated from one another. At the moment when Dante sets foot in the earthly paradise, at the summit of the mount of Purgatory, Virgil says to him:

> Non aspettar mio dir più nè mio cenno:
> Libero, dritto, sano è tuo arbitrio,

E fallo fora non fare a suo senno:
Perch'io te sopra te corono e mitrio.

*No longer expect my counsel nor my sign: for free, upright and whole is thy judgement, and it were a fault not to act according to its promptings; wherefore I crown and mitre thee over thyself.* (Purgatorio, XXVII, 139–142)

The earthly paradise is as it were the cosmic 'place' where the ray of the Divine Spirit, which pierces through all the Heavens, touches the human state, since from here on Dante is raised up to God by Beatrice. That this place should be the summit of a mountain overtopping the whole earthly region corresponds quite simply to the nature of the earthly paradise itself.

A question arises here: what is the meaning of the fact that Dante himself scales the mount of Purgatory without suffering a single one of the punishments through which others atone for their faults? Only at the last stage does he have to walk quickly through the fire so as to reach the earthly paradise (*Purgatorio*, XXVII, 10ff). Stage by stage the angels of the gates erase the marks of sin from his forehead: on reaching the summit, Virgil acknowledges his sanctity, and yet shortly thereafter Beatrice meets him with burning reproaches that move him to agonizing repentance (*Purgatorio*, XXX, 55ff). The meaning of all this can only be that the way taken by Dante, thanks to a special grace, is not a path of merit, but a path of knowledge. When Virgil says that for him there is no other way to Beatrice, to Divine Wisdom, except by passing directly through hell, this shows that knowledge of God is to be attained along the path of self-knowledge: self-knowledge implies taking the measure of the abysses contained in human nature and consciously shedding every self-deception that has its roots in the passional soul: there exists no greater self-denial than this, and hence also no greater atonement. Properly understood, what Beatrice reproaches Dante for is not some actual sin, but simply that he has lingered too long in contemplation of her reflected earthly radiance, instead of following her into the realm of the invisible. In repenting of this Dante throws off the last fetter binding him to this world. Much could be said here about the meaning of the two rivers of Paradise, Lethe and Eunoe, the first of which washes away the memory of sin, while the other restores the memory of good deeds; but we must return to our consideration of the will-knowledge theme.

Whereas, in those who sin, the will conditions the degree of their knowledge, in the elect the will flows from the knowledge of the divine order that they possess. This means that their will is the spontaneous expression of their vision of God, and for that reason the rank of their position in Heaven implies no constraint at all, as the soul of Piccarda Donati explains to the poet in the moon-heaven, in answer to his question whether the blessed in one sphere might not desire to occupy some higher sphere 'in order to behold more and be more deeply loved?'

> Frate, la nostra volontà quieta
> Virtù di carità che fa volerne
> Sol quel ch'avemo, e d'altro non ci asseta.
> Se disiassimo esser più superne,
> Foran discordi li nostri disiri
> Dal voler di Colui che qui ci cerne;
> Che vedrai non capere in questi giri
> S'essere in caritate è qui necesse.
> E la sua natura ben rimiri:
> Anzi è formale a questo beato esse
> Tenersi dentro alla divina voglia,
> Perch' una fansi nostre voglie stesse:
> Sì che come noi siam di soglia in soglia
> Per questo regno, a tutto il regno piace,
> Com' allo Re che in suo voler ne invoglia:
> In la sua volontade è nostra pace:
> Ella è quel mare al qual tutto si muove
> Ciò ch'ella cria o che natura face.

*Brother, the quality of love stilleth our will, and maketh us long only for what we have, and giveth us no other thirst. Did we desire to be more highly placed, our longings were discordant from His will who assigns us to this place. But that, as thou wilt see, cannot happen in these circles, since here of necessity love rules. And when thou dost rightly consider its nature, so wilt thou understand how it is of the essence of beatitude to exist in harmony with the divine will, so that our own wills themselves become one. Our being thus, from threshold to threshold throughout the realm, is joy to all the realm as to the king, who draweth our wills to what He willeth: in His will is our peace; It is that sea to which all moves that it createth and that nature maketh.* (*Paradiso*, III, 70–87)

Submission to the Divine will is not lack of freedom: on the contrary, the will that revolts against God falls under compulsion on that very account,[5] for which reason those who die 'in the wrath of God' are quick to reach hell, 'since divine justice spurs them on' (*Inferno*, III, 121–6), and the seeming freedom of passion turns into dependence upon the urge which, 'just as it once inclined towards sin, is now directed by divine justice towards punishment against her (the soul's) own will' (*Purgatorio*, XXX, 61–6), whereas the will of him who knows God springs from the source of freedom itself. Thus real freedom of the will depends upon its relationship with the truth, which forms the content of essential knowledge. Conversely, the highest vision of God, of which Dante speaks in his work, is in accord with the spontaneous fulfilment of the divine will. Here knowledge has become one with divine truth and will has become one with divine love; both qualities reveal themselves as aspects of Divine Being, the one static and the other dynamic. This is the ultimate message of the *Divine Comedy*, and also the answer to Dante's effort to comprehend the human being's eternal origin in the Divinity:

> Ma non eran da ciò le proprie penne;
> Se non che la mia mente fu percossa
> Da un fulgore, in che sua voglia venne.
> All'alta fantasia qui mancò possa;
> Ma già volgeva il mio disiro e velle,
> Si come ruota ch'egualmente è mossa,
> L'amor che muove il sole e l'altre stelle.

[5] The justification for the forcible defending and diffusion of a religion rests precisely on the thought that truth alone liberates while error enslaves. If man is free to choose between truth and error, then he deprives himself of freedom the moment he decides in favour of the latter.

*But not for this did my own wings suffice; yet was my spirit smitten suddenly with a flash, whereupon its will found fulfilment. Here the power of high fantasy failed; but already my desire and my will were as a wheel that turned regularly, driven by the Love which moves the sun and the other stars. (Paradiso, XXXIII, 139–145)*

Some scholars take the view that Beatrice never lived, and that everything that Dante says about her refers only to Divine Wisdom (*Sophia*). This opinion illustrates the confusion between genuine symbolism and allegory, taking the latter term in the sense attributed to it since the Renaissance: taken in that sense, an allegory is more or less a mental invention, an artificial clothing for general ideas, whereas genuine symbolism, as we have said, lies in the very essence of things. That Dante should have bestowed upon Divine Wisdom the image and name of a beautiful and noble woman is in accordance with a compelling law, not merely because Divine Wisdom, in so far as it is the object of knowledge, includes an aspect which precisely is feminine, in the highest sense, but also because the presence of the divine *Sophia* manifested itself first and foremost to him in the appearance of the beloved woman. Herein a key is provided that enables us to understand, at least in principle, the spiritual alchemy whereby the poet is able to transpose sensory appearances into supra-sensory essences: when love encompasses the entire will and causes it to flow towards the centre of the being, it can become knowledge of God. The operative means between love and knowledge is beauty: when experienced in its inexhaustible essence—which confers release from all constraints—an aspect of Divine Wisdom is already within it, so that even sexual attraction may lead to knowledge of the Divine, to the extent that passion is absorbed and consumed by love, and passion likewise transformed by the experience of beauty.

The fire that Dante has to pass through at the last stage before entering the Earthly Paradise (*Purgatorio*, XXVII) is the same as the fire in which the lustful are purged of their sin. 'This wall alone stands between thee and Beatrice,' says Virgil to Dante, as the latter shrinks from stepping through the flames (*ibid*, 36). 'While I was in them', Dante says, 'I could have wished to throw myself into molten glass to cool myself' (*ibid*, 49–50).

The immortal Beatrice greets Dante sternly at first (*Purgatorio*, XXX, 103ff), but then with fervent love, and as she leads him upwards through the heavenly spheres she unveils her beauty to him more and more, which his regard can scarcely bear. It is significant that here Dante no longer stresses the moral beauty of Beatrice—her goodness, innocence and humility—as he did in his *Vita Nuova*, but speaks quite simply of her visible beauty; what is most outward has here become the image of what is most inward, sensory observation the expression of spiritual vision.

At the beginning Dante is not yet capable of looking directly at the Divine Light, but sees it mirrored in Beatrice's eyes. (*Paradiso*, XVIII, 82–4)

> Giustizia mosse il mio alto fattore:
> Fecemi la divina potestate
> La somma sapienza e il primo amore.
> Dinanzi a me non fur cose create
> Se non eterne, ed io eterno duro:
> Lasciate ogni speranza, voi ch'entrate.

*Justice moved my exalted Maker: Divine Power made me, Wisdom supreme and primal Love. Before me were no things created, except the eternal, and eternal I endure: abandon all hope, ye that enter.* (*Inferno*, III, 1–9)

Faced with these famous words, which stand inscribed upon the gate of hell, many a present-day reader is inclined to say: *Maestro, il senso lor m'è duro*—'Master, their meaning is hard for me to understand' (*ibid*, 12), because it is difficult for him to reconcile the idea of eternal damnation with the idea of divine love—*il primo amore*. But for Dante, divine love is the origin, pure and simple, of creation: it is the overflowing of the eternal which endows the world, created 'out of nothing', with existence, and thus permits its participation in Divine Being. In so far as the world is different from God, it has as it were its roots in nothingness; it necessarily includes a God-denying element, and the boundless extent of divine love is revealed precisely in the fact that it even permits this denying of God and grants it existence. Thus the existence of the infernal possibilities depends upon divine love, while at the same time these possibilities are judged through divine justice as the negation that indeed they are. 'Before me was nothing created, except the eternal, and I endure eternally': the Semitic languages distinguish between eternity, which pertains to God alone and is an eternal now, and the endless duration which pertains to the posthumous states: the Latin language does not make this distinction, and thus Dante likewise cannot express it in words. Yet who knew better than Dante that the duration of the beyond is not the same thing as God's eternity, just as the timeless existence of the angelic worlds is not the same thing as the duration of hell, which is like a congealed time. For if the state of the damned, viewed in itself, has no end, nevertheless in God's sight it can only be finite.

'Abandon all hope, ye who enter': it could also be said, conversely: whoever still hopes in God will not need to pass through this gate. The condition of the damned is precisely hopelessness, since hope is the hand held out for the reception of grace.

To the modern reader, it seems strange that Virgil, the wise and good, who was able to lead Dante to the summit of the mount of Purgatory, should have to reside like all the other sages and noble heroes of antiquity in limbo, the ante-chamber of hell. But Dante could not transfer the unbaptized Virgil into any of the Heavens attainable through grace. If, however, we look a little more closely, we become aware of a remarkable rift in Dante's work, which seems to hint at a dimension that was not developed further: in general, limbo is described as a gloomy place, without light and without sky, but as soon as Dante, together with Virgil, has entered the 'noble castle' where the sages of old walk upon 'emerald lawns', he speaks of an 'open, luminous and high place' (*Inferno*, IV, 115ff), as though he no longer found himself in the underworld covered by the earth. Men there are 'of slow and deep gaze, of great dignity in their behaviour, and speak seldom, with mild voices' (*ibid*, 112–114). All this no longer has anything to do with hell, but neither does it lie directly within range of Christian grace.

In this connection, the question arises: did Dante adopt an exclusively negative attitude towards non-Christian religions? In a passage in the *Paradiso*, where he numbers the Trojan prince Ripheus among the elect, he speaks of the unfathomable nature of divine grace and warns us not to be precipitate in our judgement (XX, 67ff). What else could Ripheus be for Dante, other than some distant, innocent example of an extra-ecclesiastical saint? We do not say 'extra-Christian', because for Dante every revelation of God in man is Christ.

And this leads to yet another question: did Dante, in creating the *Divine Comedy*, draw consciously upon certain Islamic mystical works, which show various analogies with it? The type of epic poem describing the path of the knower of God in symbolical form, is not rare in the Islamic world. It may be surmised that certain of these works were translated into the Provençal language,[6] and we know that the community of the 'Fedeli d'Amore' to which Dante belonged, was in communication with the Order of the Temple, which was established in the East and open to the intellectual world of Islam.[7] The argument can be carried a long way, and one can find a prototype in Islamic esoteric writings for almost every important element in the *Divine Comedy*—for the interpretation of the planetary spheres as stages in spiritual knowledge, for the divisions of hell, for the figure and role of Beatrice, and much else besides. However, in view of certain passages in Dante's *Inferno* (XXVIII, 22), it is scarcely credible that he can have known Islam and recognized it as a true religion. A more likely explanation is that he drew on writings that were not themselves Islamic, but were directly influenced by Islamic doctrines,[8] and it is probable that what actually reached Dante through these channels amounted to much less than comparative research[9] would have us suppose. Spiritual truths are what they are,

[6] There exists a medieval Provençal translation of the *Mirâj*, the story of the Prophet's ascent to Heaven (*Eschiele Mahomet*, published by Múñoz Sendino and Enrico Cerulli). But this is more of a popular treatment of a theme which elsewhere provides the basis for important metaphysical and contemplative considerations.

[7] See the works of Luigi Valli, especially *Il linguaggio segreto di Dante e dei Fedeli d'Amore*, (Optima, Rome, 1928).

[8] Important in this respect is MS. Latin 3236A in the Bibliothèque Nationale in Paris, first published by M. T. D'Alverny in *Archives d'Histoire doctrinale et littéraire du Moyen Age*, 1940 (42). It has already been referred to in the author's book on alchemy. It is related to the *Divine Comedy* in many ways, and all the more remarkably in that it expressly names the founders of the three monotheistic religions, Moses, Christ, and Mohammed, as the true teachers of the way to God through knowledge.

[9] See the studies of P. Asín Palacios.

and minds can encounter one another at a certain level of insight without ever having heard of one another on an earthly plane.

What matters is not so much what Dante was influenced by as the fact that he was right: the teachings contained in his *Divine Comedy* are all valid, those in the foreground in the sense of the general Christian belief, and the more hidden ones—for example the teaching on the mutual relationship between will and knowledge discussed above—in terms of gnosis in the Christian sense of the word. It is significant in this connection that Dante was not self-deceived about his own person, and that he could observe himself from an impersonal point of view: he assessed himself correctly when he counted himself amongst the six greatest poets of all ages (*Inferno*, IV, 100–102), and he rightly allows Virgil to say of him: *Alma sdegnosa, benedetta colei che in te s'incinse!*—'Soul disdainful (of all that is vulgar), blessed be she that bore thee!' (*Inferno*, VIII, 44–45). He was equally unmistaken when he condemned the Papal policy of his time, since it led to the misfortune of the Lutheran secession and the secular explosion of the Renaissance. His chief spiritual legacy, however, lies in the symbols and imagery of his poem, which neither profane philosophical research nor any 'psychology' will ever exhaust. They bear the seal of an inspiration independent of all temporal and spatial circumstances, and the spiritual nourishment they offer is reserved for those who, as Dante says, 'in the temporal world already stretch out their necks for the bread of the angels, by which one lives here, but is never sated' (*Paradiso*, II, 10).

# 6

# Contra Teilhard de Chardin

*Below are extracts from two of the author's letters, in which he expresses his view regarding Teilhard de Chardin.*

## I

MY MAIN OBJECTION to the evolutionary doctrine of Teilhard de Chardin is as follows: if the spiritual faculty of man—the 'noetic faculty', as Teilhard de Chardin calls it—is merely a phase of a continuing biological evolution—or involution—which, seen as a whole, can be compared to a curve or a spiral, then this phase cannot step out of the whole and say: I am part of a spiral. Anything that such an evolution-bound faculty could ever grasp or express would likewise be subject to evolution, and this leads to the Marxist view that there is no truth, but only biological pragmatism and utilitarianism. It is here that Teilhard's theory breaks down completely.

The human spirit does, in fact, have the faculty of placing itself outside biological contingency, of viewing things objectively and essentially, and of making judgements. Teilhard de Chardin confuses the cerebral and 'noetic' faculties. The *Nous* (= Intellect = Spirit) is not the same as the activity of the brain; the latter 'works over', whereas the former judges and knows. The truly spiritual faculty—that of discriminating between true and false, of distinguishing the relative from the absolute—is related to the biological level, metaphorically speaking, as is the vertical to the horizontal; it belongs to another ontological dimension. And precisely because this dimension occurs in man, he is not an ephemeral biological appearance, but, in this physical and earthly world, and in spite of all his organic limitations, an absolute centre. This is also indicated by the faculty of speech, which belongs to man alone, and which, precisely, presupposes the capacity to 'objectivize' things, to place oneself behind and beyond appearances.

The terrestrial absoluity of the human state and of the human form is also confirmed by the doctrine of the incarnation of the Divine Word—a doctrine which, in Teilhard's system, loses all its meaning. If man fundamentally possesses the capacity of knowing God, in other words, if the fulfilling of the function which is his by definition is a way to God, then on the biological plane there is no occasion for a super-man. He would be a pleonasm.

The poor saints! They came a million years too soon. None of them, however, would ever have accepted the doctrine that God could be reached biologically, or again through collective scientific research.

And so I come back to my main objection: according to Teilhard's system, the 'noetic' faculty of man is related to biogenesis not as the eye is related to the other human parts, but rather as a part-process is related to a whole process—and this is something quite different. The eye can view the other limbs and organs, even if only in a mirror, but a part-process can never view the whole process of which it is a part. This has already been said by Aristotle: whoever asserts that everything is in a stream can never prove his assertion, for the simple reason that it can rest on nothing that is not itself in the stream; it is thus self-contradictory.

## II

No, it is not true that 'so long as a writer on religious subjects is affirming beliefs (whether his own or other people's) he is expressing the truth, but when depreciating other people's beliefs, his word is not to be trusted', for in that case the most erroneous of sects, including satanism, and the most absurd of personal beliefs would be justified; the 'discerning of spirits' of which the New Testament speaks would have no meaning. But perhaps the author of this remark is thinking somehow of the principle according to which a doctrinal pronouncement—not a metaphysical one but a dogmatic or moral one—may be perfectly valid within the framework of a given religion without necessarily being valid outside it and within the framework of another religion that is equally true in itself? Be that as it may, this principle does not apply to the case of Teilhard de Chardin, whose thesis on the genesis of man stands in opposition not only to the form and spirit of the Christian dogma, but also to all traditional wisdom. Let us simply say that this thesis is false, that it expresses no particle of transcendent truth. And how could it, seeing that it denies truth as such: according to Teilhard de Chardin, intelligence itself, including all that is deepest in it, all that is implicitly divine, is subject to change; it 'evolves' together with the supposed evolution of matter, so that it could have no fixed and immutable content; the spirit of man, according to Teilhard de Chardin, is entirely 'in a state of becoming'. It is here, moreover, that the Teilhardian thesis contradicts itself, for if human intelligence is no more than matter which has been in a state of progressive transformation ever since the age of the first molluscs, how could modern man, 'half-developed' as he is, possibly take in, with the eye of his understanding, the whole movement which is carrying him along? How is it possible for the essentially impermanent to judge the nature of impermanence? This argument should be enough to condemn the Teilhardian thesis. It remains to be seen why it has so much success.

The average modern man 'believes' above all in science—the science that has produced modern surgery and modern industry—and this is almost his basic 'religion'. If he considers himself a Christian at the same time, the two 'beliefs' stand in opposition to each other in his soul, and engender a latent crisis that calls for a solution. This solution is what Teilhard de Chardin seems to bring. He 'ties the two loose ends together'; but he does so, not by making, as he should, a distinction between different planes of reality—that of empirical knowledge which is exact in its way but necessarily fragmentary and provisional, and that of faith which is bound up with timeless certainties—but by mixing them inextricably together: he endows empirical science with an absolute certainty that it does not and cannot have, and he projects the idea of indefinite progress into God Himself.

He puts forward the theory of the transformation of species as a certain fact, whereas it is no more than a hypothesis, as its most serious defenders admit; no valid proof of it has ever, in fact, been made, and if in spite of everything it keeps its hold, this is because modern minds can only conceive of a genesis which takes place in time; the 'vertical' genesis of specific forms from the supra-formal and animic degrees of existence is beyond them. None the less, scientific honesty demands that one should make a distinction between proof and hypothesis, and that one should not build, as Teilhard de Chardin does, a whole philosophy—indeed, a pseudo-religion—on an entirely conjectural basis. It is not for nothing that Teilhard de Chardin was the victim of the famous Piltdown hoax—the *Eoanthropos* of unhappy memory—and that he was one of the inventors of the no less fantastic 'Sinanthropos' of Chou-Kou-Tien! But the worst and most grotesque feature of Teilhardism is the fact that it is obliged to consider the prophets and sages of ancient times as being mentally 'under-developed': are they not a little nearer to the ape than modern man is ? It is true that in this respect the thesis of Teilhard de Chardin is in no sense original; its novelty lies in its being a Trojan horse to introduce materialism and progressivism into the very bosom of religion.

# 7

# The Heavenly Jerusalem
# and the
# Paradise of Vaikuntha

W E REPRODUCE HERE a miniature of the Heavenly Jerusalem taken from a manuscript of the eleventh century, the so-called 'Apocalypse of Saint-Séver'[1] which belongs to a certain group of medieval manuscripts, mostly of Spanish origin and all stemming from a single prototype, a commentary on the Apocalypse written by the Asturian monk Beatus de Liébana towards the end of the eighth century. The same image of the Heavenly Jerusalem occurs in most of these manuscripts, with only slight variations, so that one can admit that its composition goes back to the prototype, which is now lost.

The artist made use of a kind of abstract perspective, familiar to medieval readers and viewers: he represented the heavenly city as if seen from above, with its walls projected onto the horizontal plane. In this way, he could portray the twelve gates facing the four cardinal points: east, north, west and south, according to the sacred text. (XXI, 13) The same iconographical scheme shows clearly the square form of the city: 'And the city lieth foursquare, and the length is as large as the breadth . . . ' (XXI, 16) The heavenly Jerusalem is in fact the 'squaring' of the heavenly cycle, its twelve gates corresponding to the twelve months of the year, as well as to the analogous divisions of the greater cycles, such as the precession of the equinoxes which, in the ancient world-system, is the greatest of all the astronomical cycles and therefore the largest measure of time. The Apocalypse mentions 'twelve thousand furlongs' as the measure of the city's circuit; this

---

[1] Cod. Lat. 8878 of the Bibliothèque Nationale, Paris, fol. 207v–208. The Heavenly Jerusalem from the Apocalypse of Saint-Séver (eleventh century).

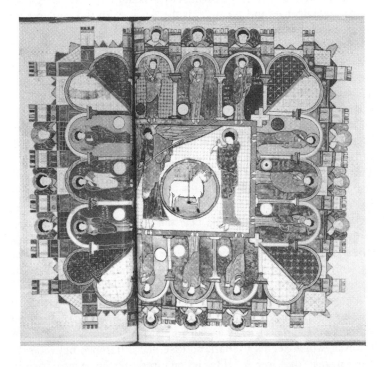

The Heavenly Jerusalem from the Apocalypse of Saint-Séver (eleventh century).

number corresponds to the 'great year' of the Persians and is in fact an approximate measure for half the equinoxial cycle, namely for the time of the reversion of the equinoxes (12960 years). Upon the walls of the heavenly city are seen twelve angels, who are the guardians of the gates (XXI, 12), and under each gate is portrayed one of the twelve apostles, whose names are written on the city's foundations. (XXI, 14) Under the gates there are also represented twelve circles or spheres with inscriptions referring to the twelve precious stones garnishing the foundations of the wall (XXI, 9). In older manuscripts of the same group, however, these circles clearly represent the pearls of which the gates are made: 'And the twelve gates were pearls: every several gate was of one pearl'. (XXI, 21)

In the midst of the city the divine Lamb is standing; on his right we see the Evangelist, and on his left the Angel with the golden reed measuring the city. (XXI, 15)

For the medieval viewer it would have been clear that the city was in fact not only a square but a cube: 'The length and the breadth and the height of it are equal'. (XXI, 16) The Heavenly Jerusalem is really a crystal, not only because of its transparent, incorruptible and luminous substance, but also because of its crystalline form. It is the 'crystallization', in the eternal present, of all the positive and essentially indestructible aspects of the temporal or changing world.

This miniature of the Heavenly Jerusalem was published in a book dealing with the symbolism of the cathedral[2], which prompted a reader in India to send the here inserted drawing of the *mandala* of the Paradise of Vaikuntha, the celestial abode of Vishnu, together with a translation of the corresponding passages of the *Skanda Purâna*.[3] The resemblance of the *mandala* with our miniature of the heavenly city is indeed surprising; it is even more complete if one compares the corresponding scriptural texts.

Like the Heavenly Jerusalem, the divine abode of Vaikuntha has twelve gates facing the four cardinal points. The *mandala* shows these in exactly the same manner as our miniature. There is one feature, however, which seems to mark an essential difference between the two images: the tree of life is pictured in the centre of the *Vaikuntha-mandala*, whereas the centre of the city of Jerusalem is the Lamb. But this difference is due to an iconographical economy only; it veils an even deeper analogy, for the Apocalypse also mentions the Tree of Life in the centre of the divine city: 'In the midst of the street of it, and on either side of the river, was there the tree of life, which

---

[2] Titus Burckhardt, *Chartres un die Geburt der Kathedrale*, Olten, 1962.

[3] For this documentation we are indebted to Miss Alice Boner, Benares, the author of important studies on Hindu sculpture and architecture; see *Principles of Composition in Hindu Sculpture*, (Leiden, 1962), dealing with the geometrical patterns (*yantras*) underlying the Hindu sculptures of the cave period, and *Silpa Prakâsa*, a manual of Hindu architecture, translated by Alice Boner and Sadâśiva Rath Śarmâ, (Leiden, 1966).

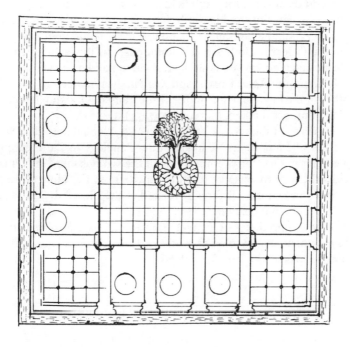

TRIPĀDA VIBHŪTI VAIKUNṬHA-MAṆIMAṆḌAPA

bare twelve manner of fruits, and yielded her fruit every month . . .'
(XXII, 2)

The central field of the *Vaikuntha-mandala* is divided into small squares; there should be $12 \times 12 = 144$ compartments according to the *Purâna*; our drawing has $13 \times 12$, probably by mistake. The same division into $12 \times 12$—and sometimes $13 \times 12$—squares marks the central field of the celestial city in some of the older manuscripts of the Beatus group[4]. The number 144 is mentioned in the Apocalypse as the measure of the city's wall (XXI,17); its nature is solar and cyclical, $144 \times 180 = 25920$ being the number of years contained in the complete cycle of the equinoxes.

The four corners of the *Vaikuntha-mandala* represent secondary shrines; they are divided into 16 compartments each, which makes 64 altogether, the number of cosmic perfection. This is also the number of squares in the chess-board, the *astapâda*, which is a *mandala* of the cosmos in the form of the battlefield of the *devas* and the *asûras*.[5]

Like the gates of the Heavenly Jerusalem in our miniatures, the gates of Vaikuntha are said to be built of crystal and gold, precious stones and pearls. Both are self-luminous: 'In this self-luminous, brilliant sanctuary no sun is shining, no moon and no stars', says the *Purâna;* and the Apocalypse: 'And this city has no need of the sun, neither of the moon to shine in it: for the glory of God did lighten it, and the Lamb is the light thereof.' (XXI, 23)

On the top of the roof of Vaikuntha is a golden pitcher filled with the Milk of Immortality. It has no direct analogy in the Heavenly Jerusalem; but it clearly reminds one of the symbolism of the Graal; incidently, we may observe that the sanctuary of the Holy Graal as described in 'Titurel', is directly related to the Heavenly Jerusalem and its cyclical implications.

We now reproduce the extract from the *Skanda Purâna* (*Utkala Khanda*, chap. 48, *Suta Samhita* and *Kapila Samhita*) and beside it the analogous passages of the Apocalypse.

---

[4] Cf. Ms. of San Isidro in León, National Library, Madrid, B. 31.
[5] See the chapter 'The Symbolism of Chess' in this book.

*Tripâda Vibhûti*
*Vaikuṇṭha-Maṇimaṇḍapa*

Behold the Temple of Gems standing on the White Island surrounded by the Ocean of Milk. In the midst of the Milk Ocean the Sacrificial Hall is made of precious stones. It is built of pure crystal and is unshakable.

*Apocalypse*

And he carried me away in the spirit to a great and high mountain, and showed me that great city, the holy Jerusalem, descending out of heaven from God,
Having the glory of God: and her light was like unto a stone most precious, even like a jasper stone, clear as crystal (XXI, 10, 11).

The interior of the Temple is in twelve by twelve parts and is shining with the fiery brilliance of the Sun.

And he measured the wall thereof, an hundred and forty and four cubits (XXI, 17).

It is resting on sixteen pillars made of emeralds and has twelve portals towards the four directions of space.

And had a wall great and high, and had twelve gates ... On the east three gates; on the north three gates; on the south three gates; and on the west three gates (XXXI, 12, 13).

Deathlessness (*amrta*), Bliss (*ânanda*), Growth or Increase (*puṣṭi*), Happiness (*tuṣṭi*), Prosperity (*puṣâ*), Delight (*rati*), Steadfastness (*dhriti*), Moon-like Lustre (*śaśinî*), Illumination (*candrikâ*), Splendour (*kânti*), Heavenly Light (*jyoti*), Fortune (*śrî*), these are the twelve guardians of the portals. These *Pratiharinîs*, who are guarding the portals are all very young and beautiful.

And at the gates twelve angels, and names written thereon, which are the names of the twelve tribes of the children of Israel (XXI, 12).
And the wall of the city had twelve foundations, and in them the names of the twelve apostles of the Lamb (XXI, 14).
And the foundations of the wall of the city were garnished with all manner of precious stones. The first foundation was jasper; the second, sapphire; the third, a chalcedony; the fourth, an emerald; the fifth, sardonyx; the sixth, sardius; the seventh, chrysolyte; the eighth, beryl; the ninth, a topaz; the tenth, a chrysoprasus; the eleventh, a jacinth; the twelfth, an amethyst (XXI, 19, 20).

The walls of the secondary shrines in the four corners are made of rubies and have perforated windows with sixteen openings
These are sixteen parts (*kalâs*), by adding which the full number of 64 *kalâs* is obtained.

The beautiful sacrificial Hall is emitting a light equal to a score of Suns, and that light will endure to the end of all the *kalpas*.

And there shall be no night there; and they need no candle, neither light of sun; for the Lord God giveth them light: and they shall reign for ever and ever (XXII, 5).

In the centre of the Hall there is the stainless Tree (of Life) arising from the shining, hundred-petalled lotus.

And he shewed me a pure river of water of life, clear as crystal, proceeding out of the throne of God and of the Lamb. In the midst of the street of it, and on either side of the river, was there the tree of life, which bare twelve manner of fruits, and yielded her fruit every month; and the leaves of the tree were for the healing of the nations (XXII, 1, 2).

Its roof has two storeys and is covered with golden tiles. Between the storeys there is a perforated wall made of pearls.

On the top of the roof is a beautiful *kalaśa*, a golden pitcher filled with the Milk of Immortality.

The flagstaff is made of coral, and the flag is motionless.

Two divine birds are sitting by the side of the *kalaśa* in perfect silence.

In this self-luminous, brilliant sanctuary no sun is shining, no moon and no stars.

And this city has no need of the sun, neither of the moon, to shine in it: for the glory of God did lighten it, and the Lamb is the light thereof (XXI, 23.)

This is the abode of *Nârâyana,* who is beyond the changeable world and beyond the unchangeable.

I worship this *Puruṣottama,* who in all the three worlds is the most difficult to approach.

# 8

# Two Examples of Christian Symbolism

*Because of their intrinsic interest and their relevance to the other themes dealt with in the present section, we reprint below two short extracts from the author's earliest book* Schweizer Volkskunst *('Swiss Folk Art').*

## The Wooden Chest

BECAUSE of its geometrical form, comprising six flat sides, which the chest (traditionally carved out of one piece of wood) has in common with the ark, the house, and the coffin, it is regarded, in the traditional lore of all peoples, as a symbol of the earth—not the earth in a geographical sense, but in a transposed sense, as a degree of existence (the terrestrial state), which supports or contains life, just as the chest contains precious possessions, and which like the ark floats on the waters of the deep. There is an inverse relationship between the symbol of the three-dimensional or six-armed cross, which represents the world as radiating outwards from a centre, and the sacred chest which, in its hexahedral, crystalline form, symbolizes the terminal stage of creation.

## Gargoyles

The purpose of the grotesque masks on the outside walls of Romanesque churches was undoubtedly that they should serve as a means of exorcism against impure spirits. The mode of action of such exorcistic masks can be readily understood if one considers how, when a man approaches a sanctuary and seeks to direct his spirit towards the highest, all the dregs in his being, owing to a natural reaction of the soul, tend to arise and seek to enter his thoughts under a multitude of guises. If, at this moment, he espies a mask which represents, with unmistakable grossness, any hidden greed, passivity or lust, he can look on them 'objectively', and laugh at them. In this way the evil spirit is exorcized and flees the scene.

These stone masks thus contribute to a process of unmasking in the soul, but on a basis that is the exact opposite of modern psychoanalysis. For whereas in the latter the one who is plagued by dubious impulses is invited to accept his complexes as himself, the medieval man, awakened by an exorcistic device, looks on the mischievous intruder as an enemy from without, as an impulse foreign to himself which, like a disease, has sought to take root in him, and which he has only to perceive with clarity in order to be freed from it. For, according to Christian doctrine, the devil cannot tolerate the truth.

# 9

# The Theological Message
# of Russian Icons

THE ART of icons is a sacred art in the true sense of the term: it is nourished wholly on the spiritual truth to which it gives pictorial expression. For this reason it is often inadequately and faultily judged when approached from the outside and with criteria borrowed from profane and purely human art.

Most studies on art place historical development in the forefront; they analyze the interplay of ethnic and geographical influences and seek thereby to explain the art itself, while the intellectual content of the pictorial representation plays a subordinate role. In the art of icons, however, it is the content that is the criterion of the form. The specifically doctrinal character of this art determines not only the iconography, but also its artistic form and general style. This is so because the meaning of an icon touches a centre so close to man's essence that it governs virtually all aspects of the work of art, from its didactic elements to the imponderables of artistic inspiration.

It is quite different in profane art, where the subject-matter of a painting merely provides an opportunity for the artist to express his own genius, which may be more vital than the subject chosen and whose richness comes from elsewhere.

It is through its content that a sacred art has access to a living and truly inexhaustible source. Hence it is in its nature to remain true to itself, even when a particular artist has not himself fully realized the spiritual depth of a given theme, and so does not draw directly from the spring of holiness, but only transmits more or less of the light that is comprised in the sacred forms sanctioned by Tradition.

Fundamentally, the icon always remains the same; changes of style arise from the meeting between the timeless spirit of tradition and circumstances conditioned by time and place, which merely cause the unfolding of diverse potentialities latent in the nature of the icon itself. As Leonid Ouspensky has rightly said[1], just as Byzantium brought theology to a certain perfection in words, so Russia has done likewise in pictures.

Nothing could be more presumptuous than the wish to replace traditional wisdom with the point of view of modern psychology, which is quite out of place here. There is just as little possibility of grasping spiritual content psychologically as of explaining the nature of beauty psychologically.

---

[1] See *The Meaning of Icons* by Leonid Ouspensky and Vladimir Lossky (St. Vladimir's Seminary Press, Crestwood, New York, 1983).

# III
# SYMBOLISM AND
# MYTHOLOGY

# 10

# The Symbolism of
# the Mirror

ROM THE RICH reservoir of symbols that are used to give expression to the mysticisms of the various world religions, we select here the symbol of the mirror, for it, more than almost any other, is fitted to express the essence of mysticism, and at the same time its essentially gnostic or sapiential character. The mirror is the most immediate symbol of spiritual contemplation, and indeed of knowledge (*gnosis*) in general, for it portrays the union of subject and object.

At the same time this example serves to demonstrate how the various meanings of a symbol, which refer to so many different levels of reality and which may sometimes seem contradictory, are inwardly coherent, and harmoniously contained within the total meaning of the image, which itself is purely spiritual.

Multiplicity of meaning inheres in the very essence of a symbol; and this is its advantage over rational definition. For, whereas the latter organizes a concept in respect of its rational connections—at the same time fixing it on a given level—the symbol, without losing an iota of its precision or clarity, remains 'open upwards'. It is above all a 'key' to supra-rational realities.

For 'supra-rational realities' we could equally well say 'supra-rational truths', and we emphasize this point, for it has for long been the custom to explain symbolism in purely psychological terms. Not that a psychological interpretation is necessarily wrong in every case, for it could be a possibility. What is absolutely false is the view that the origin of the symbol is to be found in the so-called 'collective unconscious', in other words, in a chaotic substratum of the human soul. The content of a symbol is not irrational, but supra-rational, that is to say, purely spiritual. This is no new thesis, but pertains to the science of symbolism that is present in every genuine spiritual tradition.

Our approach here is purely principial: the symbolism of the mirror is as illuminating as it is because, in a sense, the mirror is the symbol of the symbol. Symbolism indeed can best be described as the visible reflection of ideas or prototypes that cannot be fully expressed in purely conceptual terms. In this sense, St. Paul says: 'For now we see through a glass, darkly; but then face to face: now I know in part; but then shall I know even as also I am known.' (1 Cor. 13;12.)

What is the mirror in which the symbol appears as the image of an eternal prototype? Firstly the imagination, if one is thinking of the visual or 'plastic' nature of the symbol in contradistinction from abstract concepts. But in a wider sense, it is the mind which, as the faculty of discrimination and knowledge, reflects the pure Intellect. In an even wider sense, the Intellect itself is the mirror of the divine Being. Plotinus says of the Intellect (*Nous*) that it contemplates the infinite One, and from this contemplation, which can never completely exhaust its object, the world proceeds as an ever imperfect image which may be compared to a continually broken reflection.

According to a saying of the Prophet Mohammed, there is 'for every thing a means of polishing it and freeing it from rust. One thing alone polishes the heart, namely the remembrance of God (*dhikr Allâh*)'. The heart, centre of the human being, is therefore like a mirror, which must be pure, so that it may receive the light of the divine Spirit.

To this may be compared the following teaching from Northern or *Ch'an* Buddhism:

> Just as it is in the nature of a mirror to shine, so all beings at their origin possess spiritual illumination. When, however, passions obscure the mirror, it becomes covered over, as if with dust. When false thoughts, under the direction of the master, are overcome and destroyed, they cease to proclaim themselves. Then is the Intellect illumined, in accordance with its nature, and nothing remains unknown. It is like the polishing of a mirror . . . (*Tsung-mi*)

This passage might equally well have come from a Sufi treatise.

When the heart has become a pure mirror, the world is reflected in it as it really is, namely, without the distortions due to passional thought; in addition, the heart reflects Divine Truth more or less directly, firstly in the form of symbols (*ishârât*), then in the form of spiritual qualities (*sifât*) or essences (*'ayân*), which lie behind the symbols, and finally as Divine Realities (*haqâ'iq*).

This recalls the sacred mirror that plays such an important role in Taoism and Shintoism. The sacred mirror of Shintoism that is conserved in the shrine at Ise signifies both truth and truthfulness. According to the legend, the gods made this mirror in order to entice the sun-goddess Amaterasu out of the cave into which she had angrily withdrawn, and so restore light to the world. When the goddess peeped out of the cave, she saw her own light in the mirror, thought it was a second sun, and, out of curiosity, came out of the cave. Amongst other things, this indicates that the heart, through its reflective capacity—its truthfulness—attracts the divine light.

Everything that lies within the law of reflection, can also be applied to the corresponding spiritual process. It is important here to remember that the reflected image is inverted in relation to its object. Thus, for example, when divine Reality, which contains everything, is reflected, it appears as an ungraspably minute centre; the bliss of pure Being, when reflected, appears as an annihilating rigour; eternity appears as a sudden moment; and so on.

To the law of reflection also belongs the fact that, while a reflection is qualitatively similar to its object, it is materially different from it. The symbol *is* the thing symbolized only when one abstracts it from its material, or otherwise conditioned, limits, and perceives only its essence.

Yet a further characteristic of reflection is that, depending on the shape and positioning of the mirror, the object appears more completely or less completely, more clearly or less clearly. This too can be applied to spiritual reflection, and it was in this sense that the Sufi masters said that God revealed Himself to His servant in accordance with the readiness or capacity of his heart; He took on, so to speak, the form of His servant's heart, rather as water takes on the colour of the glass containing it.

In this connection, the mirror of the heart is compared with the moon, which, depending on its position in space, more or less perfectly reflects the light of the sun. The moon is the soul (*nafs*), which is illumined by the pure Spirit (*Rûh*), but, being still bound to time, its receptivity has to suffer change (*talwîn*).

The process of reflection is perhaps the most perfect image of the 'process' of knowing, which is not exhausted at the rational level. The mirror *is* what it reflects, to the extent that it reflects. As long as the heart—i.e. the cognitive Intellect—reflects the multiplicity of the world, it *is* the world, according to the way of the world, namely with the scission of object and subject, of outward and inward. To the extent, however, that the mirror of the heart reflects divine Being, it *is* precisely this, according to the undivided mode of pure Being. In this sense the Apostle Paul said: 'But we all, with open face beholding as in a glass the glory of the Lord, are changed into the same image. . . .' (2 Cor. 3;18.)

We should like now to look at the symbol of the mirror from another angle. Hasan al-Basrî, one of the earliest mystics of Islam, compares the world in its relationship to God with the reflected image of the sun that is produced by a flat surface of water. Everything that we may know from the reflected image stems from the original object; but this is completely independent from its reflection, and infinitely above and beyond it.

If we seek to understand this comparision from the standpoint of the 'unicity of existence' (*wahdat al-wujûd*)—the fundamental concept of Islamic mysticism—we must know that light stands for Being and consequently darkness stands for nothingness; visibility is existence and invisibility is absence. Now it is only what is reflected in the mirror that is visible. The presence of the mirror is revealed only through the nature of the reflection and through its pure possibility. In itself, without light, the mirror is invisible, and this means, according to the meaning of the comparison, that in itself it *is* not.

From this there is but a step to the Hindu doctrine of *Mâyâ*, the divine power by virtue of which the Infinite manifests itself in the finite by covering itself with the veil of illusion. The illusion consists in the fact that manifestation (i.e. reflection) appears as something existing outside Infinite Unity. It is *Mâyâ* that gives rise to this; and *Mâyâ*, apart from the reflections that fall upon her, is nothing other than a pure possibility or function of the Infinite.

If the universe as a whole is the mirror of God, so also is man in his original nature, since this qualitatively contains the whole universe, the mirror of the One. In this connection, Muhyi 'd-Dîn ibn 'Arabî (twelfth century) writes:

Because of His innumerable perfections, God wanted to contemplate His own Essence in an object comprising all reality, so as to manifest His own mystery to Himself . . . For a being's knowledge of himself in himself is not the same as knowledge of himself by means of something other that acts for him like a mirror. Such a mirror shows him to himself in the form corresponding to the 'plane of reflection' and the reflection resulting from it. . .

What Ibn 'Arabî has in mind is, on the one hand, the 'pure receptacle' of *materia prima* (*al-qâbil*) and, on the other, Adam; *materia prima* is in a sense the mirror that is still dark and on which no light has yet shone, while Adam is 'the very brightness of this mirror and the spirit of this form' (*Fusûs al-Hikam*, chapter on Adam).

Man is thus the mirror of God. From another, and more esoteric, point of view God is the mirror of man. Regarding this, Ibn 'Arabî writes in the same work:

Man, to whom the Essence of God offers itself to be known, does not see God; he only sees his own form in the mirror of God. It is not possible that he see God Himself, although he can know that only in Him can he behold his own form. This process takes place in the manner of one looking in a mirror; for when thou beholdest thyself in a mirror, thou seest not the mirror itself, even though thou knowest that thou beholdest thine own form only because of the mirror. God Himself provided this phenomenon as the best symbol of His Self-revelation, so that whoever receives this revelation may know that he cannot see God . . . Try for thyself whether, when thou lookest at a reflection in a mirror, thou canst see the mirror itself; thou wilt never see it. This is so true that some people, observing this law of reflection in [physical and spiritual] mirrors, have asserted that the reflected form is interposed between mirror and observer. This of course is not so; in reality it is as we have just said [namely, that the reflected form, since it does not stand between us and the mirror, does not hide it from us; nevertheless it is only thanks to the mirror that we can see the form reflected in it] . . . If thou graspest this [namely that the creature contemplating never sees the Essence itself, but only his own form in the mirror of the Essence], thou graspest the utmost limit that the creature can reach; therefore aspire not beyond it and tire not thy soul in seeking to depass this degree [in 'objective' mode], for in principle and in fact there is nothing beyond it but pure non-existence [the Essence itself being non-manifested] (*Fusûs al-Hikam*, chapter on Seth).

In the same connection, Meister Eckhart writes:

The soul contemplates itself in the mirror of Divinity. God Himself is the mirror, which He conceals from whom He will, and uncovers to whom He will . . . The more the soul is able to transcend all words, the more it approaches the mirror. In this mirror union occurs as pure undivided like-ness.

The Sufi Suhrawardî of Aleppo (twelfth century) writes that the man on the way to the Self first discovers that the whole world is contained within him, the cognitive subject; he sees himself as the mirror in which all eternal prototypes appear as ephemeral forms. Then he becomes aware that he himself has no existence; his 'I' disappears as the subject, and only God remains as the Subject of all knowledge.

Muhyi 'd-Dîn ibn 'Arabî writes further: 'God is the mirror in which thou seest thyself, and thou art His mirror in which He contemplates His names. These however are naught other than He, so that it is merely a case of the analogy of relationships being inverted' (*Fusûs al-Hikam*, chapter on Seth).

Whether God be the mirror of man or man be the mirror of God, the mirror in both cases signifies the knowing subject, which as such cannot also be the object of knowledge. In an absolute manner this is true of the Divine Subject alone, the eternal 'Witness' (*Shahîd*) of all manifested creatures; this is the infinite mirror whose 'substance' can in no wise be grasped, but which nevertheless is knowable in a certain sense, because one can know that only in it can all creatures be known.

This throws light on the otherwise obscure words that Dante puts in the mouth of Adam. Of Dante's longing, Adam says:

Perch'io la veggio nel verace speglio
Che fa di sè pareglio all'altre cose,
E nulla face lui di sè pareglio.

*I see it in the truthful mirror*
*That makes itself reflector of all other things,*
*And of which no thing makes itself reflector.*

(*Paradiso*, XXVI, 106ff)

Fârid ad-Dîn 'Attâr says:

*Come, wandering atoms, come back to your centre,*
*and become the eternal mirror which ye have seen . . .*

# 11

# The Symbolism of Water

THE MODERN ECONOMY, in spite of all the research findings at its disposal, has for a long time almost completely left out of account one of the most important bases of our life as well as of its own existence, namely the living purity of water. This fact bears witness to a unilateralness of development which, quite apart from the question of water, is also harmful to many other things, not the least of which is the psyche or soul. When the balance of Nature is not disturbed, the earth's waters themselves continually re-establish their purity, whereas, when this balance is lost, death and pollution are the result. It is thus not merely a coincidence that the 'life' of the waters is a symbol for the 'life' of the human soul.

When one considers whether there is anything that could possibly alert non-scientifically minded people to the menace of water pollution, one quickly realizes that the natural sense of beauty that enables us spontaneously to distinguish a diseased tree from a healthy one, should also be able to sound a warning here. That it has not done so—or hardly done so—comes from the fact that modern man completely separates not only 'the beautiful' from 'the useful', but also 'the beautiful' from 'the real'. This way of thinking is like a split in one's consciousness, and it is difficult to say whether it is cause or effect of a state of affairs which, on the one hand, drives man systematically to destroy, on an ever-widening front, the natural balance of things and, on the other, impels him periodically to flee the artificial world which in this way he creates. Never before have there been such enormous concentrations of buildings of stone, concrete and iron, and never before did city-dwellers, in such enormous numbers, periodically leave their homes in order to re-discover Nature at the seaside or in the mountains—that very Nature which they themselves have so inexorably banished. It would not be true to say that, in so doing, people are merely seeking to preserve their health. Many, if not all, are at the same time seeking a relaxation of soul that is accorded only by surroundings whose still unspoilt and harmonious state has ensured the preservation of such beauty as gives peace to the soul and frees the mind from the pressure of calculating thoughts. However, the same people who, when on holiday, consciously or unconsciously seek this beauty, quickly reject it as 'romanticism' whenever it stands in the way of their utilitarian interests. In this, the good or bad intention of the individual scarcely plays a role; everyone is under the pressure of economic forces, and it is usually unconscious self-defence if one hides from oneself the destructive consequences of certain developments. In the longer view, however, such an attitude is disastrous.

Beauty always represents an inward and inexhaustible equilibrium of forces; and this overwhelms our soul, since it can neither be calculated nor mechanically produced. A sense of beauty can therefore permit us the direct experience of relationships before we can perceive them, in a differentiated manner, with our discursive reason; in this, incidentally, there is a defence for our own physical and psychic well-being, something that we cannot neglect with impunity.

To this it may be objected that men have always distinguished between the useful and the beautiful; a pleasure-grove was always a luxury, while a wood was usually viewed in a utilitarian manner. It might even be said that it took modern education to create the desire to protect a given piece of nature on purely aesthetic grounds.

However, in earlier times there were also sacred groves, which no axe might fell. They catered neither for use in the usual sense of this word nor for luxury. Beauty and reality—two qualities which the modern world spontaneously separates—were (and, for men who have a pre-modern view regarding the sacred, still are) united. Even today there are sacred woods in Japan and India, just as there were in pre-Christian Europe; we mention them here only as one example of sacred nature, for there are also sacred mountains, as well as—and this touches us more closely—sacred springs, rivers, and lakes. Even within Christendom, which generally avoids the veneration of the various phenomena of Nature, there were and are springs and lakes—for example, the well at Chartres and the spring at Lourdes—which, because of their connection with miraculous events, have come to be regarded as sacred. What is important here is not that some particular mountain or spring is regarded as sacred, and therefore inviolable; but that one particular phenomenon is invariably an example of a whole range of related things, of a complete order of Nature, which for a larger or smaller community of men is of vital importance, and expresses a higher or supernatural reality: thus, for the ancient Germans, the forest was the indispensable basis of their very life, and at the same time something of a temple, a place that harboured the Divine Presence. All forest had this quality and, in this sense, was inviolable. Since, however, the forests also had to be used, there were special sacred woods whose function was to recall the principial and spiritually significant inviolability of the forest as such. The case of the sacred cow among the Hindus is similar: in reality, for the Hindus, everything living is sacred, in other words, inviolable and symbolical, for, according to their doctrine, all consciousness participates in the Divine Spirit. Since, however, it is impossible everywhere and always to avoid the killing of living creatures, the law of inviolability was in practice limited to a few symbolic species, amongst which the cow, as the incarnation of the maternal mercy of the cosmos, assumes a special position. By renouncing the slaughtering of cows, the Hindu in principle venerates all life and at the same time protects one of the most important bases of his way of life, which for thousands of years has depended on cultivation and the raising of cattle. Likewise the sacred springs, of which there were many in Medieval Christendom, drew attention to the sacredness of water as such; they were a reminder that water is a symbol of grace, something that can readily be seen in the symbolism of baptism. The sacred is that which is the object of veneration and awe; it is the reflection of something eternal, and therefore indestructible; and the inviolability which it enjoys stems directly therefrom.

Depending on which faith a people adheres to, and depending on their hereditary mentality, there are other natural or artificial things that they may regard as sacred. The four elements—air, fire, water, and earth—which are the most elementary modes of manifestation of all matter to offer themselves to our senses, are almost everywhere—with the exception of the modern, rationalistic world—endowed with the quality of sacredness; from this point of view, earth is illimitable, air is ungraspable, fire in its very nature is undefilable; only water is open to violation, and therefore commended to special protection.

To recapitulate: for pre-modern cultures, there are realities which transcend the level of mere utilitarianism and have precedence over them. These realities are in themselves of a purely spiritual or divine nature. They are however reflected in certain sensory appearances, which may consequently become the object of veneration and awe. These are then, either completely or in part (as representative symbols), withheld from the violent interference of men. Such an attitude is naturally very different from that of aesthetic sensitivity, which may also cause us, all considerations of usefulness apart, to admire and protect a natural phenomenon. But the sense of beauty is somehow contained within the veneration of the sacred; for the truly beautiful is that which lies hidden in the inexhaustible richness of harmoniously united possibilities. The same holds true for the sacred, and indeed for all phenomena and elements pertaining to the very bases of life, so that awe of the sacred also more or less directly contributes—not always in a predictable way—to the maintenance of life itself.

A few remarks should be made here regarding the elements: these have naturally nothing to do with what are called elements in modern chemistry but, as we have already said, represent the most elementary modes of manifestation in which the 'stuff on which the world is made' communicates itself to our five senses: the solid, the liquid, the aerial, and the fiery modes of manifestation. There are indeed other liquids besides water, but none has for us the same aspect of purity, and none plays such an important role in the preservation of life. Likewise there are other gaseous substances besides air, but none of them can be breathed.

Cosmically, then, the four elements are the simplest manifestational modes of matter. From an inward point of view, on the other hand, they are also the simplest images of our soul, which as such is ungraspable, but whose fundamental characteristics can be likened to the four elements. This is what St. Francis of Assisi has in mind when he praises God for the four elements, one after the other, in his famous *Canticle of the Sun*. In regard to water, he says: 'Praised be Thou, O Lord, for sister water, who is very useful, humble, precious, and chaste *(Laudato si, o Signore, per sor acqua, la quale è molto utile ed umile e preziosa e casta).*' That may sound like pure poetic allegory, but in fact it signifies very much more: humility and chastity well describe the quality of water which, in a river, takes on all forms, without thereby losing its purity. Herein also lies an image of the soul, which possesses the capacity to take in all impressions and to follow all forms while remaining true to its own undivided essence. 'The soul of man resembles water,' said Goethe, thereby reiterating an image that occurs in the Scriptures of both Near and Far East. The soul resembles water, just as the Spirit resembles wind or air.

It would lead us too far to mention all the myths and customs in which water appears as an image or reflection of the soul. An awareness that the soul recognizes itself when it beholds water—finding animation in its play, refreshment in its rest, and purity in its clarity—is perhaps nowhere more widespread than amongst the Japanese. The whole of Japanese life, to the extent that it is still formed by tradition, is penetrated by a sense of purity and pliant simplicity that finds its prefiguration in water. The Japanese make pilgrimages to the famous waterfalls of their country and will gaze for hours at the unruffled surface of a temple pond. Significant is the story of the Chinese sage Hsuyu—a recurring theme of Japanese painters—who received a message that the Emperor wished to hand over his kingdom to him; he fled to the mountains and washed his ears in a waterfall. The painter Harunobu represented him allegori-cally in the form of a young and noble maiden who, in the solitude of the mountains, washes her ear in the vertical fall of water.

For the Hindus, the water of life finds embodiment in the Ganges which, from its source in the Himalayas, the mountains of the Gods, irrigates the largest and most populous plains of India. Its water is held to be pure from beginning to end, and in fact it is preserved from all pollution by the fine sand which it drags along with it. Whoever, with repentant mind, bathes in the Ganges, is freed from all his sins: inner purification here finds its symbolic support in the outward purification that comes from the water of the sacred river. It is as if the purifying water came from Heaven, for its origin in the eternal ice of the roof of the world is like a symbol of the heavenly origin of divine grace which, as 'living water', springs from timeless and immutable Peace. Here, as in the similar rites of other religions and peoples, the correspondence of water and soul helps the latter to purify itself or, more exactly, to find anew its own—originally pure—essence. In this process, the symbol prepares the way for grace.

Water symbolizes the soul. From another point of view—but analogously—water symbolizes the *materia prima* of the whole universe. For, just as water contains within itself, as pure possibilities, all the forms which, in flowing and sparkling, it may assume, so *materia prima* contains all the forms of the world in a state of indistinction.

In the Biblical story of creation it is said that, in the beginning, before the creation of the earth, the Spirit of God moved upon the face of the waters; and the holy books of the Hindus tell us that all the inhabitants of the earth emerged from the primordial sea. In these myths, water is not meant in the ordinary sense of the word; and yet the picture they create in our imagination is in its own way correct, and as apt as possibly can be, for nothing conveys better the undifferentiated and passive unity of *materia prima*.

The myth of the creation of all things from the primordial sea finds an echo in the Koranic words: 'We have created every living thing from water'. The Biblical allegory of the Spirit of God moving upon the waters has its counterpart in the Hindu symbol of the divine swan Hamsa which, swimming on the primordial sea, hatches the golden egg of the world; and each of these allegorical representations is finally echoed in the Koran, where it is said that, at the beginning, the Throne of God was upon the water.

The opened lotus flower, the seat of Indian divinities, is also a 'throne of God' floating upon the water of *materia prima*, or upon the water of principial possibilities. This symbol, which was transmitted from Hindu to Buddhist mythology and art, brings us back from water as the image of the primordial substance of the world to water as the image of the soul. The lotus-stream of the Buddha or Boddhisattva rises up from the waters of the soul, just as the spirit, illumined by knowledge, frees itself from passive existence. Here water represents something which has to be overcome, but in which nevertheless there is good, because in it is rooted the flower whose calyx contains the 'precious jewel' of *Bodhi*, the Divine Spirit. The Buddha, the 'Jewel in the Lotus', is himself this Spirit.

That must suffice as a survey of the meanings which water can have as a symbol, though many other examples of this kind could be mentioned. But it is not merely a question of demonstrating that in all cultures that can be called pre-rationalist—and the term is not used pejoratively—water has more than a purely physical or biological meaning; the spiritual realities, of which it is the symbol, are never attached to it arbitrarily, but are directly and logically derived from its essence. The contemplative beholding of Nature which, through essential and constant appearances, perceives the timeless proto-types or causes of these appearances, is not something that is merely sentimental, nor is it bound to time and place, and this despite the fact of the modern world, from which this kind of contemplation seems to have been banished. We say 'seems', for such a contemp-lation of things is too deeply rooted in the human heart to be able to disappear completely. It even continues unconsciously, and it would not be difficult to show how the mysterious attraction of water as something sacred, as a symbolic and manifested expression of a psychic or cosmic reality, lives on in art, especially in painting and poetry. Who, when confronted with a pure mountain lake or with a spring gushing forth from the rock, has never felt at least something of the awe and veneration that are inseparable from anything sacred? The people of earlier times knew better than we that one does not disturb the balance of nature with impunity. Our superior scientific knowledge is totally insufficient to protect us from all the effects of a disturbed nature; and even if we could insure ourselves against every negative reaction on the part of the physical environment, we would still have no guarantee that the psychic or subtle world would not take its revenge on us. A glance at Asia and Africa, where the spiritual equilibrium of ancient cultures has been disturbed on all sides, and their very existence called into question, is sufficient to let us sense that it may still come to a destruction of 'living waters', in comparison with which the pollution of our physical waters will seem harmless.

In conclusion, and by way of indicating that even in modern Europe there are still sacred waters, mention should be made of Lough Derg in Donegal, the most northerly county in Ireland. In this lough is an island on which are a number of Christian shrines dating from the Middle Ages and also a cave, which represents the entry to the underworld. It is called 'St. Patrick's Purgatory', for it is said that it was here that St. Patrick, the Apostle of Ireland, made hell and the Mount of Purgatory appear to the heathen in a vision. Since the early

Middle Ages, the island has been a place of pilgrimage, with which very strict rules are associated. The pilgrims, who are brought to the island by boat, must walk on it fasting and bare-footed, and carry out certain spiritual exercises during a stay of three days. These consist principally in kneeling on the rocks and praying before a number of crosses that have been erected in honour of the most important of the Irish saints. Each time a pilgrim completes his devotion before these 'stations', set out like the beads of a rosary, he makes his way to a large rock that rises out of the water at a little distance from the shore of the island, and, after a few prayers, recites aloud the creed, looking out over the water of the lake. People who have performed this pilgrimage declare that these moments of solitude, in contemplation of the unruffled lake, surrounded by uninhabited hills, release in their hearts something that is undescribable.

# 12

# Insight into Alchemy

'To make of the body a spirit and of the spirit a body': this adage sums up the whole of alchemy. Gold itself, which outwardly represents the fruit of the work, appears as an opaque body become luminous, or as a light become solid. Transposed into the human and spiritual order, gold is bodily consciousness transmuted into spirit, or spirit fixed in the body.

For the base metal, which represents the immediate material of the work, is none other than consciousness bound to the body and as if submerged in it. This is the 'metallic body' from which must be extracted the 'soul' and the 'spirit', which are Mercury and Sulphur. If the 'body' were not an inner reality, it could not serve as the material for the spiritual work.

In the average man, 'to know' and 'to be' are as it were polarized in thought and bodily consciousness; the first represents an intelligence separated from the being of its objects, whereas the second is a passive state of being that is as if bereft of intelligence. This dichotomy is noticeable even in the dream state, in which the psychic form of the body is more or less detached from its sensory form. The return to the centre, to the heart considered as 'seat' of the spirit, is both an integration, and as it were an inversion, of the two poles: bodily consciousness in its fashion becomes intelligent: it is transmuted into a passive state of knowledge; at the same time thought—or the mental element—becomes crystallized under the lightning-like action of the spirit.

This transmutation of spirit into body and of body into spirit is to be found in a more or less direct and obvious manner in every method of spiritual realization; alchemy, however, has made of it its principal theme, in conformity with the metallurgical symbolism that is based on the possibility of changing the 'state of aggregation' of a body.

At the beginning of the work, bodily consciousness is chaotic and obscure. It is then compared to lead, and the 'régime' corresponding to this state of 'matter' is attributed to Saturn. This planet represents the principle of condensation, and it is this that explains its seemingly contradictory assignation to the metal lead (among corporeal substances) and to the reason (among the faculties of the soul): in relation to the existential dimension of the other faculties, the reason is like a point without extension. The polarity of thought and bodily consciousness—the opposition 'spirit'/'body'—is thus to be found in the nature of Saturn, and this corroborates the hostile, impeding, and even sinister character which this planet assumes in divinatory astrology.

On the plane of method, Saturnine condensation becomes concentration; the intelligence withdraws from the outward to the inward; having become a single point, it descends into the inward night of the body.

According to alchemical doctrine, every metal is constituted by the more or less perfect union of the two principles known as Sulphur and Mercury; likewise bodily consciousness, assimilated to the metal to be transformed, is woven from these two principles or subtle forces, which are both opposite and complementary: Sulphur, which is male, and Mercury, which is female, are combined in the chaotic bodily consciousness—or in the base metal—in such a way that they neutralize or impede one another.

Basilius Valentinus[1] writes: 'Wherever metallic soul, spirit, and form are to be found, there too are metallic quicksilver, sulphur, and salt . . .'[2] He thus likens Mercury to the soul and Sulphur to the spirit, and it is indeed thus that the two principles should be understood, always bearing in mind that alchemy considers them primarily as powers or forces co-operating on the same plane, namely that of 'nature'. If it happens that the same author, or other alchemists, should sometimes call Mercury 'spirit', this is because its 'volatile' nature is here being opposed to that of inert and solid bodies, and in this sense both Sulphur and Mercury are 'spirits'. Furthermore, Mercury, as 'substance' of the inner or psychic form of

---

[1] A German alchemist of the fifteenth century.
[2] See *De la grande pierre des Anciens Sages*, published together with *Les douze Clefs de la Philosophie*, translated by Eugène Canseliet (Paris, 1956).

the body, corresponds to the vital spirit, which is intermediary between soul and body.

According to Galen, the vital spirit is a very pure substance, distributed throughout cosmic space, which the heart assimilates by a process analogous to respiration, thus transforming it into animate life. It is easy to see that this corresponds to the role of *prana*, the 'vital breath', as it is conceived by the Hindus; its employment in *laya-yoga*, the 'yoga of solution', appears to be directly analogous to the use to which the alchemists put their 'universal solvent'.

Just as breathing re-establishes rhythmically the link between the physical organism and the cosmic environment, a link which the progressive solidification of bodies tends to break, so the parallel but more intimate assimilation of the vital spirit maintains the continuity between the psychic form of the body and its cosmic substance. Brother Marcanton writes on this subject:

> It is not that I do not know that your secret Mercury is an innate, universal, and living spirit, which, in the form of an aerial vapour, descends from Heaven to earth to fill its porous belly, and is then born amongst the impure Sulphurs and, in growing, passes from a volatile to a fixed nature, giving to itself a radical humid form.[3]

The 'porous belly' of the earth here corresponds to the human body; as for the 'impure Sulphurs', they are none other than gross bodies as it were enclosing their Sulphur, which is their formal principle. In allying itself with the psychic form of the body, Mercury is so to speak solidified, while at the same time constituting its 'radical humid', in other words its *hylé* or plastic substance.

As regards ordinary mercury, it is noteworthy that, alone amongst the metals known to Antiquity and the Middle Ages, it normally occurs in liquid form, and it evaporates under the action of the craftsman's fire; it is thus both a 'body' and a 'spirit'. Through it gold and silver can be liquefied; in metallurgy, it is also used to extract the noble metal from a mixture of impure and insoluble minerals; the amalgam is exposed to the fire which expels the mercury and lays bare the gold.

Just as common mercury forms an amalgam with gold, so subtle

[3] *La Lumière sortant par soi-même des Tenèbres*, Paris, 1687.

Mercury contains the germ of spiritual gold; the vital breath, while being 'humid' by nature—which is that of the feminine cosmic energy (the *Shakti* of the Hindu doctrine)—is the vehicle of the fiery principle of life. Reduced to its universal prototype, Mercury corresponds to the primordial ocean of Hindu mythology, namely *Prakriti*, which carries *Hiranyagharba*, the golden egg of the world.

In conformity with this universal prototype, Mercury includes a maternal aspect; more precisely, it is itself the maternal aspect or power of the *materia* of the animic world. For this reason certain alchemists, somewhat disconcertingly, give it the name *menstruum*; by this they mean the uterine blood that nourishes the embryo as long as it does not flow outwards and become corrupted; Mercury indeed nourishes the spiritual embryo enclosed in the Hermetic vessel.

It is through bodily consciousness, apparently closed in on itself, and in the most intimate depths thereof, that the alchemist recovers the cosmic substance Mercury. In order to 'capture' it, he will use as support some bodily function such as respiration, and this is significant for all the spiritual arts related to alchemy; taking a physical modality as its starting-point, consciousness—which is essentially intelligence—ascends through its own 'existential enve-lopes' to arrive at the universal reality of which the modality in question is a reflection or echo. Such an integration cannot however, be achieved without some kind of grace; moreover it presupposes a sacred framework, as well as an attitude that excludes any promethean or egoistic adventure.

Mercury is thus, at one and the same time and depending on its various planes of manifestation, the subtle 'breath' animating the body, the restless substance of the soul, the lunar power, the *materia* of the whole animic world, and finally *materia prima*. Just as the universal energy which the Hindus call *Shakti* possesses not only a maternal but also a terrible and destructive aspect, so Mercury is both 'water of life' and 'deadly poison'; in other words, its 'humid' nature is either generating or dissolving, depending on the circum-stances.

'Shun the mixture,' wrote Synesius,[4]

¹ Greek alchemist. He is perhaps identical with Bishop Synesios of Cyrene (379–415), a disciple of Hypatia, the Platonist of Alexandria. See *Bibliothèque des Philosophes Chimiques*, Paris, 1742.

and take its simple (*sic*), for this is its quintessence. Observe that we have two bodies of great perfection (gold and silver, or heart and blood) filled with quicksilver. So draw your quicksilver thence, and you will make of it a medicine which is called quintessence, and has a permanent and ever victorious power. It is a living light that illumines every soul that has once beheld it. It is the knot and bond of all the elements, which it contains within itself, just as it is the spirit that nourishes and vivifies all things, and by means of which nature acts in the universe. It is the strength, the beginning, the middle, and the end of the work. To tell you all in a few words, know, my son, that the quintessence and hidden reality of our stone is but our glorious, heavenly and viscous soul which by our mastery we derive from the mine[5] which alone engenders it. It is not in our power to make this water by any art, since nature alone can beget it. And this water is the sharp vinegar that makes a pure spirit from the body of gold. And I tell you, my son, take no account of any other things, for they are vain, but only of this water, which burns, whitens, dissolves, and congeals. It is also this water that decomposes and makes to germinate . . .

Although Mercury, after the fashion of universal substance, contains in potency all natural qualities—it is also often represented as androgynous—it is polarized in relation to Sulphur, and is manifested as cold and humid, while Sulphur is manifested as warm and dry. It should be noted here that warmth and dryness, which are the two masculine qualities, correspond to expansion and solidification, and that the two feminine qualities, humidity and cold, represent solution and contraction. In a sense, Sulphur imitates, in a dynamic and indirect way, the action of the formal principle, or essence, which 'deploys' forms and 'fixes' them in a certain plane of existence. On the other hand solution and contraction, which pertain to Mercury, express the receptivity of the feminine or plastic principle, its faculty of assuming all forms without being held by them, and its delimiting or separative action, which is an aspect of *materia*. In the crafts, the analogy between Sulphur and the formal

[5] According to Morienus, it is man who is the mine of the thing with which Mastery is accomplished. (*Dialogue du roi Khalid avec l'ermite Moriénus* in *Bibliothèque des Philosophes Chimiques*.)

principle is evinced in Sulphur's colouring action: thus the combination of common sulphur and mercury produces cinnabar, in which the liquid mercury is both fixed and coloured by sulphur. In metallurgical symbolism, colour is analogous to quality, and thus to form, in the traditional meaning of this term. However it should be stressed that cinnabar is only an imperfect product of the principles concerned, just as common sulphur and mercury are not identical with the two alchemical principles they symbolize.

In the first phase of the work, it is the solidifying or coagulating action of Sulphur which is opposed to the liberation of Mercury, just as the contracting action of Mercury neutralizes Sulphur. The knot is loosened by the growth of Mercury: to the extent that Mercury dissolves the imperfect coagulation—the 'base metal'—the expanding warmth of Sulphur comes into play in its turn. At the beginning Mercury works against the solidifying power of Sulphur; but after that, it awakens its generative strength, which manifests the true form of gold. This is analogous to the amorous combat between man and woman; it is the feminine fascination that dissolves the 'solidification' of the virile nature and awakens its power. It is sufficient here to remark that it is this fascination, spiritually canalized, which plays a certain role in Tantric methods.

In *Les Noces Chymiques de Christian Rosencreutz*, Johann Valentin Andreae[6] narrates the following parable:

> . . . a beautiful unicorn, white as snow, and wearing a gold collar inscribed with certain signs, advanced towards the fountain and, bending on its front legs, knelt as if to do obeisance to the lion who stood upright on the fountain. This lion, who because of his complete immobility seemed to be of stone or brass, forthwith seized a naked sword which he held in his claws, and broke it in twain; I think the two halves fell into the fountain. Then the lion continued to roar until a white dove, carrying an olive branch in its beak, flew towards him as fast as it could; she gave the branch to the lion who swallowed it and became quiet once more. Then with joyous bounds the unicorn returned to her place.

The white unicorn, a lunary animal, is Mercury in its pure state. The

[6] 1586–1654. Book published by Chacornac, Paris, 1928.

lion is Sulphur which, being identified with the body of which it is the formal principle, appears at first as immobile as a statue. By the homage of Mercury he wakes and begins to roar. His roaring is none other than his creative power: according to the *Physiologus*, the lion vivifies the stillborn cubs by his voice. The lion breaks the sword of reason and the pieces fall into the fountain where they dissolve. He does not stop roaring until the dove of the Holy Spirit gives him to eat the olive branch of knowledge. This seems to be the meaning of this parable, of which Johann Valentin Andreae was certainly not the author.

In certain conditions, Sulphur, when fettered, is the reason and contains the gold of the spirit in a sterile state. This gold first has to be dissolved in the fountain of Mercury, in order to become the living 'ferment' which will transform other metals into gold.

The first action of Mercury is to 'whiten' the body. Artephius[7] wrote:

The whole secret . . . is that we should know how to extract from the body of Magnesia the non-burning quicksilver, which is Antimony, and the Mercurial Sublimate; in other words, it is necessary to extract an incombustible living water, and then congeal it with the perfect body of the Sun, which dissolves in it into a white substance like cream, until it all becomes white. However, because of the decomposition and solution it undergoes in this water, the Sun will first lose its light; it will be obscured and blackened; then it will rise above the water, and gradually a white colour and substance will float on the surface; this is what is called whitening the red brass, philosophically sublimating it, and reducing it to its primary matter, namely incombustible white sulphur and fixed quicksilver. Thus the humid is terminated; in other words, gold, our body, having undergone repeated liquefaction in our dissolvent water, is converted and reduced to sulphur and fixed quicksilver. In this way the perfect body of the sun takes life in this water, and is vivified and inspired; it will grow and multiply in its own kind like all other things . . .

[7] A medieval alchemist of whose life nothing is known. 'Artephius' is probably a pseudonym. (*Bibliothèque des Philosophes chimiques*.)

The sun referred to by Artephius, which has to die and be dissolved in the mercurial water[8] before being reborn, represents individual consciousness bound to the body, the bodily ego as it were, which is gold or sun only in the latent state. Alchemists often give the name 'gold' or 'sun' to what is merely virtually gold.

The 'whitening' of the 'body', which follows the 'blackening', is sometimes described as a dissolving of the body in the mercurial water, and sometimes as a separating of the soul from the body. What this means is that the reduction of bodily consciousness to its psychic substance causes the soul to withdraw from the sensory organs and as it were expand in a 'space' that is both inward and unlimited. 'It ascends from Earth to Heaven,' says the Emerald Tablet, 'and redescends from Heaven to Earth, thus receiving the power of both higher and lower things.' In the same sense, one speaks of a sublimation that has to be followed by a new coagulation.

When the inner consciousness is thus reduced to its primary matter, the equivalent of the moon or silver, Sulphur is revealed in its true nature, which is a power emanating from the mysterious centre of the being, from its divine essence. This is the roaring of the solar lion, which is like a sonorous light or a luminous sound. Sulphur 'fixes' the fluid and ungraspable substance of Mercury by giving it a new form which is both body and spirit.

Artephius wrote:

> . . . natures change each other, because the body incorporates the spirit, and the spirit changes the body into a spirit both coloured and white . . . boil it in our white water, namely Mercury, until it is dissolved in blackness; then, through continuous decoction, the blackness will disappear, and finally the body thus dissolved will ascend with the white soul [bodily consciousness reabsorbed into the soul], and the one shall be merged with the other, and they shall embrace each other in such a way that they can nevermore be separated; then the spirit is united to the body (by a process inverse to the first) with true harmony, and they become a single permanent thing (the body 'fixing' the spirit, and the spirit turning bodily consciousness into a pure spiritual state); this is the solution

---

[8] Or in Antimony, which is also a dissolvent and which, in spiritual alchemy, is a synonym for Mercury.

of the body and the coagulation of the spirit, which are one and the same operation.

Most alchemists speak only of Sulphur and Mercury as the constituent natures of gold; others, like Basil Valentine, add a third, namely Salt. In the crafts, Sulphur is the cause of combustion and Mercury of evaporation, whereas Salt is represented by ash. If Sulphur and Mercury are 'spirits', Salt is the body, or more accurately, the principle of corporeality. In a certain sense, Sulphur, Mercury, and Salt correspond respectively to the spirit (or the spiritual essence), the soul, and the body in man, or alternatively, to the immortal soul, the vital breath, and the body.

If the distinctions between these three natures do not always seem clear in the descriptions of the alchemical work, this results from their not being considered in themselves, but only through their actions on the cosmic plane or, more exactly, on the subtle or animic plane, where their forces intermingle in countless ways. Because of the complexity of the domain in question, it is the most 'archaic' descriptions of the work that are the most accurate, because their symbolism is all-inclusive; as is said in the Emerald Tablet, Sulphur (solar power) and Mercury (lunar power) are respectively the 'father and mother' of the alchemical embryo. The 'wind' (the vital breath, which is the second nature of Mercury) has 'carried it in its womb'. The 'earth' (the body) is its 'nurse'.

When the body—or, more exactly, bodily consciousness—is purified of all passional 'humidity'—and in this connection it corresponds to 'ashes'—it helps to retain the 'fugitive' spirit; in other words, it becomes the 'fixative' of spiritual states which the mental faculty cannot maintain by itself. This is so because the body is the 'lower' that corresponds to the 'higher', according to the words of the Emerald Tablet.

The spiritual state that finds its 'support' in the body nevertheless has no common measure with the latter; it is as if a pyramid, inverted and of unlimited extension, sought to support itself with its point on the earth; it goes without saying that this image, which suggests a state of instability, is valid only from the point of view of extension.

In sacred art, the human likeness which most directly expresses the 'spiritualization of the body and the incorporation of the spirit' is that of the Buddha: the analogy with alchemical symbolism is all the more striking in that this image comprises solar attributes—halo and rays—and is often gilded. We have in mind especially the Mahayana statues of the Buddha, the best of which express in the plastic quality of their outward appearance that plenitude which is both immutable and intense and which the body contains but cannot circumscribe.

Basil Valentine compares the result of the conjunction of spirit and body to the 'glorious body' of the resurrected.[9]

Morienus[10] says:

> In such a one as shall have truly known how to cleanse and whiten the soul and make it ascend on high; and shall have guarded his body well and removed from it all darkness and blackness along with any bad odour; the soul will be able to be restored to its body, and at the hour of their reuniting, great wonders will appear.

And Rhases[11] writes:

> Thus each soul reunites with its first body; and in no way can it unite with any other; from thenceforth they will never again be separated; for then the body will be glorified and brought to incorruption and to unutterable subtlety and lustre, so that it will be able to penetrate all things, however solid, since its nature will then be that of a spirit.

---

[9] *Op. cit.* This is comparable to the role played by the immortality of the body in Chinese alchemy.

[10] The *Dialogue du roi Khalid avec l'ermite Moriénus* is perhaps the first alchemical text translated from Arabic into Latin.

[11] Rhases is undoubtedly the Greco-Latin form of the Arabic Razî, the full name being Abu Bakr ar-Razî (826–925). (*Bibliothèque des Philosophes chimiques.*)

# 13

# The Symbolism of Chess

IT IS KNOWN that the game of chess originated in India. It was passed on to the medieval West through the intermediary of the Persians and the Arabs, a fact to which we owe, for example, the expression 'checkmate' (German *Schachmatt*), which is derived from the Persian *shâh*: 'king' and the Arabic *mât*: 'he is dead'. At the time of the Renaissance some of the rules of the game were changed: the 'queen'[1] and the two 'bishops'[2] were given a greater mobility, and thenceforth the game acquired a more abstract and mathematical character; it departed from its concrete model, strategy, without however losing the essential features of its symbolism. In the original position of the chessmen, the ancient strategic model remains obvious; one can recognize two armies ranged according to the battle order that was customary in the ancient East: the light troops, represented by the pawns, form the first line; the bulk of the army consists of the heavy troops, the war chariots ('castles'), the knights ('cavalry'), and the war elephants ('bishops'); the 'king' with his 'lady' or 'counsellor' is positioned at the centre of his troops.

The form of the chess-board corresponds to the 'classical' type of *Vâstu-mandala*, the diagram which also constitutes the basic lay-out of a temple or a city. It has been pointed out[3] that this diagram

[1] In Oriental chess this piece is not a 'queen' but a 'counsellor' or 'minister' to the king (in Arabic *mudaffir* or *wazîr*, in Persian *fersan* or *fars*). The designation 'queen' in the Western game is doubtless due to a confusion of the Persian term *fersan*, which became *alferga* in Castilian, and the old French *fierce* or *fierge* for 'virgin'. Be that as it may, the attribution of such a dominant role to the king's 'lady' corresponds well with the attitude of chivalry. It is significant also that the game of chess was passed on to the West by that Arabo-Persian current that also brought with it heraldic art and the principal rules of chivalry.

[2] This piece was originally an elephant (Arabic *al-fîl*) which bore a fortified tower. The schematic representation of an elephant's head in some medieval manuscripts could be taken either for a 'fool's cap' or a bishop's mitre: in French the piece is called *fou*, 'fool'; in German it is called *Läufer* 'runner'.

[3] See the author's *Sacred Art in East and West* (Perennial Books, London, 1986), Chapter 1, 'The Genesis of the Hindu Temple'.

symbolizes existence conceived as a 'field of action' of the divine powers. The combat which takes place in the game of chess thus represents, in its most universal meaning, the combat of the *devas* with the *asûras*, of the 'gods' with the 'titans', or of the 'angels'[4] with the 'demons', all other meanings of the game deriving from this one.

The most ancient description of the game of chess which we possess appears in 'The Golden Prairies' by the Arab historian al Mas'ûdî, who lived in Baghdad in the ninth century. Al-Mas'ûdî attributes the invention—or codification—of the game to a Hindu king 'Balhit', a descendent of 'Barahman'. There is an obvious confusion here between a caste, that of the Brahmins, and a dynasty; but that the game of chess has a brahminic origin is proved by the eminently sacerdotal character of the diagram of 8 × 8 squares (*ashtâpada*). Further, the warlike symbolism of the game related it to the Kshatriyas, the caste of princes and nobles, as al-Mas'ûdî indicates when he writes that the Hindus considered the game of chess (*shatranj*, from the Sanskrit *chaturanga*[5]) as a 'school of government and defence'. King Balhit is said to have composed a book on the game of which 'he made a sort of allegory of the heavenly bodies, such as the planets and the twelve signs of the Zodiac, consecrating each piece to a star . . .' It may be recalled that the Hindus recognize eight planets: the sun, the moon, the five planets visible to the naked eye, and *Râhu*, the 'dark star' of the eclipses;[6] each of these 'planets' rules one of the eight directions of space. 'The Indians', continues al-Mas'ûdî, 'give a mysterious meaning to the re-doubling, that is to say to the geometrical progression, effected on the squares of the chess-board; they establish a relationship between the first cause, which dominates all the spheres and in which everything finds its end, and the sum of the squares of the chess-board . . .' Here the author is probably confusing the cyclical symbolism implied in the *ashtâpada* and the famous legend accord-

---

[4] The *devas* of Hindu mythology are analogous to the angels of the monotheistic traditions; it is known that each angel corresponds to a divine function.

[5] The word *chaturanga* signifies the traditional Hindu army, composed of four *angas* – elephants, horses, chariots and soldiers.

[6] Hindu cosmology always takes account of the principle of inversion and exception, which results from the 'ambiguous' character of manifestation: the nature of stars is luminosity, but as the stars are not Light itself, there must also be a dark one.

ing to which the inventor of the game asked the monarch to fill the squares of his chess-board with grains of corn by placing one grain on the first, two on the second, four on the third, and so on up to the sixty-fourth square, which gives the sum of 18,446,744,073,709,551,616 grains. The cyclical symbolism of the chess-board resides in the fact that it expresses the unfolding of space according to the quaternary and octonary of the principal directions ($4 \times 4 \times 4 = 8 \times 8$), and that it synthesizes, in crystalline form, the two great complementary cycles of sun and moon: the duodenary of the zodiac and the 28 lunar mansions; furthermore, the number 64, the sum of the squares on the chess-board, is a sub-multiple of the fundamental cyclic number 25920, which measures the precession of the equinoxes. We have seen that each phase of a cycle, 'fixed' in the scheme of $8 \times 8$ squares, is ruled by a heavenly body and at the same time symbolizes a divine aspect, personified by a *deva*.[7] It is thus that this *mandala* symbolizes at one and the same time the visible cosmos, the world of the Spirit, and the Divinity in its multiple aspects. Al-Mas'ûdî is therefore right to say that the Indians explain, 'by calculations based on the chess-board, the march of time and the cycles, the higher influences that are exerted on this world, and the bonds that attach them to the human soul . . .'

The cyclical symbolism of the chess-board was known to King Alphonsus the Wise, the famous troubadour of Castile, who in 1283 composed his *Libros de Acedrex*, a work which draws largely from Oriental sources.[8] Alphonsus the Wise also describes a very ancient variant of the game of chess, the 'game of four seasons', which takes

---

[7] Certain Buddhist texts describe the universe as a board of $8 \times 8$ squares, fixed by golden cords; these squares correspond to the 64 *kalpas* of Buddhism (see *Saddharma Pundarika*, Burnouf, *Lotus de la bonne Loi*, p. 148). In the *Ramayana*, the impregnable city of the gods, *Ayodhyâ*, is described as a square with eight compartments on each side. We also recall, in the Chinese tradition, the 64 signs which derive from the 8 trigrams commented on in the *I-Ching*. These 64 signs are generally arranged so as to correspond to the eight regions of space. Thus we again encounter the idea of a quaternary and octonary division of space, which summarizes all the aspects of the universe.

[8] In 1254 St. Louis, King of France, forbade chess to his subjects. The saint had in mind the passions that the game could unleash, especially as it was frequently combined with the use of dice.

place between four partners, so that the pieces, placed in the four corners of the chess-board, move in a rotatory direction, analogous to the movement of the sun. The 4 × 8 pieces must have the colours green, red, black, and white; they correspond to the four seasons: spring, summer, autumn, and winter; to the four elements: air, fire, earth, and water; and to the four organic 'humours'. The movement of the four camps symbolizes cyclical transformation.[9] This game, which strangely resembles certain 'solar' rites and dances of the Indians of North America, brings into relief the fundamental principle of the chess-board.

The chess-board can be considered as the extension of a diagram formed by four squares, alternatively black and white, and constitutes in itself a *mandala* of Shiva, God, in his aspect of transformer: the quaternary rhythm, of which this *mandala* is, as it were, the 'spatial' coagulation, expresses the principle of time. The four squares, placed around an unmanifested centre, symbolize the cardinal phases of every cycle. The alternation of the black and white squares in this elementary diagram of the chess-board[10] brings out its cyclical significance[11] and makes of it the rectangular equivalent of the Far-Eastern symbol of *yin-yang*. It is an image of the world in its fundamental dualism.[12]

If the sensible world in its integral development results to some extent from the multiplication of qualities inherent in space and time, the *Vâstu-mandala* for its part derives from the division of time by space: one may recall the genesis of the *Vâstu-mandala* from the

---

[9] This variant of chess is described in the *Bhawisya Purana*. Alphonsus the Wise also speaks of a 'great game of chess' which is played on a board of 12×12 squares and of which the pieces represent mythological animals; he attributes it to the sages of India.

[10] Given that the Chinese chess-board, which likewise had its origin in India, does not possess the alternation of two colours, it is to be assumed that this element comes from Persia; it nevertheless remains faithful to the original symbolism of the chess-board.

[11] It also makes of it a symbol of inverse analogy: spring and autumn, morning and evening, are inversely analogous. In a general manner the alternation of black and white corresponds to the rhythm of day and night, of life and death, of manifestation and of reabsorption in the unmanifest.

[12] For this reason the type of *Vâstu-mandala* which has an uneven number of squares could not serve as a chess-board: the 'battlefield' which the latter represents cannot have a manifested centre, for symbolically it would have to be beyond oppositions.

never-ending celestial cycle, this cycle being divided by the cardinal axes, then crystallized in a rectangular form.[13] The *mandala* is thus the inverted reflection of the principial synthesis of space and time, and it is in this that its ontological significance resides.

From another point of view, the world is 'woven' from the three fundamental qualities or *gunas*[14] and the *mandala* represents this weaving in a schematic manner, in conformity with the cardinal directions of space. The analogy between the *Vâstu-mandala* and weaving is brought out by the alternation of colours which recalls a woven fabric of which the warp and the woof are alternately apparent or hidden.

Moreover, the alternation of black and white corresponds to the two aspects of the *mandala*, which are complementary in principle but opposed in practice: the *mandala* is on the one hand *Purusha-mandala*, that is to say a symbol of the Universal Spirit (*Purusha*) inasmuch as it is an immutable and transcendent synthesis of the cosmos; on the other hand it is a symbol of existence (*Vâstu*) considered as the passive support of divine manifestations. The geometric quality of the symbol expresses the Spirit, while its purely quantitative extension expresses existence. Likewise its ideal immutability is 'spirit' and its limiting coagulation is 'existence' or *materia*; here it is not *materia prima*, virgin and generous, that is being referred to, but *materia secunda*, 'dark' and chaotic, which is the root of existential dualism. In this connection one may recall the myth according to which the *Vâstu-mandala* represents an *asûra*, personification of brute existence: the *devas* have conquered this demon and have established their 'dwelling-places' on the stretched-out body of their victim; thus they confer their 'form' upon him, but it is he who manifests them.[15]

This double meaning which characterizes the *Vâstu-Purusha-mandala*, and which, moreover, is to be found in every symbol, is in a sense actualized by the combat that the game of chess represents.

---

[13] See the author's *Sacred Art in East and West*, Chapter 2, 'The Foundations of Christian Art' (Perennial Books, London, 1986).

[14] See René Guénon, *The Symbolism of the Cross* (Luzac, London, 1958).

[15] The *mandala* of 8×8 squares is also called *Manduka*, 'the frog', by allusion to the 'Great Frog' (*maha-manduka*) which supports the whole universe and which is the symbol of obscure and undifferentiated *materia*.

This combat, as we have said, is essentially that of the *devas* and the *asûras*, who dispute the chess-board of the world. It is here that the symbolism of black and white, already present in the squares of the chess-board, takes on its full value: the white army is that of Light, the black army that of darkness. In a relative domain, the battle which takes place on the chess-board represents, either that of two terrestrial armies each of which is fighting in the name of a principle,[16] or that of the spirit and of darkness in man; these are the two forms of the 'holy war'; the 'lesser holy war' and the 'greater holy war', according to a saying of the Prophet Mohammed. One will see the relationship of the symbolism implied in the game of chess with the theme of the *Bhagavad-Gîtâ*, a book which is likewise addressed to *Kshatriyas*.

If the significance of the different chessmen is transposed into the spiritual domain, the king becomes the heart, or spirit, and the other pieces the various faculties of the soul. Their movements, moreover, correspond to different ways of realizing the cosmic possibilities represented by the chessboard: there is the axial movement of the 'castles' or war chariots, the diagonal movement of the 'bishops' or elephants, which follow a single colour, and the complex movement of the knights. The axial movement, which 'cuts' through the different 'colours', is logical and virile, while the diagonal movement corresponds to an 'existential'—and therefore feminine—continuity. The jump of the knights corresponds to intuition.

What most fascinates the man of noble and warlike caste is the relationship between will and destiny. Now it is precisely this that is so clearly illustrated by the game of chess, inasmuch as its moves always remain intelligible without being limited in their variation. Alphonsus the Wise, in his book on chess, relates how a king of India wished to know whether the world obeyed intelligence or chance. Two wise men, his advisers, gave opposing answers, and to prove their respective theses, one of them took as his example the game of chess, in which intelligence prevails over chance, while the other

[16] In a holy war it is possible that each of the combatants may legitimately consider himself as the protagonist of Light fighting the darkness. This again is a consequence of the double meaning of every symbol: what for one is the expression of the Spirit, may be the image of dark 'matter' in the eyes of the other.

produced dice, the symbol of fatality.[17] Al-Mas'ûdî writes likewise that the king 'Balhit', who is said to have codified the game of chess, gave it preference over *nerd*, a game of chance, because in the former intelligence always has the upper hand over ignorance.

At each stage of the game, the player is free to choose between several possibilities, but each movement will entail a series of unavoidable consequences, so that necessity increasingly limits free choice, the end of the game being seen, not as the fruit of hazard, but as the result of rigorous laws.

It is here that we see not only the relationship between will and fate but also between liberty and knowledge; except in the case of inadvertence on the part of his opponent, the player will only safeguard his liberty of action when his decisions correspond with the nature of the game, that is to say with the possibilities that the game implies. In other words, freedom of action is here in complete solidarity with foresight and knowledge of the possibilities; contrariwise, blind impulse, however free and spontaneous it may appear at first sight, is revealed in the final outcome as a non-liberty.

The 'royal art' is to govern the world—outward and inward—in conformity with its own laws. This art presupposes wisdom, which is the knowledge of possibilities; now all possibilities are contained, in a synthetic manner, in the universal and divine Spirit. True wisdom is a more or less perfect identification with the Spirit (*Purusha*), this latter being symbolized by the geometrical quality[18] of the chessboard, 'seal' of the essential unity of the cosmic possibilities. The Spirit is Truth; through Truth, man is free; outside Truth, he is the slave of fate. That is the teaching of the game of chess; the *Kshatriya* who gives himself over to it does not only find in it a pastime or a means of sublimating his warlike passion and his need for adventure, but also, according to his intellectual capacity, a speculative support, and a 'way' that leads from action to contemplation.

---

[17] The *mandala* of the chessboard, on the one hand, and dice, on the other, represent two different and complementary symbols of the cosmos.

[18] We may recall that the Spirit or the Word is the 'form of forms', that is to say the formal principle of the universe.

# 14

# The Sacred Mask

THE MASK is one of the most widespread and doubtless one of the most ancient modes of sacred art. It is to be found as much in the most elaborated of civilizations, such as those of India and Japan, as among the so-called primitive peoples. The only exception is that of the civilization attached to Semitic monotheism, although in fact the mask has been preserved in the folklore of Christian peoples as well as among certain Moslem peoples,[1] and this at times in forms whose symbolism is still evident.[2] Indeed, the tenacity of their survival in the face of all modern thought proves indirectly their sacred origin.

For Christianity, as for Judaism and Islam, the ritual use of the mask can only be a form of idolatry. But in fact the mask is linked not with idolatry but with polytheism, if one understands by this term not paganism, but a spiritual vision of the world that spontaneously personifies cosmic functions without ignoring the single and infinite nature of Supreme Reality.

This vision implies a conception of the 'person' that is somewhat different from that familiar to us from monotheism. It derives from the expression *persona* itself. We know that in the ancient theatre, derived from the sacred theatre of the Mysteries, this word designated both the mask and the role.[3] Now the mask necessarily

---

[1] Especially among the Moslems of Java and Black Africa. The mask is also to be found among the Berbers of North Africa, where it has a carnivalesque character.

[2] The grotesque mask—of an 'apotropeic' character and used above all in the solsticial masquerades—as well as the fairy mask, and even the heroic mask, are to be found among the Germanic peoples. The heroic mask also features in Spanish folklore.

[3] *Persona* has been derived from *personare*, 'to sound through'—the mask being literally the mouthpiece of the cosmic Essence that is manifested through it—but according to Littré this etymology is doubtful for phonetic reasons. Even so it retains a certain value from the point of view of significant coincidences—which are by no means accidents—in the sense of the Hindu *nirukta*.

expresses not an individuality—whose representation scarcely requires a mask—but a type, and hence a timeless reality, cosmic or divine. The 'person' is thus identified with the function, and this in turn is one of the multiple masks of the Divinity, whose infinite nature remains impersonal.

There is a hierarchy of functions and thus of divine 'persons'; but their very multiplicity means that no single one of them can be regarded as the unique and total mask of the infinite Divinity. The Divinity can clothe itself in one mask or another in order to reveal itself more directly to the worshipper; or alternatively the latter can choose one particular mask as his support and way of worship; he will always end by finding in it every celestial dignity, for each of the universal qualities essentially contains the others. This explains the apparently fluctuating character of the ancient pan-theons.[4]

The essence of the universal qualities is one; this is what monotheism seeks to affirm when it proclaims the unicity of the divine 'person'. It is as if it made use of the idea of the person—the only idea that a polytheism that has become forgetful of the Absolute can still grasp—in order to affirm the unity of the Essence. On the other hand, monotheism had to make a distinction between the person and his various functions and qualities, a distinction that is indeed evident since it is similar to that which exists between the human subject and his faculties. Nonetheless it remains true that the personal divinity is always conceived by means of one or other of His qualities, which on the plane of manifestation are distinguishable and even sometimes mutually exclusive. They can never all reveal themselves at the same time, and where they coincide—in the undifferentiated plenitude of their common essence—one can no longer truly speak of a person, since this essence is beyond all distinctiveness, and thereby beyond the person. But the distinction between the personal God and the impersonal Essence pertains to the domain of esoterism, and thus rejoins the metaphysics that underlies traditional polytheism.[5] Be all that as it may, by denying the

[4] We have in mind the fact that a subordinate god can sometimes 'usurp' the highest role.

[5] In Moslem esoterism, for example, the multiple gods of the polytheists are often compared to divine names; paganism, or polytheism in the restrictive sense of the term, thus corresponds to a confusion between the 'name' and the 'named'.

multiplicity of persons, monotheism also had to reject the ritual use of the mask.

But to return to the sacred mask as such: it is above all the means of a theophany; the individuality of its wearer is not simply effaced by the symbol assumed, it merges into it to the extent that it becomes the instrument of a superhuman 'presence'. For the ritual use of the mask goes far beyond mere figuration: it is as if the mask, in veiling the face or the outward ego of its wearer, at the same time unveiled a possibility latent within him. Man really becomes the symbol that he has put on, which presupposes both a certain plasticity of soul and a spiritual influence actualized by the form of the mask. In addition, a sacred mask is generally regarded as a real being; it is treated as if it were alive, and it is not put on until certain rites of purification have been performed.[6]

Moreover, man spontaneously identifies himself with the role that he plays, one that has been imposed on him by his origin, his destiny, and his social ambience. This role is a mask—most often a false mask in a world as artificial as our own, and in any case one that limits rather than liberates. The sacred mask, on the contrary, along with all that its wearing implies as regards gestures and words, suddenly offers one's 'self-consciousness' a much vaster mould and thereby the possibility of realizing the 'liquidity' of this consciousness and its capacity to espouse all forms without being any one of them.

Here we should make an observation: by 'mask' we mean above all an artificial face that covers the face of its wearer. But in many cases—for example in the Chinese theatre or among the North American Indians—a simple painting of the face has the same function and the same efficacy. Usually the mask is complemented by the dressing or ornamentation of the whole body. Furthermore, the ritual usage of the mask is mostly accompanied by sacred dancing, whose symbolic gestures and rhythm have the same purpose as the mask, namely the actualizing of a superhuman presence.

The sacred mask does not always suggest an angelic or divine presence: it can also be the support of an 'asuric' or demonic

---

[6] The same is true for the making of masks among most of the African peoples: the sculptor of a sacred mask has to undergo a certain ascetic discipline. See Jean-Louis Bédouin, *Les Masques* (Les Presses Universitaires, Paris, 1961).

presence, without this necessarily implying any deviation; for this
presence, malefic in itself, can be tamed by a higher influence and
captured with a view to expiation, as in certain lamaist rites. Also
worthy of mention, as a well-known example, is the combat between
the *Barong* and the sorceress Rangda in the sacred theatre of Bali: the
*Barong*, who has the form of a fantastic lion, and is commonly
considered as the protective genius of the village, is in reality the solar
lion, symbol of divine light, as is expressed by his golden ornaments;
he has to confront the sorceress Rangda, personification of ten-
ebrous forces. Both of these masks are supports for subtle influences
that are communicated to all who participate in the drama; between
the two a real combat develops. At a given moment, young men in a
trance throw themselves upon the sorceress Rangda in order to stab
her; but the magical power of the mask forces them to turn their *kris*
on themselves; finally the *Barong* repulses the sorceress Rangda. In
reality she is a form of the goddess Kali, of the divine power
envisaged in its destructive and transforming function, and it is by
virtue of this implicitly divine nature of the mask that its wearer can
assume it with impunity.

The grotesque mask exists at many different levels. It generally
possesses an 'apotropeic' power, for, in unveiling the true nature of
certain evil influences, it puts them to flight. The mask 'objectivizes'
tendencies or forces whose danger is increased to the extent that they
remain vague and unconscious; it reveals to them their own ugly and
despicable face in order to disarm them.[7] Its effect is thus psychological, but it goes far beyond the plane of ordinary psychology, since
the very form of the mask and its quasi-magical efficacy depend on a
science of the cosmic tendencies.[8]

The 'apotropeic' mask has often been transposed to the sculptural
decoration of temples. When its grotesque and terrifying character is
conceived as an aspect of the divine destructive power, it is in its turn
a divine mask. The Gorgoneion of archaic Greek temples must no
doubt be interpreted in this way, and this is also the meaning of the

[7] The healing masks of the Iroquois—called 'false faces'—are a well known and
very typical example of the function in question; strangely enough, they recall certain
popular masks of the Alpine countries.
[8] This was one of the first themes dealt with by Titus Burckhardt in a published
work; see pages 110–1 of this book.

*Kâla-mukha*, the composite mask that adorns the topmost point of the niches in Hindu architecture.[9]

The sacred mask necessarily borrows its forms from nature, but it is never 'naturalistic', since its purpose is to suggest a timeless cosmic type. It achieves this purpose either by emphasizing certain essential features or by combining different but analogous forms of nature, for example human and animal forms, or animal and geometrical forms. Its formal language is much less often addressed to the emotive sensibility than one might be tempted to think: the ritual masks of the Eskimos, for example, or of the Indians of the north-west coast of America, or of certain African tribes, are intelligible only to those who are familiar with all their symbolic references. The same can be said about the masks of the Hindu sacred theatre: the mask of Krishna, as it is represented in southern India, is like an assemblage of metaphors.

As regards masks of animal form, the following may be said: the animal is in itself a mask of God; what looks at us from its face is less the individual than the genius of the species, the cosmic type, which corresponds to a divine function. One might also say that in the animal the different powers or elements of nature assume the form of a mask: water is 'personified' in the fish, the air in the bird; in the buffalo or bison the earth manifests its generous and fertile aspect, and in the bear it shows its darker face. Now these powers of nature are divine functions.

Nevertheless, dances with masks of animal forms can have a practical purpose, namely that of conciliating the genius of the species hunted. This is a magical action, but one that can well be integrated with a spiritual vision of things. Since subtle links between man and his natural ambience exist, one can make use of them just as one makes use of physical conditions. What is important from the spiritual point of view is an awareness of the real hierarchy of things. Certainly the ritual use of the mask can degenerate into magic pure and simple, but this happens much less frequently than is generally assumed.

For the Bantu, as for other African peoples, the sacred mask

[9] See A. K. Coomaraswamy ('Svayâmatrinnâ: Janua Coeli' in *Selected Papers*, vol. 1, Princeton, N.J. 1976), 'The Face of Glory', and also my book *Sacred Art in East and West*, p. 36.

represents the animal totem that is considered as the tribe's ancestor. Obviously it is not a question here of the natural ancestor, but of the timeless type from which the ancestors received their spiritual authority. The animal of the mask is thus a supra-terrestrial animal, and this is indicated in its half-animal, half-geometrical form.[10] Likewise the anthropomorphic masks of 'ancestors' do not merely evoke an individual; they represent the cosmic type or function of which the ancestor was the human manifestation: in the case of peoples where the spiritual filiation coincides in practice with an ancestral descendence, the ancestor who is at the origin of this descendence necessarily assumes the role of solar hero, half-human, half-divine.

In a certain sense, the sun is the divine mask *par excellence*. For it is like a mask in front of the divine light, which would blind and consume earthly beings if it were unveiled. Now the lion is a solar animal, and the mask in the form of a lion's head is the image of the sun. This same mask is also to be found on fountains, and the jet of water that gushes from it symbolizes the life that comes from the sun.

The custom of covering the face of a dead man with a mask was not exclusive to the ancient Egyptians; and the primal meaning of this custom must have been the same everywhere: by its symbolic form—sometimes resembling the sun[11]—this mask represented the spiritual prototype into which the dead man was supposed to reintegrate himself. The mask covering the face of Egyptian mummies is usually regarded as a stylized portrait of the dead man, but this is only partially the case, although this mask did in fact become, towards the end of the ancient Egyptian world and under the influence of Greco-Roman art, a veritable funerary portrait. Prior to this decadence, it was a mask that showed the dead man not as he was but as he had to become. It was of a human face that in a sense approximated to the unchanging and luminous form of the stars. Now this mask played a specific role in the posthumous evolution of the soul: according to Egyptian doctrine, the lower subtle modality of

---

[10] It may be that the Egyptian images of gods with a human body and an animal head derive from the ritual use of the mask. These gods correspond to angels; according to St. Thomas Aquinas, each angel occupies the rank of an entire species.

[11] See Jean-Louis Bédouin, *op. cit.*, pp. 89 ff.

man, which the Hebrews call the 'breath of the remains'[12] and which normally dissolves after death, can be held and fixed by the sacred form of the mummy. This form—or this mask—thus plays, in relation to this assemblage of diffuse and centrifugal subtle forces, the role of a formative principle: it sublimates this 'breath' and fixes it, making of it a kind of link between this world and the soul of the dead man, a bridge by means of which the incantations and offerings of the survivors can reach the soul, and by means of which its blessing can reach them. This fixation of the 'breath of the remains' is moreover produced spontaneously on the death of a saint, and it is this that makes a relic what it is: in a saint, the lower psychic modality or bodily consciousness had already been transformed during his lifetime; it has become the vehicle of a spiritual presence with which it will imbue the relics and the tomb of the holy personage.

It is probable that in the beginning the Egyptians consecrated only the mummies of men of high spiritual dignity, since there is a danger in retaining the psycho-physical modality of just anyone. As long as the traditional framework remained intact, this danger could be neutralized; the danger arises only when men of a totally different civilization, and completely ignorant of subtle realities, break the seals of the tombs.

Typical stylization of the human face is also to be found in the masks of *Nô*, the ritual theatre of Japan, where the intention is both psychological and spiritual. Each type of mask manifests a certain tendency of the soul; it lays this tendency bare, showing what is either fatal or generous within it. Thus the play of the masks is the play of the *gunas*, the cosmic tendencies, within the soul.

In *Nô*, the differentiation of types is obtained by extremely subtle methods; the more the expression of a mask is latent and immobile, the more it is living in its play: each gesture of the actor will make it speak; each movement, causing the light to glide over its features, will reveal a new aspect of the mask; it is like a sudden vision of a depth or of an abyss of the soul.

[12] See René Guénon, *L'Erreur spirite*, chapter 7.

# 15

# The Return of Ulysses

**E**VERY PATH leading towards spiritual realization requires of man that he strip himself of his ordinary and habitual ego in order that he may truly become 'himself', a transformation which does not take place without the sacrifice of apparent riches and of vain pretensions, and thus not without humiliation, nor without a struggle against the passions of which the 'old ego' is woven. This is why one finds, in the mythology and folklore of almost all peoples, the theme of the royal hero who returns to his own kingdom under the guise of a poor stranger, or even of a juggler or a beggar, in order, after many trials, to re-conquer the property which legitimately is his and of which a usurper had dispossessed him.

Instead of a kingdom to be re-conquered—or perhaps in parallel to this theme—the myth often speaks of a marvellously beautiful woman who is to belong to the hero capable of liberating her from the physical or magical fetters by means of which a hostile power holds her prisoner. If, in the myth, this woman is already the hero's wife, the idea that she belongs to him by right is reinforced, as is also the spiritual meaning of the myth according to which the wife, freed from hostile forces, is none other than the soul of the hero, unlimited in her essence, and feminine, because complementary to the hero's virile nature.[1]

We find all these mythological themes in the last part of the *Odyssey*, the part that describes Ulysses' return to Ithaca and to his own home, which he finds invaded by young suitors for his wife's hand, who squander his possessions and force him to undergo all kinds of humiliations until the moment that he makes himself known, not only as the master of the house but also as their implacable and quasi-divine judge.

[1] One particular case is the Hindu myth of Râma and Sîtâ: Sîtâ, liberated from the demons, is repudiated by Râma in spite of her fidelity.

It is also this part of the epic that includes the most direct allusions to the spiritual domain, allusions that prove that Homer was aware of the deep meaning of the myths that he was transmitting or adapting. These openings are nevertheless rare and as if neutralized by a sort of naturalistic tendency that seeks to adhere to modalities that are only too human. What a contrast with the great Hindu epics such as the *Mahâbhârata*, for example, or even with Germanic mythology, in which it is precisely the improbable, the excessive, the discontinuous, and even the monstrous that signalize the presence of a transcendent reality!

The last cantos of the *Odyssey*, moreover, constitute part of the essential narrative of the poem, for it is as guest of the Phaeacians that Ulysses relates his adventures since leaving Troy; and this he does in such a way that all his wanderings are presented retrospectively as a long and painful return to his homeland, one that had been several times delayed by the insubordination or folly of his own companions; for it was they who, while Ulysses was asleep, had opened the flasks in which Aeolus, the god of winds, had enclosed the unfavourable winds before entrusting them to the safe-keeping of the hero. The demonic forces thus imprudently let loose drive his little fleet far from its destination. It was also these companions who killed the sun god's sacred cattle, thus incurring his curse. Ulysses is forced to visit the Hyperborean regions, there to consult the ghost of Tiresias before regaining the way to his homeland. He alone is saved, without his companions; shipwrecked and bereft, he finally reaches the island of the Phaeacians, who receive him warmly. They convey him to Ithaca and deposit him, sleeping, on the shore. Thus Ulysses reaches his much longed-for homeland without knowing it; for when he awakes, he does not at first recognize the country, veiled as it is in mist, until Athena, his divine protectress, lifts the fog and shows him his native land.

At this point occurs the famous description of the cave of Nymphs, in which Ulysses, on Athena's advice, hides the precious gifts received from the Phaeacians. According to Porphyry, the disciple and successor of Plotinus, this cave is an image of the whole world and we will see below on what this interpretation is based.[2] One thing

---

[2] See Porphyry, *De Antro Nympharum* Station Hill Press (Barrytown, N.Y. 1983).

is certain: Ulysses' visit to the cave marks the hero's entry into a sacred space; henceforth the island of Ithaca will no longer merely be the hero's native land, but will be as it were an image of the centre of the world.

All the same, Homer no more than touches on this dimension; as always, when he speaks of spiritual realities, he expresses himself by means of allusion:

> At the head of the harbour is an olive-tree with long leaves,
> And close to that is a pleasant and shadowy cavern
> Sacred to the nymphs who are called Naiads.
> And in it there are bowls and amphoras
> Of stone. And bees store up their honey in them.
> There are also high stone looms in it, where the nymphs
> Weave purple mantles, a wonder to behold,
> And ever-flowing waters are there. It has two doors,
> One toward the North, accessible to men,
> And the other one divine is toward the South, nor may men
> Approach by that one, but it is a path for immortals.
>
> *Odyssey*, XIII, 102–112.[3]

According to Porphyry, the stone of which the cave and the objects contained within it are made represents the substance or plastic matter of which the world is a coagulation, for stone has no form other than that which is imposed on it. The same is true for the waters that gush forth from the rock: they too are a symbol of substance considered, in this case, in its original purity and fluidity. The cave is dark because it contains the cosmos in potency, in a state of relative indifferentiation. The garments that the Nymphs weave on their high stone looms are the garments of life itself, and their purple colour is that of blood. As for the bees that deposit their honey in bowls and stone amphoras, they are, like the Naiads, pure powers in the service of life, for honey is an incorruptible substance. Honey is also the essence, or the 'quintessence', that fills the receptacles of 'matter'.

Like the great cave of the world, the sacred cave has two doors: the

[3] Adapted from the translation by Albert Cook (W. W. Norton & Co., New York, 1967).

northern one is for the souls which once more descend into becoming, and the southern one is for the souls which, immortal or immortalized, ascend towards the world of the gods.[4] These are the two solsticial doors, *januae coeli*, which are really two doors in time, or indeed out of time, for they correspond to the two turning points in the annual cycle, the two moments of immobility between the expanding and contracting phases of the sun's movement. In order to understand Homer's allusion, one must carefully note the fact that the 'place' of the winter solstice, Capricorn, is situated in the southern hemi-cycle of the sun's orbit, while the 'place' of the summer solstice, Cancer, is situated in the northern or boreal hemi-cycle.

Porphyry also reminds us that the sacred olive tree that grows close to the cave is the tree of Minerva and that its leaves turn round in winter, obeying the annual cycle of the sun. Let us add that this tree is here the image of the tree of the world, whose trunk, branches, and leaves represent the totality of beings.[5]

There is one thing Porphyry does not mention, and that is that the sacred cave is above all a symbol of the heart. And it is in this context that Ulysses' gesture of entrusting all his treasures to the guardianship of the divine Naiads acquires its full significance: from this moment he is like one who is 'poor in spirit': outwardly poor, but inwardly rich.[6] Athena, through her magic, confers on him the appearance of a poor old man.

The fact that Ulysses is the protégé of Pallas Athena, the goddess of wisdom, forces us to believe that the guile he exhibits on every occasion and which is almost his most salient characteristic, did not, in the spiritual cosmos of the Greeks of Antiquity, play the same negative role that it did for a Christian like Dante, who places Ulysses in one of the most terrible regions of hell, as a liar and deceiver *par excellence*. For the Greeks, Ulysses' guile amounted to a capacity to

---

[4] According to Hellenic eschatology, the only alternative is between deliverance by divinization and a return to becoming; it does not conceive of the permanent dwelling of souls in paradise, this possibility arising only in the shadow of a saviour or mediator.

[5] Let us note that the olive tree is a sacred tree not only for the 'pagan' world, but also for Judaism and Islam.

[6] In Islamic esoterism, initiates are called the 'poor towards God' (*fuqarâ ilâ 'Llâh*).

dissimulate and persuade which in itself was positive; it was the sign of a sovereign intelligence, and almost a magic of the spirit that could penetrate and fathom others' thoughts. Let us refer to Porphyry, who analyzes the spiritual and moral nature of Ulysses in the following way:

> He could not easily free himself from this life of the senses, given that he had blinded it [in Polyphemus] and set about annihilating him with one single blow . . . For he who dares to do such things is always persecuted by the wrath of the gods, both marine and material.[7] Therefore he must first propitiate them with sacrifices, then with trials of mendicancy and other acts of perseverance, sometimes combating the passions, sometimes using incantations and dissimulations, and by those very means passing through all modalities in order finally to escape from his rags and make himself master of all.[8]

The inhabitants of Ithaca believe that Ulysses is dead; Penelope herself, the ever faithful wife, doubts if he will ever return. In fact, he has already returned, a stranger in his own home, and as if dead to this life. In begging alms from the suitors who are abusing his property, he puts them to the test, and he suffers this test himself. Before he had come, they were relatively innocent; now they burden themselves with faults through their outrages towards the stranger, and Ulysses is justified in his intention to destroy them.

According to a more inward aspect of things, the prideful suitors are the passions which, in the hero's very heart, had taken possession of his inward birthright and were seeking to seize his wife, the pure and faithful depth of his soul. However, stripped of the false dignity of his ego, having become poor and a stranger to himself, he sees, without illusion, these passions for what they are, and decides to fight them to the death.

In order to provoke an ordeal, Ulysees himself suggests to his wife that she invite the suitors to an archery contest. It consists in bending

---

[7] An allusion to the anger of Poseidon, god of the ocean, whose son, Polyphemus, Ulysses had blinded. According to Porphyry, the ocean represents universal substance in its terrible aspect.

[8] Porphyry, *op. cit.*

the sacred bow belonging to the master of the house and in shooting an arrow through the holes in twelve axes lined up and planted in the ground.

The contest takes place on the feast of Apollo, for the bow is the weapon of the sun-god. One may recall in this connection the analogous trials which, according to Hindu mythology, were undergone by certain *avatâras* of Vishnu, such as Râma and Krishna, and even the young Gautama Buddha: it is always the bow of the sun-god that they bend.

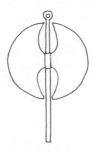

*Cretan double axe*

The twelve axes planted in the ground (through the holes in which the arrow had to be directed) represent the twelve zodiacal constellations, which measure the path of the sun. The axe is a symbol of the axis, as its name in English indicates, and the hole in the axe, which must have been situated at the top of the handle,[9] corresponds to the 'axial' door of the sun at the time of the solstice. Now there are only two solstices in the year, but each month corresponds in principle to a lunar cycle, analogous to the solar cycle, and including in its turn an 'axial' passage that in a sense mirrors the solstice, whence the line of twelve axes. Their number in any case made the trial more difficult.

[9] Some interpret this text to mean that the axes were without handles and were planted in the soil by their blades, the hole through which the arrow had to pass being precisely that into which the handle was normally fixed. But this means that the arrow would have to be shot at a height of only two hands above the ground, which in practice would be impossible. It may thus be assumed that the hole in question was situated at the upper end of the axe and was normally used to hang the axe on the wall.

We do not know for certain the shape of the axes Homer had in mind; they may have been simple war axes, or they may have had the form of Cretan axes with double blades. In the latter case their axial and lunar significance would be particularly evident, for the two blades of the *bipennis* resemble the two opposing phases of the moon—waxing and waning—between which indeed is located the celestial axis.

The trajectory of the arrow thus symbolizes the sun's path; one might object that this path is not a straight line but a circle; now the sun's path is not situated solely in space but also in time, which can be compared to a straight line. Furthermore, the arrow in itself symbolizes the ray which the sun-god hurls into the darkness.

The power of the sun is both sound and light: when Ulysses alone succeeds in bending the sacred bow and causes its string to vibrate 'with the voice of a swallow', his enemies shudder and fearfully anticipate the terrible end that he has in store for them, even before he has revealed to them his true nature, that of the hero under Athena's protection.

The description of the massacre which follows is so horrible that it would revolt us, were it not for the fact that Ulysses incarnates light and justice, whereas the suitors represent darkness and injustice.

It is only after killing the suitors, and purifying the house from bottom to top, that he makes himself known to his wife.

Penelope, as we have said, represents the soul in its original purity, as the faithful wife of the spirit. The fact that each day she weaves her nuptial garment and each night undoes it again—in order to deceive her suitors—shows that her nature is related to universal substance, the principle both virginal and maternal of the cosmos: like her, Nature (*physis* in Hellenism and *Mâyâ* in Hinduism) weaves and dissolves manifestation following a never-ending rhythm.

The so much longed-for union between the hero and his faithful wife thus signifies the return to the primordial perfection of the human state. Homer indicates this clearly, and through Ulysses' own mouth, when the latter names the signs by means of which his wife will recognize him: no one except him and her knew the secret of their marriage bed: how Ulysses had built it and made it immobile; with his own hand he had walled in their nuptial chamber around an old and venerable olive-tree, whose trunk he had then cut to the height of a bed, carving out of the firmly rooted part a support for the couch that was made of plaited strips. As in the description of the Nymphs' cave, the olive-tree is the tree of the world; its oil, which nourishes, heals, and fuels lamps, is the very principle of life, *tejâsa* in Hindu terminology. The trunk of the tree corresponds to the axis of the world, and the bedstead carved in this trunk is symbolically situated at the centre of the world, the 'place' where opposites and complementaries, such as active and passive, man and woman, spirit and soul, unite. As for the nuptial chamber built around the tree, it represents the 'chamber' of the heart, through which passes the spiritual axis of the world, and within which is accomplished the marriage of spirit and soul.

# 16

# The Sun Dance

*What follows is a personal description of the author's friendship with Thomas Yellowtail, a Medicine Man of the Crow Indians, and of his attendance at a Sun Dance held on the Reservation of the Crow Indians in Montana.*

## FIRST MEETING WITH YELLOWTAIL

WE MET YELLOWTAIL for the first time in the Hôtel des Champs Elysées in Paris. He was there with a group of Indian dancers who were travelling together, not so much to earn money as to see foreign lands. Our friend Frithjof Schuon had told us of the authentic nature of the dances being performed, and the fact of staying in the same hotel as the group of Indians gave us the opportunity of making their acquaintance. Amongst the Indians, Yellowtail, who at that time was not yet a medicine man, stood out by his strong personality. I had never before seen a man who was so strong and at the same time so gentle. He was slow in his movements, with an almost hieratic slowness, and had an expression of serenity and strength. Whenever one spoke of spiritual realities, his face would light up.

We spoke to him about the meaning of the gestures and costumes of certain dances, and he confirmed what we said, with some surprise. Towards midnight of the same evening he sent a messenger who directed us to his room where he had lit a ritual fire on a copper tray that he had found in the hotel. He explained to us that he was going to celebrate the rite of the full moon, which recapitulated, in brief, the Sun Dance.

Yellowtail opened his medicine bundle and took out several objects that were the vehicles of a subtle force, such as animal skins, birds' feathers, and stones of unusual colours, which he placed around the fire. Then he burnt some sweet grass and said: 'With this eagle's feather, which I pass over the sacred fire, I shall purify each one of you; then I shall raise my voice to the great spirit, that he may give you an understanding of our religion. You will receive this understanding in the form of a dream.' Then he hung an eagle-bone whistle around his neck and, rising up, turned successively to the four directions of space, praying aloud in the language of the Crow Indians. Finally he whistled several times, reproducing the whistling voice of the eagle.

Each of us later had a dream which symbolically revealed one or other aspect of the tradition of the Plains Indians. At that point we had already left Paris; but Yellowtail, with a few members of his family, unexpectedly visited us in Switzerland. The bond of friendship—and more than friendship—remains, and we have subsequently met one another on both continents more often than we would have believed possible.

## THE SUN DANCE

After crossing the immense plain of Wyoming, we reached the reservation of the Crow Indians by the end of the afternoon. It was the second day of the summer solstice, and that very evening the Sun Dance was to begin. We were surrounded by hillsides covered with flowers; no sign of the sacred site could be seen until we crossed the raised edge of a high plateau where the sacred tree of the preceding year—now a leafless skeleton—was outlined against the sky. A little further on stood the newly built Sun Dance lodge. The sacred tree was already in place; there were twelve radially arranged beams, whose upper ends were supported in the fork of the tree, and whose lower ends rested on the surrounding fence of small fir-trees that had been stripped of their bark. Yellowtail, the medicine man, was there with a few other Indians. He had just attached the two great symbols: the bison's head, which was hung from the trunk of the tree, and the eagle, which was placed on one of the radial beams and which swayed gently in the breeze.

The lodge was thus almost entirely complete on our arrival. The first part of the rites, concerning the felling of the tree and its erection in the centre of the enclosure, had already taken place. The impression of primordiality that emanated from the lodge was accompanied by an atmosphere of coolness and the fragrance of resin. The sacred enclosure was in the form of a vast circle, the eastern portion of which, facing the rising sun, remained open. I could not prevent myself from embracing Yellowtail, who smiled and said *Ahó* ('it is good').

Hours were spent waiting. At dusk the dancers entered the lodge, after marching round it in two opposed movements. A large drum had been installed and five singers took up their positions round about it. The chants that rose towards the star-filled heavens were melodies without words, apparently imitations of the voices of nature. Each melody, which we could barely differentiate from the one that went before, proceeded like a cascade: it would begin with a high note and then move down until it became low and harsh, like an echo that grows stronger as one gets nearer.

The dance lasted three days and three nights, and during this time the dancers fasted; when they were exhausted, they would rest for a few moments in the shade of the fir-trees and then immediately resume the movement of the dance. This movement took place between a given point on the surrounding fence of fir-trees and the sacred tree in the centre, each dancer moving back and forward on his own radial pathway. When he approached the sacred tree, his pace would accelerate; then, having felt the coolness that always surrounded the tree—so it was explained to us—he moved backwards with small steps towards his position on the surrounding fence.

From the second day onwards, certain alleviations are provided for the dancers by members of their families: aquatic plants, rushes and reeds are intertwined from one fir-tree to the next, forming little areas of cover that provide some shade, and sacred sage, which grows profusely in the region, is scattered in the dancers' paths. There were at least sixty dancers, including both men and women, the latter taking up positions alongside each other near the opening at the eastern side of the lodge.

During the night a fire is kept going inside the lodge. It is situated on the axis that links the sacred tree to the point on the horizon at which the sun rises. As soon as it is dawn, the dancers prepare themselves for the most important rite, the greeting of the rising sun. Yellowtail says a long prayer in his native tongue and sings four sacred chants without words. The dancers receive the first ray of sunlight standing in a row, and intensify the sound of their eagle-bone whistles. One might say that their whistling is made visible by the vibration of the eagle-down attached to their whistles. The dancers, the upper parts of whose bodies are bare during the day, cover their shoulders with blankets to shield themselves from the cold wind blowing across the prairie—a sharp contrast to the intense heat of the sun that lasts throughout the whole day and causes considerable suffering to the dancers exposed to it. But the suffering was much greater in olden times when leather thongs, inserted under the skin of the dancers' chest or back, attached them to the trunk of the tree. There is as it were a reminder of this custom in the sometimes rapid, sometimes measured movements of the dance. On the movement away from the centre, the leather thong would pull on the skin until it broke. But in these inward and outward movements there is also the expression of a spiritual movement which first quickly grasps its object, and then slowly assimilates it by taking up a certain distance from it. Moreover, each participant in the dance has to a certain extent his own particular movement. I remember especially a woman of about forty years of age who accomplished her inward and outward movements with a small number of majestic steps.

On the trunk of the tree are painted three rings which correspond to the three worlds. The eagle dominates all three of these worlds, whereas the bison is associated with the earth; his heavy head can be seen amidst the foliage that faces the sun; sacred sage has been put in his mouth and clay on his cheeks because, as our Indian friends explained to us, the bison in anger causes the earth to tremble. The eagle and the bison are the two symbols that most often appear inwardly to Sun Dance participants when they faint under the heat of the sun or are ravished by an ecstasy. The eagle dominates the tree as the Spirit dominates the Cosmos. 'The sacred eagle is called Poor Eagle,' Yellowtail told us. This is no doubt because the cosmic Spirit is situated directly beneath the Great Spirit.

As mentioned above, the second day of the Sun Dance is the day of alleviations. It is also the day of supernatural manifestations. It is then that members of the dancers' families ornament the dancers in accord with the Indian art of painting, the purpose of which is to 'fix' the presence of certain cosmic powers in the body of their protégé. Since the dancers perform the dance with the upper part of their bodies bare, this lends itself to symbolical painting. Sometimes a simple sign—a ring round about an eye, or a zigzag of lightning along an arm—suffices to associate the one thus ornamented with the vision that he has most often received in dreams.

During all these ceremonies, the drum beating and the monotonous chanting continue unceasingly both day and night. The rhythm is rapid and reminds one of thunder; thunder is also identified with the eagle, which otherwise is manifested in the strident sound of the whistles. The eagle is the spirit, and the spirit is the heart. The wide prairie provides so to speak primordial and immediately convincing symbols of all spiritual realities. When, after sunset, one approaches the lodge, still enlivened by the rhythm of the drum and the whistling of the eagle bones and its foliage trembling in the wind, one has the impression of being in the presence of a great living creature endowed with magical strength. From the dance itself there emanates a powerful magic that resonates in the heart for days and days.

The second day is also the culmination of the dance. The third day is the day of cures. From morning onwards, a crowd of people, including entire families of white farmers, come to the Sun Dance site and patiently wait for Yellowtail to let them share in the healing power with which the sacred tree is as it were filled as a result of the rite of which it has been the centre. Yellowtail heals in the name of the eagle who is his particular protector, and also in the name of the otter. He touches the trunk of the sacred tree with an eagle feather, and then with it he strokes the sick parts of the patient's body; as he does this he holds up an otter's skin. In reality all these gestures are addressed to the archetype of the protecting animal; with the Indians the function of healer is of necessity part of the spiritual rank of the one who is invested with it. Essentially the Indian seeks the harmony of nature, as well as the harmony of his own people with their cosmic ambience.

The third day ends with the giving of presents to clan relatives who have offered special prayers for the dancers; this exchange is an expression of the harmony between creatures.

A long prayer is said on behalf of the sponsor, who has undertaken to cover the costs of the rite and who during it has offered ritual prayers alongside Yellowtail, the Medicine Man. Finally a ritual meal of bison meat is offered to all present.

Yellowtail, in full vigour in spite of his age, could not but be exhausted by the dance and the fast, and we suggested to him that we should camp in a forest in the Bighorn Mountains so that he could rest. He agreed and we left almost immediately. Before choosing our camp-site, we climbed to the ridge of the mountain which, on our side, rose gently; on the other side was a deep gorge. On the ridge is situated the famous 'Medicine Wheel', the meaning of which, according to the tradition of his tribe, Yellowtail explained to us: a man who was suffering from a disease of the skin had withdrawn to the solitude of the mountain, there to express in stone the outline of the Sun Dance. Twenty-eight radii joined the rim of the wheel to its axis; these are the twenty-eight mansions of the moon. Four heaps of stones indicated the cardinal directions; they looked like four shrines. According to Yellowtail, the maker of the sacred wheel was able to sleep there by covering himself with fir twigs. The construction of the wheel was accompanied by an invocation to the Great Spirit and when it was completed (it was about the same size as a Sun Dance lodge) its maker was cured.

On leaving the Medicine Wheel, we went down again to the spot where the great rivers of the mountains leave the edge of the forest (in which they have created large swamps) and where deer, as silent as shadows, move to and fro. We set up our tents near the water, in a place called Dead Swede. Seated at our camp-fire, we listened to the Medicine Man: he gave us the history of the transmission of the powers of healing from one medicine man to another by means of a 'chain' starting with the mysterious 'Little People' and ending with Yellowtail himself. As in many of the Indian traditions, it is lightning that forges the link between the world of men and the world of the spirits. The power of healing is included in the spiritual power, while being vehicled to a greater or lesser extent by natural objects, such as stones or plants. In this connection, Yellowtail told me that no medicine is effective if it does not comprise both herbs and prayer. According to his own experience, the double effect of the medicines prepared in this way sometimes exceeds by far the expectations of the medicine man using them.

He also told us the name of the genius who is the guardian of these powers; he is called 'Seven Arrows', a name which is a symbol of the Centre: according to tradition, an 'arrow' signifies a direction of space. There are firstly the four arrows of the cardinal directions; then there are the Zenith and the Nadir, which make six. The seventh is in reality not a direction, but the Centre itself, from which the other directions emanate.

# IV
# ISLAMIC THEMES

# 17

# The Traditional Sciences
# in Fez

*This chapter is the text of an address given by the author to members of staff and former students at the University of Al-Qarawîn in Fez, Morocco, in Autumn 1972.*

**T**RADITIONAL SCIENCE (*al-'ilmu 't-taqlîdî*) and modern science have little or nothing in common; they do not have the same root and do not bear the same fruits. To say tradition is to say transmission; it is a question of essential transmission of non-human origin, one destined to ensure the continuity of a spiritual influence and of an integral science which, should they ever be lost, could not be reconstituted by human efforts. Completely different is the nature of modern science, which is founded on sensory experience, and thus on something which in principle is accessible to everyone, so that this science can always be reconstituted from scratch, provided that one can accumulate sufficient experimental data. This condition however is difficult to fulfil, since scientific data and the conclusions drawn from them are accumulated in such a progression that it has become impossible for anyone to grasp them all. Experimentation on the basis of the senses, practised methodically and as if it were the only approach to reality, gets bogged down in the indefinite multitude of physical phenomena and thereby runs the risk of forgetting its own point of departure: man in his integral nature, man who is not only a physical datum but, at one and the same time, body, soul, and spirit (*jasad, nafs, rûh*).

If one should ask modern science, what is man? it will either remain silent through awareness of its own limits, or it will reply by saying that man is an animal with particularly well-developed cerebral faculties. And if one should raise the question as to the origin of this animal, it will speak to you about an infinitely long chain of coincidences, accidents, and chances. As much as to say that the existence of man has no meaning.

If on the other hand one should ask traditional science, what is man?, it will reply by means of metaphors—e.g. Biblical and Koranic stories about the creation of Adam—which one might be tempted to cast aside as outworn mythology, if one did not divine that these sacred accounts are the vehicle of a profound vision of man, too profound in fact to be encapsulated in rational definitions. The first thing we gather from accounts of this kind is that man has a unique cause, situated entirely beyond contingency, and that his existence on earth has a meaning. This meaning—or this vision of man—has nothing to do with an empirical science; one could not reconstitute it from experiments and reasonings, for it concerns man, not in respect of his spatial and temporal existence, but 'in respect of eternity', if one may venture to express it thus.

Tradition in all its forms is essentially a remembrance (*dhikrâ*) of this timeless vision of man and his origin—whether it be a question of the transmission of sacred laws and customs, or of their spiritual significance—to the extent that this can be transmitted from one man to another, in other words, to the extent that masters are authorized to expound it and disciples are ready to receive it.

These somewhat general observations were necessary in order to situate our theme and above all to make clear what is meant by 'traditional science'. Even in the earlier part of this century, many branches of Islamic science—which had reached its peak during the Middle Ages—were no longer part of the instruction offered in the great mosque of Al-Qarawîn. Already in the fourteenth century Ibn Khaldun had complained about a certain intellectual impoverishment in the field of the Islamic sciences, and the decline continued during the following centuries, up to the time of the arrival of the French in Morocco. However, the progressive reduction of the domains covered by traditional science was not uniquely due to decadence; it was the exclusive domination of Malikism that had simplified the study of law, while Asharism had eliminated Hellenistic philosophy. And, in a more general manner, there is in the genius of the Maghreb a tendency to reduce things to the essential and to the rigorously necessary. The teaching of history, for example, had come to be concerned only with sacred history, that of the origins of Islam, because it was considered that only sacred history—which expressed timeless truths (*haqâ'iq*)—deserved to be retained. As for astronomy, it had been reduced to the calculations necessary for the establishment of the Moslem calendar and the hours of prayer. In spite of these reductions—and perhaps also because of them—the corpus of sciences taught at the great mosque of Al-Qarawîn in the 1930s constituted a perfectly homogeneous whole, whereas modern university instruction is divided into different disciplines which are often divergent among themselves. At Al-Qarawîn, all the branches of learning: language, logic, law, moral philosophy, and theology converged toward one and the same end; and it could also be said that they derived from one and the same source, namely the Koran and the *hadîth* (traditions of the Prophet), which are the foundation of both the spiritual order and the social order in Islam.

One might be astonished at the zeal of the grammarians who would hold forth for hours, or even days, on one single verb, or one single grammatical form. And yet it is perhaps not so astonishing that a language that had served as the vehicle of a divine revelation—and had thereby retained a depth and a fineness that profane languages had long since lost—should be cherished as the most precious of possessions.

One might also be astonished at the meticulousness with which the specialists in *hadîth* examined the 'chain of transmission' (*isnad*) of every saying of the Prophet; their memory in this field was indeed prodigious. And yet it is hardly astonishing that, for sayings on which depend the very life of both the community and each individual soul, the proofs of authenticity had to be scrupulously weighed.

But there was something else that might understandably astonish or even dismay the uninformed observer, namely the apparently rationalistic and in any case frankly legalistic style generally attaching to instruction given in the great mosque. Sometimes the courses, which took the form of a dialogue between master and pupil, would resemble a legal discussion. It is true that juridical thought had its wholly legitimate place in this instruction, since the *sharî'ah* is a law, and the legal science that derives from it constituted the principal object of study for the majority of students. Nevertheless, in the theological domain (*kalam*), legalistic thought with its pros and its contras—its *law kâna, in kâna,* and *lam yakun*—could give the impression of rationalism, that is to say of a mode of thought exclusively made up of alternatives, and for this reason much too schematic to be adequate for its object: Infinite Reality. All the same, it was only a provisional rationalism, a rationalism on the surface, for undoubtedly none of the *'ulamâ* who used this method of argumentation would have dreamt of making human reason the measure of all things, as in fact modern science believes it can do. The difference between the two points of view, that of Islamic law (*fiqh*) and that of modern rationalism (be it philosophic or merely scientistic), is basically the following: for *fiqh*, reason does not include all reality, far from it, but represents it after its fashion and to the extent that it opens itself to divine revelation; on the other hand, for philosophic and scientific rationalism, everything must be explainable by reason, and by it alone, even though one does not know what this reason is, nor why it should possess this quasi-absolute right with regard to reality.

Let us note that, among the best of the learned men of Fez, the juridical routine was tempered by a lively awareness of human fragility, and thus by a sort of constant prudence, which conferred on them much dignity. And it was perhaps this virtue that had the greatest influence on their pupils, as well as on the simple men of the people who would come to listen to courses given at Al-Qarawîn, while remaining seated at a respectful distance from the man of learning who was surrounded by his regular students.

In a general manner, the open and generous character of the instruction had a benefic influence on the whole town. The relationship between professor and student was a human one: not impeded by regulations, but based on reciprocal trust. Very often both master and disciple worked only for the love of the science. Many of the professors received only a very modest salary or none at all; some of them lived from a trade which they would practise in addition to their teaching function, or from gifts made to them by rich citizens.

From time to time, classical works of Sufism (*at-Tasawwuf*) were read and commented on at Al-Qarawîn. One such work was 'The Revivification of the Religious Sciences' (*Ihyâ 'ulûm ad-dîn*) of Al-Ghazâlî, and it was not the first time in Morocco that this work played the role of conciliator between law (*fiqh*) and mysticism (*tasawwuf*), between outward science (*'ilm az-zâhir*) and inward science (*'ilm al-bâtin*). In general, however, the professors at the university of Al-Qarawîn were very reserved regarding anything that had to do with Sufism. During the period of the French protectorate this attitude was reinforced by the political opposition between the university circles and the Sufi brotherhoods (*turuq*), an opposition which the colonial administration exploited to the limit. The brotherhoods do indeed derive from Sufism, of which they represent, in a sense, the popular form; nevertheless they constitute groups that are too large not to be subject to political pressures. This danger was all the greater in that many of these brotherhoods no longer had true spiritual masters at their head, but purely nominal leaders, mostly descendants of the founder of the brotherhood; physical heredity, however, is not a guarantee of spirituality. The true spiritual masters—and there still were such—remained aloof from politics and from the great collective movements and were surrounded by only a small number of disciples; it was in these more or less isolated circles that true *tasawwuf* was taught.

On the other hand, there were always scholars at Al-Qarawîn who, without necessarily adhering to Sufism, recognized its validity, for the simple reason that *fiqh* clearly did not embrace all the dimensions of religion (*ad-dîn*). We may recall in this connection the three dimensions of the Islamic religion—'submission' (*al-islâm*), 'faith' (*al-îmân*), and 'virtue' or 'excellence' (*al-ihsân*)—established by the famous 'Gabriel *hadîth*'.[1] The first two dimensions comprise respec-

---

[1] The full form of this *hadîth*, reported by Omar, is as follows: 'One day when we were with the Messenger of God, there came unto us a man whose clothes were of exceeding whiteness and whose hair was of exceeding blackness, nor were there any signs of travel upon him, although none of us had seen him before. He sat down knee unto knee opposite the Prophet, upon whose thighs he placed the palms of his hands, saying: "O Mohammed, tell me what is the surrender unto God (*al-islâm*)." The Prophet answered: "The surrender is that thou shouldst testify that there is no god but God and that Mohammed is God's Apostle, and that thou shouldst perform the prayer, bestow the alms, fast Ramadan and make, if thou canst, the pilgrimage to the Holy House." He said: "Thou hast spoken truly" and we were amazed that having questioned him he should corroborate him. Then he said: "Tell me what is faith (*îmân*)," and the Prophet answered: "It is that thou shouldst believe in God and His Angels and His Books and His Apostles and the Last Day, and that thou shouldst believe that no good or evil cometh but by His Providence." "Thou hast spoken truly,"

tively the prescribed actions and the dogmas—and these are precisely the domain of scholastic science—whereas the third
dimension, spiritual virtue, refers to the contemplative life. According to the Prophet's own words, *al-ihsân* consists in the following:
'That thou shouldst worship God as if thou sawest Him, for if thou
seest Him not, verily He seeth thee.' These few words summarize a
far-reaching inward practice, one whose development is in principle
unlimited, since its object is infinite, and which presupposes, not a
more or less dialectical knowledge, but a 'science of the heart'.

The presence of man—body, soul and spirit—in the act of worship
opens onto the presence of God in man, if it be permitted to express
in these terms a complete spiritual universe that is too subtle and
too rich to be defined lightly. In a certain sense, the whole of
Islamic mysticism (*tasawwuf*) is developed from the fundamental
requirement for sincerity (*ikhlâs*): 'to worship God as if thou sawest
Him' is to worship Him sincerely; now this effort logically leads to a
'conversion' (*tawbah*) of the whole being, and this brings about a sort
of reversal of the subject-object relationship in one's inward vision:
until then man saw everything with the eye of his individual ego, his
passional soul, and everything for him was inevitably coloured by
this; henceforward man sees his own ego with the eye of the spirit,
which transcends it and judges it; as the *hadîth* teaches: 'He who
knows his own soul, knows his Lord.' (*Man 'arafa nafsa-hu, fa-qad
'arafa Rabba-h.*)

In order to express things as simply as possible, we could also put it
as follows: in Islam, the believer is saved basically by the double
testimony, that 'there is no god but God', and that 'Mohammed is the
Messenger of God', the first testimony in a sense including the
second. What Sufism (*tasawwuf*) does is to give to this testimony all
the meaning that it can possibly have, and to demand at the same time
that the believer be completely sincere. This amounts to saying that,

he said, and then: "Tell me what is excellence (*ihsân*)." The Prophet answered: "It is
that thou shouldst worship God as if thou sawest Him, for if thou seest Him not, verily
He seeth thee." Then the stranger went away, and I stayed there long after he had
gone, until the Prophet said to me: "O Omar, knowest thou the questioner, who he
was?" I said "God and His Prophet know best, but I know not at all." "It was Gabriel,"
said the Prophet. "He came to teach you your religion".' Translated by Martin Lings.
See *A Sufi Saint of the Twentieth Century* (London, Allen & Unwin, 1971).

for *tasawwuf,* all things are finally effaced before the Absolute: the world, which is but its reflection, and the ego, which is both its reflection and its veil (*hijâb*); the reflection because, like all things, it has its existence from God, and the veil because it attributes to itself *a priori* an absolute character that belongs to God alone: 'there is no god but God' (*lâ ilâha illâ 'Llâh*).

As we have said, the brotherhoods represent the popular form of *tasawwuf,* a fact which does not exclude the existence, in their midst, of authentic spiritual treasures. Some fundamental classics of *tasawwuf* like the *Hikam* of Ibn 'Atâ'i 'Llâh were read and commented on to the members of such brotherhoods (*fuqarâ,* the 'spiritually poor'), and the poems of Ibn al-Fârid, Shushtari and other great Sufis, which were sung at *majâlis* (spiritual meetings for the 'remembrance of God' [*dhikr*]), expound the highest spiritual truths; these are sometimes better understood by simple and apparently uncultivated men than by the educated, because the intelligence of the heart and the intelligence of the brain are not the same thing.

Morocco has always been a land of Sufis; it received a rich heritage of spiritual masters who, in the twelfth and thirteenth centuries, came over from Spain and settled in North Africa. At the very time when Europe was undergoing the effects of the French revolution, a major victory for materialism, Morocco was enjoying a new flowering of the contemplative life: masters such as Al-'Arabî, ad-Darqâwî and Al-Harrâq continued to represent the purest of classical Sufism.

Traditional medicine, which had been taught on the margin of the official courses at Al-Qarawîn, was banished by the French protectorate. The contempt of modern Europeans for 'medieval' and 'backward' sciences inevitably had its effect. Nevertheless, this medicine continued to be practised clandestinely. Has it now entirely disappeared? It would be a matter for regret if it has, for this science—which the Arabs inherited from ancient Greece, but which they considerably enriched—possessed (over and above its long and rich experience) a synthetic vision of man, compared with which the impoverished viewpoint of modern science can be seen for what it is.

It was moreover this viewpoint of synthesis that constituted the link that attached Greco-Arab medicine to the intellectual world of Islam. Unity-totality-equilibrium: these are the reference points of Islamic thought, and it was equilibrium, precisely, that was the principle of this form of traditional medicine. According to its perspective, the whole of nature and *a fortiori* the human organism are ruled by the law of equilibrium. There are four radical humours which, analogous to the four elements, are subtly combined in the various vital functions; any rupture of equilibrium in the relationship of these humours causes an illness. The art of the doctor in Greek medicine was to help nature to recover its original equilibrium. Nature acts by complementary forces: it tempers heat with cold, and dryness with humidity; or expansion with contraction, and solution with coagulation; the doctor does the same, using whatever in nature corresponds to these forces. The *materia medica* generally consisted of vegetable substances, preferably plants which were also foodstuffs and which the body would absorb spontaneously. Many of these means are still to be found in popular medicine.

Having referred to traditional medicine, we must also mention alchemy, which is also a science or an art of pre-Islamic origin which has been spiritually integrated into Islam. False ideas regarding alchemy—which was practised in Fez until relatively recently—are common. It is usually regarded as a superstitious practice that seeks—on a basis of complete self-deception—to transmute lead and other base metals into gold. In actual fact, true alchemy was often concealed behind this caricatural appearance. For true alchemy, the lead or other base metal that was to be transmuted into gold was only the symbol—a very adequate one—of the human soul sunk in the darkness and chaos of the passions, while gold represented the original nature of man, in which even the body is ennobled and transfigured by the life of the spirit. Every base metal, image of a certain state of the soul, is considered as a 'sick gold', while gold itself corresponds to the perfect equilibrium of the natural forces; here we encounter once more the same principles as govern traditional Greek medicine. True alchemy might be described as a 'medicine' of total man: body, soul and spirit. But why did one use metallurgical symbols and descriptions of strange chemical procedures in order to express realities of a completely different order? Doubtless because the 'professions using fire'—metallurgists, smelters, enamellers, potters, etc.–exist, and because their procedures lend themselves quite naturally, and providentially, to the expression of certain very intimate states and transformations of the soul.

We have seen that science and art are often the two faces of one and the same tradition; medicine, for example, is both a science and an art; alchemy calls itself a 'royal art', and *tasawwuf* is a spiritual art. Likewise, the traditional plastic arts—architecture, sculpture, mosaics, etc.—presuppose a certain knowledge which, without being explicit, nevertheless also pertains to the domain of traditional science.

It is particularly significant that proficiency in a traditional art concerns both the technical solution and the aesthetic solution of a given problem; thus, the procedure enabling one to trace the outline of an arch concerns both its stability and its elegance. In traditional art, beauty and use go hand in hand; they are two inseparable aspects of perfection, as envisaged by tradition: 'God prescribed perfection for all things' (*Inna 'Llâha kataba 'l-ihsâna 'alâ kulli shay*), according to the *hadîth*. Here again we encounter the term *ihsân*, which in Sufism may be translated as 'spiritual virtue', or simply as 'virtue', and which includes the ideas of beauty and perfection.

In art and craftsmanship—in a traditional context, the two are not distinguishable—it often happens that instruction is not transmitted by means of words. The apprentice sees his master at work, and imitates him. But it is not merely a case of methods of work; the good craftsman is distinguished by a whole cluster of human values: patience, discipline, sincerity. It is difficult to overestimate the pedagogic quality of art (or craft) in the traditional sense of the terms. In a Fez of not so long ago, we knew men well-versed in one or other of the sciences—for example law (*fiqh*) or spirituality (*tasawwuf*)—and more particularly men who saw in the most modest aspects of their profession a means of spiritual perfection (*ihsân*).

How can tradition, in a plastic art, be reconciled with creative freedom, without which art is not art? Through tradition, the artist has at his disposal a set of models or typical forms which he will use or adapt according to the circumstances, or more exactly, according to the particular goal of the work. In adapting, he creates, but this creation obeys certain laws: the models or typical forms are the elements of a language that possesses its grammar and syntax; mastery in a given art is to be able to express oneself freely while obeying the rules of the language—or rather: it is to be able to express oneself freely thanks to the resources of the language. If the expression is just and adequate to the goal of the work, it is nourished by a sort of inspiration that arises from the supra-individual depth of the tradition; for just as Islamic science has its roots in the Koran (on which it is a more or less direct commentary), so the typical forms of Islamic art are rooted in the spirit of Islam, of which they are as it were the visible traces; now Islam, like all the great spiritual traditions of humanity, was not 'invented' by man.

# 18

# The Prayer of Ibn Mashîsh
# (As-Salât al-Mashîshîyah)

THE MOROCCAN SUFI 'Abd as-Salâm ibn Mashîsh[1], the master of Abu'l Hasan ash-Shâdhilî—founder of the Shâdhilî order—was the spiritual pole (*qutb*) of his age. He died in 1228, in his hermitage on Mount al-'Alam, in the Rif mountains; his tomb on the summit of this mount is one of the most venerated places of pilgrimage in the whole of the Maghrib.

Only one text by him remains, the famous prayer on the Prophet, which is recited in all the brotherhoods of Shâdhilî filiation, and which is as it were a summary of the Sufi doctrine of Universal Man (*al-insân al-kâmil*). We give here a translation of this prayer, followed by a commentary on all the difficult passages.

It should be recalled that every prayer on the Prophet refers implicitly to the Koranic injunction: 'God and His angels bless the Prophet; O ye who believe, bless him and wish him peace.' (XXXIII, 56)

The Arabic verb *salla*, which we translate here as 'to bless', also means 'to pray'; the word *salât*, from the same root, means prayer (more particularly the ritual prayer), if the action comes from man; it means blessing, or effusion of grace, if the action comes from God.[2]

⊠

'O MY GOD (*Allâhumma*), bless him from whom derive the secrets and from whom gush forth the lights, and in whom rise up the

---

[1] There also exists the form Ibn Bashîsh ('son of a man with a serene countenance'), which indeed seems to be the original Arabic form of this patronymic, the *mîm* of ibn Mashîsh (or ben Mashîsh) being explained by the assimilation—typically Maghribî—of the *bâ* to the preceeding *nûn*, or simply by the easy change from one labial to another. Mecca, originally Becca, is a well-known example of the latter.

[2] On the general meaning of the prayer on the Prophet, see: Frithjof Schuon, *Understanding Islam* (Allen & Unwin, Mandala Books, London, 1976).

realities, and into whom descended the sciences of Adam, so that he hath made powerless all creatures, and so that understandings are diminished in his regard, and no one amongst us, neither predecessor nor successor, can grasp him.

'The gardens of the spiritual world (*al-malakût*) are adorned with the flower of his beauty, and the pools of the world of omnipotence (*al-jabarût*) overflow with the outpouring of his lights.

'There existeth nothing that is not linked to him, even as it was said: Were there no mediator, everything that dependeth on him would disappear! (Bless him, O my God), by a blessing such as returneth to him through Thee from Thee, according to his due.

'O my God, he is Thine integral secret, that demonstrateth Thee, and Thy supreme veil, raised up before Thee.

'O my God, join me to his posterity and justify me by Thy reckoning of him. Let me know him with a knowledge that saveth me from the wells of ignorance and quencheth my thirst at the wells of virtue. Carry me on his way, surrounded by Thine aid, towards Thy presence. Strike through me at vanity, so that I may destroy it. Plunge me in the oceans of Unity (*al-ahadîyah*), pull me back from the sloughs of *tawhîd*, and drown me in the pure source of the ocean of Unicity (*al-wahdah*), so that I neither see nor hear nor am conscious nor feel except through it. And make of the Supreme Veil the life of my spirit, and of his spirit the secret of my reality, and of his reality all my worlds, by the realization of the First Truth.

'O First, O Last, O Outward, O Inward, hear my petition, even as Thou heardest the petition of Thy servant Zachariah; succour me through Thee unto Thee, support me through Thee unto Thee, unite me with Thee, and come in between me and other-than-Thee: Allâh, Allâh, Allâh! Verily He who hath imposed on thee the Koran for a law, will bring thee back to the promised end (Koran, XXVIII, 85).

'Our Lord, grant us mercy from Thy presence, and shape for us right conduct in our plight (Koran, XVIII, 10).

'Verily God and His angels bless the Prophet; O ye who believe, bless him and wish him peace (Koran, XXXIII, 56).

'May the graces (*salawât*) of God, His peace, His salutations, His mercy and His blessings (*barakât*) be on our Lord Mohammed, Thy servant, Thy prophet and Thy messenger, the unlettered prophet, and on his family and on his companions, (graces) as numerous as the even and the odd and as the perfect and blessed words of our Lord.

'Glorified be thy Lord, the Lord of glory, beyond what they attribute unto Him, and peace be on the Messengers. Praise be to God, the Lord of the worlds (Koran, XXXVII, 180–182).'

⊠

*O my God* (Allâhumma), *bless him from whom derive the secrets and from whom gush forth the lights.*

There is a complementarism between the 'secrets' (*asrâr*) and the 'lights' (*anwâr*), for the first are latent predispositions, of man or of the cosmos, while the second are 'emanations' or 'flashes' of Being which echo the 'secrets' by actualizing their potentialities without ever yielding up their ultimate depth.

The name 'secret' (*sirr*) is given to the innermost part of the soul, the 'locus' or organ of contemplation of the 'lights'. 'The Divine Lights', writes the sufi Ibn 'Atâ'i 'Llâh in his *Hikam*, 'abound according to the purity of the secret'. This is similar to a mirror that reflects the divine realities and polarizes them in a certain fashion according to its own predisposition (*isti'dâd*).[4]

In so far as the 'secret' is situated on the side of the potentialities, it plays a passive role with regard to the 'lights', which are like prolongations of the *fiat lux*; but in its unfathomable depth, it is identified with the 'immutable essence' (*al'ayn ath-thâbitah*) of the being, i.e. with the archetype which 'undergoes' no act exterior to itself, since it contains eminently and indistinctly everything that the individual consciousness realizes in existential and successive mode.

This enables us to consider the relationship between 'secrets' and 'lights' in all its universal breadth, the first corresponding to the archetypes, and the second to the divine Qualities, which are the very sources of Existence. According to one aspect of things, the 'lights' confer existence on the 'secrets', the latter as such being non-manifested; by manifesting the 'secrets', the 'lights' also veil them.

---

[1] See on this subject: Muhyi 'd-dîn ibn 'Arabî, *La Sagesse des Prophètes* (*Fusûs al-Hikam*), translated by Titus Burckhardt (Albin Michel, Paris, 1955), chapter on Seth. For an English version of the French translation, see *The Wisdom of the Prophets* (Beshara Publications, 1975).

And according to another aspect, complementary to the preceding one, the 'secrets' polarize the 'lights' by differentiating the single light of Being.

The archetypes, indistinctly contained in the Divine Essence, are distinguished first of all, in a principial manner, in the First Intellect (*al-'aql al-awwal*), and it is through it that they shine as it were into the cosmos; thus they 'derive' from it and, from this starting-point, are 'split up'.[5] Likewise the Divine Light is broken by the prism of the Intellect into multiple 'lights'.

The First Intellect is like the 'isthmus' (*barzakh*) between the two 'seas' of the uncreated and the created, of pure Being and Existence, the latter being relative. According to a saying of the Prophet, the Intellect is the first thing that God created; nevertheless it does not differ from the Spirit (*ar-Rûh*), which comprises both a created, or angelic aspect, and an uncreated, or divine, aspect.[6] In a certain sense, the Intellect is like the consciousness of the Spirit and the Spirit is like the life of the Intellect. If, in Islam, one does not speak of the 'Divine Intellect', whereas one speaks of the 'Divine Spirit', this is because it is only the latter that 'emanates' from God, rather like a breath that passes through all the degrees of Being; the Intellect, for its part, is so to say static, and cannot be defined but by its object: if this be the created universe, the Intellect is itself created, whereas it is neither created nor 'intellect' when it has for its immediate object the Absolute, for in this relationship no quality of its own distinguishes it from the Divine Essence; it *is* that which it knows.[7]

---

[5] The Arabic verb *inshaqqat*, used in our text, possesses both of these meanings.

[6] On the angelic aspect of the Spirit, 'Abd al-Karîm al-Jîlî writes: 'This is the Angel that the Sufis call: the Truth whereby (things) are created. It is also the Reality of Mohammed (*al-haqîqat al-muhammadîyah*). God looked upon this Angel while looking upon Himself; He created it from His Light and created from it the world . . .' (*Al-insân al-kâmil*, chapter on *ar-rûh*). On the divine aspect of the Spirit, he writes: 'The Holy Spirit (*rûh al-quds*) is the Spirit of spirits; it transcends Existence, so that it is not permitted to call it created, for it is a particular aspect of God, by virtue of which the world subsists. It is spirit, but not like other spirits, for it is the Spirit of God, and it was this Spirit that was breathed into Adam . . .' (*ibid.*, chapter on *rûh al-quds*).

[7] 'Know that God manifested this intellect like a unique essence subsisting by itself, limited (*mutahayyiz*) according to a certain school and non-limited according to another, this latter opinion being the more just . . .' (Muhyi 'd-dîn Ibn 'Arabî, 'The White Pearl' [*ad-Durrat al-baidâ*]).

The two 'faces' of the Intellect, one turned towards God and the other towards the world, are indicated in the saying of the Prophet: 'The first thing that God created was the Intellect (*al-'aql*). He said to it: receive (or turn towards me, *iqbal*), and it received; then he said to it: transmit (or turn away, *idbar*), and it transmitted.' The following saying of the Prophet also refers to the Intellect, symbolized by the supreme Calamus (*al-qalam al-a'lâ*): 'The first thing that God created was the Calamus. He said to it: Write! It replied: What shall I write? Write, said God, My knowledge of My creation until the day of resurrection.' From this it results that the Intellect is created in so far as it is a cosmic instrument, while the science that it transcribes—or the knowledge that it refracts—is divine in essence.

Thus, the First Intellect is the universal Mediator, and it is with this that the Prophet is identified by the very secret of his function.

*In whom rise up the realities, and into whom descended the sciences of Adam.*

The First Intellect is to the whole cosmos what the reflected intellect is to man. Thus, the man whose intimate consciousness is the First Intellect itself, is both a man and total cosmic being; his heart is the heart of the universe, and all the elements of the cosmos are like modalities, not of his individual nature, but of his intellectual and universal nature; he is 'Universal Man' (*al-insân al-kâmil*). It is in him that the realities (*haqâ'iq*) 'rise up' by the reintegration of all things in Unity, a reintegration perpetually operated by the Intellect, and it is in him too that the realities 'descend' by the reflection of . universal truths in the human mind: according to the Koran, God taught Adam the 'names' of all things (II, 30).

*So that he hath made powerless all creatures, and understandings are diminished in his regard, and so that no one amongst us, neither predecessor nor successor, can grasp him.*

The Whole causes its part to be powerless, in that the part can never embrace the whole. This is true of 'Universal Man' who, according to this perspective, is none other than Mohammed: Mohammed, as the last prophet in time and the 'seal' of the prophetic function, represents—by virtue of the inverse analogy between Heaven and Earth—the most complete earthly manifestation of the Universal Mediator, the First Intellect; in the other religions the pre-excellence of the respective founder has as its basis some other metaphysical relationship, such as 'Incarnation' or 'Illumination'.[8]

*The gardens of the spiritual world* (al-malakût) *are adorned with the flower of his beauty, and the pools of the world of omnipotence* (al-jabarût) *overflow with the outpouring of his lights.*

The Universal Mediator, the First Intellect, is like a mirror that reverberates the Divine Beauty. According to Plotinus—whose doctrine was confirmed and completed by the Sufis—the First Intellect (*nous*) unceasingly contemplates the One, while projecting, without being able to exhaust them, the contents of its contemplation into the Universal Soul, which for its part contemplates the First Intellect. It is in the Universal Soul that the gardens of *al-malakût* are situated. As for the 'pools' of the world of omnipotence (*al-jabarût*), they are the 'reservoirs' of non-manifestation, contained in Pure Being, from which Existence gushes forth, which in its original purity is none other than the 'Light of Mohammed' (*an-nûr al-muhammadî*). According to a saying of the Prophet, 'God took a handful of His light, and said to it: be Mohammed!'

*There existeth nothing that is not linked to him, even as it was said: Were there no mediator, everything that dependeth on him would disappear! (Bless him, O my God), by a blessing such as returneth to him through Thee from Thee, according to his due.*

According to the Sufis, the blessing or effusion of graces (*salât*) that God heaps upon the Prophet is nothing other than the irradiation (*tajallî*) of the Divine Essence, which eternally pours into the cosmos, of which Mohammed is the synthesis. To ask for the blessing of God on the Prophet is thus to conform with the divine act and intentionally to participate in it; also, tradition provides the assurance that whoever blesses the Prophet attracts upon himself the blessing of the entire universe.[9]

---

[8] In a certain sense, the name of each of the great divine messengers is the name of the Universal Mediator, but none is such in the same respect as others. 'Universal Man is the pole around whom revolve the spheres of existence from the first to the last. He has been one alone since the beginning of the universe and he is manifested in the various religions, on each occasion being named in respect of a particular manifestation and to the exclusion of the others. His original name is Mohammed ... In each case he bears that name that corresponds to his manifestation on that occasion; I met him in the form of my spiritual master Sharaf ad-Dîn Ismâ'il al-Jabartî ...' ('Abd al-Karîm al-Jîlî, *op. cit.*, chapter on *al-insân al-kâmil*).

*O my God, he is Thine integral secret, that demonstrateth Thee, and Thy supreme veil, raised up before Thee.*

The 'essential reality' (*haqîqah*) of the Mediator, his root in God, if it may be so expressed, is nothing other than the first divine self-determination (*ta'ayyun*), Being (*al-wujûd*), in so far as it is in a certain fashion detached from Non-Being (*'adam*). This first determination, which includes all others, is in itself a secret or a mystery; for how can the Undetermined determine itself? On the one hand, the first determination 'demonstrates' God, for the Undetermined is incomprehensible; on the other hand, it veils Him by limiting Him in a certain manner; it reveals Him and veils Him at one and the same time.[10]

*O my God, join me to his posterity[11] and justify me by Thy reckoning of*

[9] The following are a few sayings of the Prophet in this connection, transmitted by various chains: '(The Archangel) Gabriel—peace be upon him—came to me and said: "O Mohammed, no one shall bless thee without seventy thousand angels blessing him; and he whom the angels bless will be of the people of Paradise." "If anyone bless me out of veneration, God—may He be exalted—will create from his words an angel whose two wings will stretch from east to west, whose two feet will be placed on the seventh nether-earth and the nape of whose neck will be bent beneath the divine throne, and God will say to the angel: bless my servant, as he blessed My Prophet! And he will bless him until the day of resurrection." "If anyone bless me once, God will bless him ten times; if anyone bless me ten times, God will bless him a hundred times . . ." "No servant of God shall bless me but his blessing shall haste from his mouth, traverse every land and every sea, every east and every west, and shall say: 'I am the blessing of so-and-so, son of so-and-so, who blessed Mohammed, the elect, the best of the creatures of God'." "Then shall there remain nothing that will not bless him, this servant. And God will create from this blessing a bird with seventy thousand wings, on each wing there will be seventy thousand faces, in each face there will be seventy thousand mouths, and each mouth will have seventy thousand tongues; each one of them will praise God in seventy thousand languages; and God will inscribe for him the rewards for all of that".' All these allegories express the incalculable reciprocity between the singular man and Universal Man.

[10] This can also be said of *mâyâ*, according to the Vedantic doctrine. The origin of *mâyâ* is an unfathomable secret, since it is neither real like the Absolute, nor unreal like nothingness. It is thus that the Sufis envisage the 'Reality of Mohammed' (*al-haqîqat al-muhammadîyah*), as first existential determination.

[11] It is obviously a question of spiritual posterity. It may be mentioned that 'Abd as-Salâm ibn Mashîsh was himself a descendent of the Prophet, through Idrîs, the holy founder of Fez. The existence of countless saints issued from the physical posterity of the Prophet proves that this posterity is like the *materia prima* of a spiritual kinship, when vocation and personal effort actualize its potentialities.

*him. Let me know him with a knowledge that saveth me from the wells of ignorance and quencheth my thirst at the wells of virtue. Carry me on his way, surrounded by Thine aid, towards Thy presence. Strike through me at vanity, so that I may destroy it.*

These last words are a paraphrase of the Koranic verse: 'But we shall hurl the truth (*al-haqq*) against vanity (*al-bâtil*), so that it will shatter it, and behold it vanisheth.' (XXI, 18).[12]

*Plunge me in the oceans of Unity* (al-ahadîyah), *pull me back from the sloughs of* tawhîd.

Since *at-tawhîd* normally signifies the attestation of Unity or, by extension, union with God, Ibn Mashîsh's petition is paradoxical; what he has in view in this petition is the confusion of the created with the uncreated; it is as if he said: preserve me from the pitfalls that the doctrine of Unity, improperly understood, extends towards the 'drunken', who no longer know how to distinguish between Lord and servant.

*And drown me in the essence (or the source)* [*ʿayn*] *of the ocean of Unicity* (al-wahdah), *so that I neither see nor hear nor am conscious nor feel except through it.*

This is an allusion to the 'holy saying' (*hadîth qudsî*): 'My servant ceaseth not to draw nigh unto Me until I love him; and when I love him, I am the hearing whereby he heareth and the sight whereby he seeth and the hand whereby he smiteth and the foot whereupon he walketh; and if he asketh something of me, I will certainly give it to him.' According to this image of union, the servant does not cease to be servant, but his human nature is as if penetrated and enveloped by Divine Reality.

In Unity in the sense of *al-ahadîyah*, all traces of the creature or the servant are effaced, whereas in Unicity in the sense of *al-wahdah*, the creature appears in God; multiplicity in unity and unity in multiplicity.

*And make of the Supreme Veil the life of my spirit, and of his spirit the secret of my reality, and of his reality all my worlds.*

This means: grant that the first of all determinations, Being, be the very essence of my spirit, that the Universal Mediator be the secret of

---

[12] *Al-bâtil*, which we translate as 'vanity', signifies everything that is false, ephemeral and illusory.

my spiritual reality (*haqîqah*), and that his own spiritual reality may assimilate into itself all the modalities of my existence.

*By the realization of the First Truth.*

Concerning which the Koran says: 'We created not the Heavens and the earth and all that is between them save with Truth' (xv, 85). God Himself is called 'the Truth' (*al-Haqq*).

*O First, O Last, O Outward, O Inward.*

These divine names are mentioned in the Koran in this same order.

*Hear my petition, even as Thou heardest the petition of Thy servant Zachariah,*

who implored God not to leave him without heir; God fulfilled his desire, despite the age and barrenness of his wife (Koran, III, 37ff).

*Succour me through Thee unto Thee, support me through Thee unto Thee, unite me with Thee and come in between me and other-than-Thee:*[13] *Allâh, Allâh, Allâh! Verily He who hath imposed on thee the Koran for a law, will bring thee back to the promised end* (Koran, XXVIII, 85).

The last phrase is a verse from the Koran, addressed to the Prophet on the occasion of the emigration (*hijrah*) to Medina. Here it refers to the exile of the spirit in the world: God promises to whoever invokes Him that He will bring him back to his true homeland, eternity or God Himself.

*Our Lord, grant us mercy from Thy presence, and shape for us right conduct in our plight* (Koran, XVIII, 10).

According to the Koran, this is the prayer uttered by the seven sleepers of Ephesus, at the moment of their taking refuge in the cave. The cave is the image par excellence of the isolation (*khalwah*) of the contemplative within himself.

*Verily, God and His angels bless the Prophet; O ye who believe, bless him and wish him peace* (Koran, XXXIII, 56).

*May the graces* (salawât) *of God, His peace, His salutations, His mercy and His blessings* (barakât) *be on our Lord Mohammed, Thy servant, Thy prophet and Thy messenger, the un-lettered prophet, and on his family and on his companions, (graces) as numerous as the even and the odd and as the perfect and blessed words of our Lord.*

---

[13] This echoes the Koranic verse (VIII, 24): 'God cometh in (*yahwul*) between man and his own heart'. This root is the origin of the Sufi term *hâl*.

The graces that God heaps on His first and all-inclusive creature are as numberless and without end as are His creative words.

*Glorified be thy Lord, the Lord of Glory, beyond what they attribute unto Him, and peace be on the Messengers. Praise be to God the Lord of the worlds* (Koran, XXXVII, 180–182).

# 19
# Concerning the *Barzakh*

**A** VERY EXPLICIT example of the double meaning of symbols[1] is provided by the use of the expression *barzakh* in Islamic esoterism. In Islamic theology the word *barzakh* is generally taken to mean a certain intermediate state in the posthumous evolution of the human being. But esoterism gives it a much less restricted meaning, while moreover basing itself strictly on the metaphysical interpretation of the Koranic verses containing the term *barzakh*. One of these verses is from the sura *Ar-Rahmân*: 'He bringeth forth the two seas, which meet; between them is an isthmus (= *barzakh*), which they do not go beyond'. Another verse is from the sura *Al-Furqân*: 'He it is who bringeth forth the two seas; one is fresh and drinkable, the other is salt and bitter; and He hath made between the two an isthmus (= *barzakh*) and a closed barrier'.

According to interpretations well-known in Sufism, the two seas symbolize respectively Quiddity and the Qualities,[2] or, according to other interpretations, the non-manifested and the manifested, the formless and the formal, immediate knowledge and theoretical knowledge, etc. In short, the two seas can represent two more or less exalted, but always consecutive, degrees in the hierarchy of Being (*wujûd*).

As for the *barzakh*, which, seen 'from the outside', must necessarily have the definite meaning of 'partition' or 'separative element', it cannot be merely this for a perspective which applies to it the principle of non-otherness. Looking at it in regard to its ontological situation, if one may so put it, it appears as a simple partition only

---

[1] See René Guénon, *The Reign of Quantity and the Signs of the Times* (Baltimore, Maryland, Penguin Books, 1972), chapter 30, 'The Inversion of Symbols'.

[2] These terms are explained in the book *De l'Homme Universel* (*al-insân al-kâmil*) by 'Abd al-Karîm al-Jîlî, translated by Titus Burckhardt (Paris, Dervy-Livres, 1975). English edition, *Universal Man*, translated by Angela Culme-Seymour (Sherborne, Beshara Publications, 1983).

from the point of view of the degree of lesser reality, whereas seen 'from above', it is the very mediator between the two seas.

It can thus be compared to a prism which breaks down the integral light of a higher world into the varied colours of a lower world, or again to a lens which concentrates the rays from above by filtering them through a single point of inversion.

The *barzakh* is thus separation only in that it is itself the starting point of a separative perspective, in the eyes of which it appears to be a limit. And this finds an analogy in what is called the 'blind spot' in the physical eye, at the very place where the optic nerve perforates it.

These considerations regarding the two complementary aspects of the *barzakh* sufficiently explain why in Sufism this expression is sometimes used synonymously with *qutb*, 'pole'.

'What is called the *barzakh* of a given realm of existence,' says the Shaikh Si Mohammad Tadilî of Jadîda, 'is nothing other than the pole that governs this realm and gives it its growth.'

As can be seen from the use of the expression 'growth', the Shaikh Tadilî had above all in mind the cosmological applications of the theory of the *barzakh*:

'In the image of the hierarchy of the worlds contained in the *kawn al-kabîr*,[3] every world or every degree of human individuality is presided over by a *barzakh*, in the same way as every human faculty is governed by a certain pole.'

This is most easily seen in the faculties of mental conception, in which the *barâzikh* (plural of *barzakh*) constitute the pivots of the complementaries 'subject' and 'object', as well as in the faculties of sense perception.

The Shaikh Tadilî also says: 'All the *barâzikh* of man depend on his central *barzakh*, which is the heart (*qalb*),[4] mediator between the domain of the Spirit (*Rûh*) and that of the individual soul (*nafs*).'

Moreover, the physical aspect of the heart very clearly expresses

---

[3] The macrocosm. According to a Sufi saying, 'the cosmos is like a big man and man is like a little cosmos'.

[4] In this connection it is very significant that the root of the word *qalb*, QLB, implies the idea of 'turning upside down', whereas the root QBL implies that of 'placing one in front of the other', whence the expression *qiblah* (ritual orientation); the word *qalb*, moreover, also has the meaning of 'mould', given the inversion of 'negative' and 'positive' in the process of moulding.

the different characteristics of the *barâzikh*, for, according to Shaikh Tadilî, 'these *barâzikh* of the human hierarchy can be symbolically represented as so many imperceptible points from which a luminous vibration emanates, alternately of concentration and of expansion, continuously and spontaneously. Each pulsation of the *barzakh* produces a transformation of the vital light. In order that this transformation does not become upset and does not, through individual negligence, become fatally "downward-tending", it must always be determined by spiritual orientation and sustained by means such as *dhikr* (incantation) or by methods that depend on the science of respiration.' These methods are based, from a certain point of view, on the analogy between the phases of respiration and the pulsation of the *barâzikh*.

As for the *dhikr*, it should be noted that this word also means 'recall' or 'remembrance', which allows us to see analogies between incantation and the call to the *barzakh* of memory, situated between the 'seas' of remembrance and forgetfulness.[5]

The two-faced nature of Janus which is characteristic of the *barzakh*, its double function in a vertical sense of junction and separation, is expressed on the horizontal plane by the alternations of expansion and contraction. These are obviously aspects of the same complementarism. Reduced to an elementary logical expression, these dualities can be represented respectively by affirmation and negation.

This leads us to a corresponding application of the formula of the *Shahâdah*,[6] which itself can be called the doctrinal *barzakh* par excellence.

The *Shahâdah* is generally divided into two parts, of which the first, the *Lâ ilâha*, is called *an-nafy*, negation or *as-salb*, suppression, and the second, the *illâ 'Llâh*, is called *al-ithbât*, affirmation.

---

[5] The use of tense in the Arabic language pertains to the same order of analogies: it is not the present tense of the verb that is used to symbolize the eternal, but the past definite, or rather what corresponds to this in Arabic.

[6] The 'testimony'; in other words, the fundamental formula *Lâ ilâha illâ 'Llâh*, 'There is no divinity but The Divinity'. The word-for-word translation is as follows: *Lâ* = no; *ilâha* = divinity; *in* = if and *lâ* = not (contracted into *illâ*); *Allâh* = The Divinity. According to Arab grammarians, the name *Allâh* was originally composed of the definite article *Al* and the noun *ilâhu* (nominative of *ilâha*).

But in order to apply the *Shahâdah* even more explicitly to the theory of the *barzakh*, it must be divided into three parts: *Lâ ilâha, illâ,* and *Allâh*.[7] And in order better to understand the *barzakh illâ,* which is situated between the 'sea' of negation, *Lâ ilâha,* and the 'sea' of affirmation, *Allâh,* it should be broken down into its constituent elements: the particle *in* (= if), which expresses a condition, and *lâ* (= no), which expresses a negation.

Now, when one has understood that the particle *in* is a conditioned affirmation, since it gives back reality to *ilâhun* (nominative of *ilâha*)[8] on condition that this is not other than the reality of *Allâh,* it will be seen that the affirmation and the negation are present in the *illâ* in the reverse order to the affirmation and the negation which so to speak 'frame' the whole formula.

This reversal is naturally not a simple question of the order of words, for, as we have just indicated, the particle *in* is the 'point of reflection' for the grace of Allâh which reaches as far as the illusory *ilâhun*; one can see this if one replaces the term *ilâha* by any positive notion whatsoever; this will then be denied in so far as it affirms itself, at least illusorily, alongside the ipseity of Allâh, and it will be affirmed in so far as it is identified essentially or principially with the ipseity of Allâh. On the other hand, the second element of the *illâ,* the negative particle *lâ,* is in a sense the 'point of reflection' of the first part of the *Shahâdah,* namely the negation *Lâ ilâha*: the first *Lâ* of the formula denies the notion of 'divinity' expressed by the indeterminate form *ilâhun,* whereas the second *lâ* singles out this same notion in the determinate form *Allâh* ('The Divinity'), which symbolizes here non-comparability, and not determination in the restrictive sense of this term.

Thus the expression *illâ* demonstrates very clearly the two functions of the *barzakh*; the first consists in mediation in an 'ascending' sense, in other words in the passage from the manifested to the non-manifested, a passage or transformation which always traverses the blind spot of an extinction, or of a death; while the second is that this point is the point of reversal of relationships.

The *Shahâdah* shows that these two apparently opposed aspects

---

[7] 'There is no divinity'; 'if it is not'; 'The Divinity'.

[8] *Ilâhun* = divinity, *al-ilâhu* = The Divinity; *ilâha* = the accusative of negation.

can be integrated into the conception of 'non-otherness', a conception which obviously transcends the domain of reason and which thus gives to its expression, the *Shahâdah*, a certain appearance of pleonasm.[9]

The different aspects of the *barzakh* are further represented in the diagram of the Seal of Solomon, and this leads us to consider the relationship of the *barzakh* with *al-insân al-kâmil*, 'Universal Man', who, by expressing the constituent analogy of the microcosm and the macrocosm, is truly the *barzakh* par excellence or, what amounts to the same thing, the symbol par excellence.

Universal Man, in Islam, is *Muhammadun*, who includes in himself all *hamd*,[10] the positive aspect of existence. His role as *barzakh* is expressed by the second of the two *Shahâdatâni: Muhammadun rasûlu 'Llâh*, 'Muhammad (is) the messenger of Allâh'.

When one compares the two fundamental formulas: *Lâ ilâha illâ 'Llâh* and *Muhammadun rasûlu 'Llâh*, one sees that, in the first, the *barzakh* appears above all in its transforming aspect (*illâ* = if it is not), and, in the second, in its aspect of mediator and conserver (*rasûl* = messenger).

We must also mention here a Sufi interpretation of the following verse from the sura *Ar-Rahmân*: 'He bringeth forth the two seas, which meet; between the two is an isthmus (*barzakh*) which they do not go beyond.' The interpretation in question is related to Universal Man and consists in the affirmation that the Prophet is the 'isthmus', and that the 'two seas' are respectively *Sayyidnâ 'Alî* and *Sayyidatnâ Fâtima*.[11]

The *Risâlatu 'l-Qushairîyah* (the Qushairî Epistle), the famous treatise of Shaikh Abû 'l-Qâsim al-Qushairî,[12] contains amongst

[9] This has given rise to a number of fantastic translations of the *Shahâdah*, of which one of the least false is the following: 'there is no god except Allâh', a translation which, by its inadequacy, has induced many people to see in the *Shahâdah* only the affirmation of a very simplistic 'monotheism'.

[10] The most essential names of the Prophet are: *'Abd Allâh*, 'servant of Allâh'; *Ahmadun*, 'the best of glorifiers'; and *Muhammadun*, 'the best of the glorified'. *Ahmadun* is considered as the esoteric aspect of *Muhammadun*.

[11] *'Alî* is the esoteric *Khalîfah* (= lieutenant) par excellence, Fâtima is the daughter of the Prophet and the wife of *'Alî*.

[12] Al-Qushairî was a disciple of Abû 'Alî ad-Daqqâq and lived from 986 to 1074 A.D.

other things a compendium of certain 'technical terms' peculiar to Sufism. Orientalists have sought to see in these a kind of religious psychology and this is because, in fact, some of the terms commented on by Qushairî pertain to the symbolism of the sentiments. It is not wrong to see in this a 'psychology', in other words a science of the human psyche, since the development and control of the psychic elements or energies necessarily form an integral part in the method or 'way' (tarîqah), but it would be wrong not to be aware of the symbolical perspective implied in this Sufi science of the psyche, a perspective that gives it all its spiritual significance.

If we apply the considerations regarding the barzakh that have been formulated above to some sections of the Qushairî Epistle, the essentially metaphysical nature of what some have called a 'religious psychology' will be readily apparent.

We have seen that the double nature of the barzakh is reflected at a cosmic level by the alternation of the two phases of concentration and expansion. In the realm of the emotions, these two phases can be seen most directly in the two primordial ways in which the psyche reacts to what it considers to be 'reality': on the one hand, with fear, which is a contraction towards the centre of consciousness, and on the other hand with joy or hope, which is an expansion.[13]

Now when it is a question of consciously integrating these two phases into the universal order, they can no longer be related to something that could be conceived of as being exterior to themselves. When fear (al-khawf) and hope (ar-rajâ) are oriented towards Allâh or Universal Essence, they are not for that reason effaced from the psychic domain, but they are in a certain sense rhythmized, being no longer subject to disordered impulses; it could be said that they are determined, in a certain fashion, by the 'Present' in time, and by the 'Centre' in space, the pole which rules them and the end towards which they tend having become one and the same reality.

---

[13] This expansion which is proper to joy is expressed in a completely spontaneous manner in Arabic in the verb insharaha 'to rejoice', which literally means 'to expand', in speaking of the breast filled with joy. The verb inbasata, which also means 'to rejoice', also possesses, etymologically speaking, a meaning of 'expansion'. For the analogy between fear and contraction one could cite verbal images from several languages; let us note only, as a particularly clear example, the relationship between the German word Angst, 'fear', and the Latin word angustus, 'narrow'.

If the phases of fear and hope are thus determined and absorbed by the permanent actuality of the immediate present, in such a way that the *faqîr*[14] who realizes them has become the 'son of the moment' (*ibnu 'l-waqt*), they will manifest more essential aspects, and they can be denoted by expressions that have a more general cosmological meaning, such as 'contraction' (*qabd*) and 'expansion' (*bast*).[15]

They can then be transformed into the complementary states of *haibah*, an expression which can be approximately translated as 'terror of majesty', and of *uns*, 'intimacy'.

Whereas it is said of the two phases 'contraction' and 'expansion' (*qabd wa bast*) that one is in proportion to the other—which indicates that they must be considered as being manifested on the same plane   it is said of the state of *haibah* that it is identified with that of *ghaibah*, 'absence' or 'rapture'. It is here that a passage from the horizontal to the vertical takes place; and by inversion, through the narrow door of the *barzakh*, absence (in the world of *farq*, or separativity) becomes Presence (*Hudûr*) (in the world of *jam'*, or union).

Al-Qushairî quotes the following words of al-Junaid:[16] 'The fear of Allâh contracts me (*qabd*), hope directed towards Him enlarges me (*bast*); the Truth (*haqîqah*) unites me, and Justice (*haqq*) separates me. If He contracts me through fear, He extinguishes me from myself (*afnanî 'annî*), and if He enlarges me through hope, He returns me to myself. If He unites me by the Truth, He puts me into His Presence (*ahdaranî*), and if He separates me by Justice, He makes me witness of the other-than-myself, and veils me thus from Him.'

---

[14] The 'poor' in Allâh or for Allâh.

[15] Among the names of Allâh are: *al-Qâbid*, 'He who contracts' or 'He who grips', and *al-Bâsit*, 'He who enlarges'.

[16] Abû 'l-Qâsim al-Junaid, who came from a Persian family, lived in Baghdad, where he died in 910 A.D. He was one of the very great masters, and was called the 'lord of the troop' and 'peacock of the wise'.

# 20

# Extracts from the Commentary on the Divine Names by the Imam Ghazali[1]

*(al-maqsad al-asnâ fî sharhi asmâ' illâhi 'l-husnâ)*

THE INFINITELY GOOD, the Merciful (*Ar-Rahmân, Ar-Rahîm*).

The Divine Mercy is perfect, in the sense that it responds to every need. It is universal, in the sense that it is lavished both on those who deserve it and those who do not deserve it.

Of the two Names mentioned, the first (*Ar-Rahmân*) is not capable of any relative applications; it pertains to *Allâh* alone. Because of this fact, it approximates, in usage, to the Name *Allâh*. 'Say: invoke *Allâh* or invoke *Ar-Rahmân*, whichever ye invoke, to Him are the most beautiful Names'[2] (Koran).

The participation of the 'servant' ('*abd*, the contingent being, inasmuch as he is determined—*marbûb*—by the 'Lord' [*Rabb*], Absolute Being, inasmuch as He determines contingencies) in the quality of *Ar-Rahîm* consists in active generosity. His participation in the quality of *Ar-Rahmân* is the comprehension of all human imperfections as being aspects of his own soul.

⊠

[1] The famous Sufi and theologian Abû Hâmid at-Tûsî al-Ghazâlî (1058–1111).

[2] According to a temporal symbolism used in Islamic theology, God 'was' *Ar-Rahmân*—He who is infinitely good in Himself—'before' creation, whereas he is *Ar-Rahîm*—He who manifests His mercy—'since' creation. 'Before' thus refers to the Principle in itself, and 'since' (or 'after') to manifestation. Christianity uses an analogous temporal symbolism, but as it were in an inverse way: Christ is at the centre of time, the reign of the 'Old Covenant' referring to the human and the earthly, and the reign of the 'New Covenant' referring to the Divine and the Heavenly.

The King (*Al-Malik*).

*Al-Malik* is He who, by His Being and His qualities, is independent of all existence, while everything that exists depends on Him in every respect.
Participation in this divine quality is the state of prophethood.

⊠

The Holy (*Al-Quddûs*).

*Al-Quddûs* is He who is free from every perceptible, imaginable, and conceivable quality.
Participation in this divine quality relates to the state of purity and spiritual solitude.

⊠

Peace (*As-Salâm*).

*As-Salâm* is He who is free from all imperfections and diminishments. There is no integrity except through *Allâh*.
Participation in this divine quality is spiritual re-integration (of the contingent in the Absolute, by the return of existential disequilibria into the Divine Equilibrium, *As-Salâm*).[3]

⊠

The Faithful (*Al-Mu'min*).

---

[3] Disequilibrium is an effect of cosmic exteriorization, pure Existence corresponding to equilibrium or indifferentiation. This distinction between 'outward disequilibrium' and 'inward equilibrium' is also to be found in the division of the human world into the 'region of Islam' (*dâr al-islâm*) and the 'region of war' (*dâr al-harb*). *Al-Islâm* is conformity to *as-Salâm*, which is the goal; this is prefigured on earth by the Kaaba, which is *dâr as-salâm*, 'house of peace' or 'region of peace' (Koranic expression). In the human microcosm, this house of peace—or this Kaaba—is represented by the heart. One can understand why Râbi'a al-Adawîya omitted performing the pilgrimage to Mecca, given that she had carried out the 'pilgrimage to the heart'; in other words: had attained the 'peace' that 'pre-exists' beneath the tumult of exteriorized existence. Furthermore, if one recalls that the goal of a just war is true peace, it is easy to understand the role of the 'holy war' of the soul: the inward 'war' is in fact the abolition of another war, the one waged by earthly passions against the immortal soul and against the pure intellect.

*Al-Mu'min* is He who gives safety.

The servant who participates in this quality gives safety to other creatures; he is their refuge and their model.

⊠

The Guardian (*Al-Muhaimin*).

*Al-Muhaimin* is He who guards (or protects) creatures by his foresight, his masterfulness, and his conserving power. This Name thus contains, in a synthetic manner, aspects of prescience, powerfulness, and penetration. This is why it is counted amongst the Names revealed by the ancient sacred Books.

Participation in this divine quality relates to the state of vigilance, continual wakefulness, and spiritual supervision.

⊠

The Eminent (*Al-'Azîz*).

*Al-'Azîz* is He who at one and the same time is eminent, rare, precious, and hard of access. It would be impossible to apply this Name wherever any one of these aspects was lacking. Thus, for example, the sun is eminent, it is unique of its kind, but it is not difficult of access (i.e. by vision); therefore the Name *al-'Azîz* cannot be applied to the sun.

The perfection of rarity is (metaphysically) identifiable with Unicity.

The servant who participates in this divine quality is comparable to the rare great spiritual masters.

⊠

The Restorer (*Al-Jabbâr*).

*Al-Jabbâr* is He whose ordaining will penetrates and permeates everything, without His being Himself touched by anything (since nothing is outside of Him and consequently He is impassible).

The servant who participates in this quality is not subject to the influence of anyone else; he impresses his nature on every other creature, and is recognized only by the one who has undergone the extinction (*fanâ*) of his individuality.

⊠

The Proud (*Al-Mutakabbir*).

*Al-Mutakabbir* is He who looks on all things as being negligible in relation to Himself, and who sees neither greatness nor eminence but in His own essence (*dhât*).

The application of this quality to the servant is spiritual dignity (in other words, the concentration of the powers of the soul on the heart-intellect, and so on the Self, whence the impression of a proud attitude with regard to the appearances from which the spirit is detached).

⊠

The Creator (*Al-Khâliq*); the Producer, or He who realizes or develops creation (*Al-Bâri'*); and He who gives form, who fashions the creature (*Al-Musawwir*).[4]

Some people think that these three names are synonyms, all expressing equally the creative action; but this is not so: everything that proceeds from non-existence (*'adam*) to existence (*wujûd*) is the object firstly of divine determination (*tadqîr*),[5] then of divine manifestation (*ijâd*),[6] and finally of divine fashioning (*taswîr*).[7] Allâh is Creator (*Khâliq*) inasmuch as He assigns to each thing its existential measure (*qadr*); He is Producer (*Bâri'*) inasmuch as He realizes existence, and He is He-who-gives-form (*Musawwir*) inasmuch as He ordains manifested forms in perfect beauty. Let us cite as a parable the construction of a house: first of all, the architect sketches its proportions and determines the amount of building materials that will be necessary, then the mason erects the building, and finally the craftsman embellishes it . . .

As for the name 'He who gives form' (*Al-Musawwir*), it designates God inasmuch as He confers on things a perfect order and forms full

---

[4] This ternary of Divine Names is mentioned in this order in the Koran.

[5] This is the assignation of the 'existential measure', of the 'capacity' to receive to a greater or lesser degree the fullness of Being. It is this 'capacity' (*qadr*) that is subsequently developed under the action of *Al-Bâri'*. The creative action is thus analogous to the principial determination of the possibilities of manifestation in the Divine Intellect

[6] Literally: 'existentiation'.

[7] This word also signifies artistic activity, expecially drawing.

of beauty. This is one of the aspects of divine activity. In order to grasp its meaning completely, it is necessary to know the form of the world in its totality and in detail, for the whole world is formed on the model of a single person, whose members are coordinated with a view to a single goal.

The participation of the 'servant' in this divine name, is that man should inwardly represent to himself the whole cosmos, until he embraces its form as if he were looking at it.[8] From this global vision he will descend towards the contemplation of particular forms, considering, for example, the bodily human form with its members and organs; when he has understood their principle of formation, their composition, and the differences between them, he will raise his attention to the consideration of the cognitive and volitive qualities of which these organs are the instruments; in like manner he will contemplate the form of animals and plants, in their double aspect, outward and inward,[9] and to the extent of his own understanding, until he conceives in his heart the soul and the form of everything. Now all this refers only to the knowledge of physical forms, which has no more than a relative significance in comparison with the knowledge of the spiritual order; this latter comprises the hierarchy of Angels; it also discerns the various functions of the Angels ruling the movements of the stars, the effects of Grace in the heart of man, and the impulsions of instinct in the animals.[10] Man thus participates in

---

[8] This presupposes an inclusive and homogeneous conception of the physical cosmos, such as was possessed by all the traditional civilizations. A 'vision' of this kind will always be but a symbol; it can never be more than that. Whatever progress may have been made in modern cosmography, the totality of the physical world will always outstrip by far our means of investigation. The ancient and medieval conceptions of the world corresponded to a natural experience; because of this, they were the vehicle of a qualitative synthesis of the total cosmos, whereas modern conceptions of the sidereal universe are too indirect and too abstract to provide a support for contemplation; at the same time, they imply a materialistic point of view that creates a monstrous disproportion between surrounding reality and the human subject: one forgets that every conception of the world is basically but a content of the human mind and that its intrinsic truth cannot be superior to that of its intellective 'mirror'.

[9] This means that animal and vegetable forms must be understood both in respect of their objective formal characteristics and as manifestations of diverse modalities of consciousness.

[10] These are the impersonal, non-mental, and non-individual modes of universal Intelligence. The ternary mentioned by Al-Ghazâlî is rich in meaning.

this divine name by assimilating the intelligible form that corresponds to the existential form; for science is none other than an inward form analogous to the form of the object of knowledge.[11] The knowledge that God has of forms is the cause of the existence[12] of these forms in the essences (*al-a'yân*), and the forms contained in the essences are the cause of the actualization of the intelligible forms in the heart of man. It is in this way that the 'servant' realizes science by virtue of the divine name 'He-who-gives-form' (*Al-Musawwir*). By the assimilation of the intelligible forms, man himself becomes 'he-who-gives-form' (*musawwir*),[13] although this quality only belongs to him in a contingent manner. In reality, each of these forms is only actualized in man by a divine creative act, and not by individual creation;[14] nevertheless, the servant opens himself to the influx of the Divine Mercy (*Rahmah*), for 'God does not change what a people has received, unless they themselves change what they carry within them' (Koran); in the same sense, the Prophet said: 'Verily in the course of earthly existence, your Lord exhales certain breaths of mercy; will ye then not be ready to receive them?'[15]

As for the two names The Creator (*Al-Khâliq*) and the Producer (*Al-Bâri'*), the 'servant' only participates in them in a very indirect and distant manner, by the development of his strength, founded on his science . . . There exist divine names—indeed most of them—which in reality apply to God alone, such as the names The Creator and The Producer, which can only be attributed to the individual in a contingent and provisional manner, and there are others—like The

[11] This simple truth is in practice ignored by modern science. The definition given by Al-Ghazâlî applies to speculation. As for knowledge or gnosis (*al-ma'rifah*), it is the identification of the intellect with the essence of the object.

[12] That is to say, of the reality of these forms, for the contents of the immutable essences (*al-a'yân ath-thâbitah*) are not manifested as such; they have no 'existence' but only a principial 'permanence' (*thubût*).

[13] A term that also means 'artist'. One can see here the link attaching true art to sacred science.

[14] Individual creation is only realized within the framework of divine creation and represents no more than a prolongation of the latter.

[15] In connection with the divine name in question, this saying of the Prophet contains an allusion to the nature of art considered according to the traditional point of view, in other words, as both an art and a science: true art is to realize the prolongation of the divine creative act in the creative activity of man.

Patient (*As-Sabûr*) and The Grateful (*Ash-Shâkir*)—which are really names of the creature and apply to God only in a provisional and entirely symbolic manner . . .

⊠

He who is full of forgiveness (*Al-Ghaffâr*).

This is He who manifests beauty and hides ugliness, such as the ugliness of sins, which He hides by 'covering' them with a veil in this present world and by effacing their consequences in the world to come, for 'forgiveness' (*al-ghafr*) literally means the act of 'covering' (*as-sitr*). God 'forgives' firstly by covering the ugliness of the entrails by the beauty of bodily form, then He 'forgives' by hiding the seat of abject thoughts and bad suggestions, so that no one can detect them, and finally He forgives by the remission of sins[16] . . . Moreover, God has promised (in the Koran) that He will transform the moral ugliness of man into beauty, by covering it with the clothing of virtue, if man remains firm in his faith.[17]

The participation of the 'servant' in this divine name is that he should 'cover' in others what he must hide in himself.[18] For the Prophet—on him be Blessings and Peace—has said: 'If someone covers the shame of a believer, God will cover his own shame on the

[16] Sin or transgression is a rupture of the normal equilibrium of the being. By divine forgiveness—which is an expression of the undifferentiated plenitude of Being—transgression is as it were 'drowned' in the integral cosmic equilibrium.

[17] 'Verily, We shall transform their ugliness into beauty' (Koran). By the reintegration of the being into the Edenic state, which is the plenitude of human possibilities, accidental deviations are neutralized and brought back to their positive aspect: transgression as such is a confusion between good and evil or real and unreal; its ontologically positive content is the aspiration towards the good or the real, on condition however that the transgression, insofar as it is something obscure, does not represent the deep-seated and fundamental tendency of the being; in this case, reintegration into the Edenic state is impossible. Love also possesses the virtue of transforming into beauty what, outside itself, can appear as an ugliness. It is in this way that the animal aspect of sexual love is transformed into beauty.

[18] According to the Islamic perspective, it is not meritorious to confess one's sins publicly, if they have not been made public by someone else, for it is a lack of generosity and respect for one's neighbour to display one's own ugliness before him; moreover, to reveal this may corrupt others. It is a case of hiding one's sin in the hope that God will also hide it by forgiving it.

day of judgement'. Slander, spying, vengeance, and the retribution of evil by evil are at the extreme opposite of this quality; on the contrary, it belongs to the man who divulges only the good that creatures possess. Every creature possesses perfections and imperfections, beauties and uglinesses; whoever disregards their uglinesses and mentions only their beauties, truly participates in the Divine Forgiveness.[19] It is related that Jesus—on whom be peace—was travelling with his disciples, and that they passed by a dead dog, the evil smell from which was unbearable. 'How foul-smelling is this carcass!' exclaimed the disciples. But Jesus replied: 'How beautiful is the whiteness of its teeth!'

⊠

The Dominator, He who subdues (*Al-Qahhâr*).

This is the one who breaks the pride of his adversaries by destroying them and abasing them; there is nothing, outside God, that is not dominated by His power and that is not impotent in His grip.[20]

[19] The imitation of divine forgiveness does not exclude, in the spiritual man, discrimination and discernment, nor, in the case of the monarch responsible for social order, the administration of justice, just as the meaning of the divine name 'He who is full of forgiveness' does not exclude the meanings of the divine names The Judge (*Al-Hakam*) and The Wise (*Al-Hakîm*). Discrimination applies to ideas and actions insofar as they express truths or errors, and not to the essences of individual beings. With regard to social justice, as it is prescribed by Moslem law, it refrains from uncovering, by constraint, individual motives and acts that can remain hidden without prejudice to the safety of others. A distinction is made between infractions of the 'rights of God' and infractions of the 'rights of man'. In the case of the first, the judge can be clement, supposing that God may have forgiven the accused. In a general way, witnesses are not encouraged to give evidence against the accused, and the latter is invited to deny his crime, if the rights of others have not been infringed through it; if in spite of this, the crime is proved, judgement will be executed with rigour. This practice takes as its model the Prophet's way of acting.

[20] The first and most universal of the constraints undergone by the creature is the impossibility, for him, of approaching the Essence (*Ahadîyah*) in its transcendent and absolute Unity. Indeed, the Essence can only be known by the Essence; as a spiritual state, this knowledge implies the annihilation (*mahw*) of the creature. According to this meaning, the divine aspect of the One-who-subdues (*Qahhâr*) flows directly from Unity, which includes everything, so that nothing is situated 'outside' It, and It Itself for this reason cannot be reached 'from the outside'; in other words, God cannot be 'grasped', because it is He who 'grasps' all things.

The dominator amongst men is he who subdues his enemies. Now, the enemy of man is his own soul (*nafs*) contained between his sides.[21] It is his enemy because of satan who deceives it. To the extent that man subdues the desires of his soul he conquers satan, who leads to ruin, by means of the passions of the soul. One of the snares of satan is sexual appetite; he who is no longer subject to this desire, can no longer be caught by this snare, and the same is true for him who subdues it by religious disciplines and by the criteria of reason.[22] Whoever dominates the passions of his soul, dominates the whole world; no one can overcome him, since the worst that someone else can do him is to kill his body; now the death of his body will be life for his spirit, for the one who causes his passions to die while he is living, lives when he dies. 'Think not that those who have been killed in the way of God are dead; they live and receive their nourishment from their Lord . . .' (Koran).

### Postscriptum

The total number of Divine names is ninety-nine. Those not included in the translated extracts from Al-Ghazâlî's work given above are the following:
*Al-Wahhâb* (The Giver); *Ar-Razzâq* (The Provider); *Al-Fattâh* (The Opener [of the inward eye] of the way to success and victory); *Al-'Alîm* (The Omniscient); *Al-Qâbid* (He who contracts, The Straitener); *Al-Bâsit* (He who expands, The Munificent); *Al-Khâfid* (The Abaser); *Ar-Râfi'* (The Exalter); *Al-Mu'izz* (The Honourer, The Enhancer); *Al-Mudhill* (He who humbles); *As-Samî* (The All-Hearing); *Al-Basîr* (The All-Seeing); *Al-Hakam* (The Arbitrator, the Decider); *Al-'Adl* (The Just); *Al-latîf* (The Benign, The Subtle, The All-Penetrating); *Al-Khabîr* (He who is aware of everything); *Al-Halîm* (The Indulgent); *Al-'Asîm* (The Immense, The Magnificent); *Al-Ghafûr* (The All-Forgiving); *Ash-Shakûr* (The Grateful); *Al-'Alî* (The Most High); *Al-Kabîr* (The Great); *Al-Hafîz* (The All-Preserver); *Al-Muqît* (The Nourisher, The Giver of

---

[21] In other words, the passional soul which is identified with the 'flesh'.

[22] The most perfect domination of the soul is to know its own nature. In this case, man, intellectual by nature, 'includes' his soul as God 'includes' the world.

Strength); *Al-Hasîb* (The All-Calculating); *Al-Jalîl* (The Majestic); *Al-Karîm* (The Generous); *Ar-Raqîb* (The All-Observant); *Al-Mujîb* (The Answerer of prayers); *Al-Wâsi'* (The Vast, The All-Containing); *Al-Hakîm* (The Wise); *Al-Wadûd* (The Loving-kind); *Al-Majîd* (The All-Glorious); *Al-Bâ'ith* (The Raiser of the dead, The Sender); *Ash-Shahîd* (The Universal Witness); *Al-Haqq* (The Truth); *Al-Wakîl* (The Guardian, The Reliable); *Al-Qawîy* (The Strong); *Al-Matîn* (The Firm, The Steadfast); *Al-Walîy* (The Patron, The Helper); *Al-Hamîd* (The Praised); *Al-Muhsī* (The Knower of each separate thing); *Al-Mubdi'* (The Beginner, The Cause); *Al-Mu'îd* (The Bringer-back, The Restorer); *Al-Muhyî* (The Life-Giver); *Al-Mumît* (The Slayer); *Al-Hayy* (The Living); *Al-Qayyûm* (The Self-Existing, the All-Sustaining); *Al-Wâjid* (The Finder, The Resourceful); *Al-Mâjid* (The Magnificent); *Al-Wâhid* (The Unique); *As-Samad* (The Eternal, He who has absolute plenitude); *Al-Qâdir* (The All-Powerful); *Al-Muqtadir* (The All-Determiner); *Al-Muqaddim* (He who brings forward, The Promoter); *Al-Mu'akhhir* (The Postponer); *Al-Awwal* (The First); *Al-Akhir* (The Last); *As-Zâhir* (The Outward); *Al-Bâtin* (The Inward); *Al-Wâlî* (The Ruler); *Al-Muta'âlî* (The Exalted, the Sublime, The Transcendent); *Al-Barr* (The Doer of Good); *At-Tawwâb* (The Ever-relenting, He who makes repentance easy); *Al-Muntaqîm* (The Avenger); *Al-Afûw* (The Effacer of sins); *Ar-Ra'ûf* (The All-Pitying); *Mâliku 'l-Mulk* (The King of Absolute Sovereignty); *Dhû 'l-Jalâli wa l-Ikrâm* (The Lord of Majesty and Generosity); *Al-Muqsit* (The Equitable, The Requiter); *Al-Jâmi'* (The Assembler, The Uniter); *Al-Ghanîy* (The Rich); *Al-Mughnî* (The Enricher); *Al-Mâni'* (The Preventer, The Shielder); *Ad-Dârr* (The Punisher, He who harms); *An-Nâfi'* (He who benefits); *An-Nûr* (Light); *Al-Hâdî* (The Guide); *Al-Badî* (The Absolute Cause); *Al-Bâqî* (The Permanent, The Everlasting); *Al-Wârith* (The Heir, The Inheritor); *Ar-Rashîd* (The Right in Guidance); *As-Sabûr* (The Patient).

# 21

# The Role of the Fine Arts
# in Moslem Education

ET US START by considering the place that Islamic art
occupies in modern academic teaching, for it is through that
teaching—or more specifically through the disciplines of
archaeology and the history of art—that many Moslem
students make their first contact with the artistic legacy of Islam.
Archaeology and the history of art are two branches of one single
science which originated in eighteenth-century Europe as a sister to
humanistic philosophy, an agnostic philosophy which reduces all
spiritual values to their purely human aspect. One may therefore
wonder whether this science—which has incontestably accumulated
a great deal of valuable data and also contributed to the preservation
of many precious monuments—is able to understand, not only the
outward history of Islamic art, but also its spiritual content.

Archaeology and the history of art are both founded on the
historical analysis of works of art. Such an analysis may well deliver
objective results, but it does not necessarily lead to an essential view
of things. On the contrary, it has a tendency to stop short at details at
the expense of more comprehensive views, rather as if a man who
looked at a stone wall tried to understand the *raison d'être* of the wall
by tracing back each individual stone to its origin. This is exactly what
has happened with many scholars who have tried to explain the origin
of Islamic art by tracing back each of its elements to some precedent
in Byzantine, Sassanid, Coptic or other art. They have lost sight of
the intrinsic and original unity of Islamic art. They have forgotten the
'seal' that Islam conferred on all borrowed elements.

It is true that the history of art received many new impulses from
studying the art of oriental civilizations. However, it has by no means
freed itself from certain prejudices stemming from its very origin, the
most deeply rooted of these being the habit of judging the value of a
work of art by the degree of its real or presumed 'originality' or by

virtue of its 'revolutionary' character; as if the essential quality of a work of art were not its beauty, and as if beauty were not independent of the psychological dramas of the moment. But most historians of art are primarily interested in the individuality of the artist; they are not directly concerned with the spiritual truth which an art may convey. What they try to capture is the psychological impulse that has led to such and such an artistic expression. Now this individualism or psychologism, as we may call it, is as far as can be from the spirit of Islamic art, which never became the stage for individual problems and experiences. The Moslem artist, by his very *islâm*, his 'surrender' to the Divine Law, is always aware of the fact that it is not he who produces or invents beauty, but that a work of art is beautiful to the degree that it obeys the cosmic order and therefore reflects universal beauty: *al-hamdu li-'Llâhi wahda-hu*. This awareness, while excluding all prometheanism, by no means diminishes the joy of artistic creativity, as the works themselves testify. Rather, it confers on Islamic art a serene and somehow impersonal character. For the Moslem mind, art reminds man of God when it is as impersonal as the laws that govern the movement of the heavenly spheres.

For modern 'psychologism', therefore, Islamic art is a closed book, even more so since it hardly offers anything analogous to the representation of human beings found in European art. In Western civilization, influenced as it is both by Greek art and by Christian iconography, the image of man occupies the central position in all visual art, whereas in the world of Islam the image of man plays a secondary role and is altogether absent from the liturgical domain. The Islamic negation of anthropomorphic art is both absolute and conditional: it is absolute with regard to all images that could be the object of worship, and it is conditional with regard to art forms imitating living bodies. We refer to the saying of the Prophet in which he condemned artists who try to 'ape' the creation of God: in their afterlife they will be ordered to give life to their works and will suffer from their incapacity to do so. This *hadîth* has been interpreted in different ways. In general it has been understood as condemning an intrinsically blasphemous intention, and therefore Islam tolerates anthropomorphic art forms on condition that they do not create the illusion of living beings. In miniature painting, for instance, central perspective suggesting three-dimensional space is avoided.

From the European point of view, the Islamic restriction on figurative art seems excessive. It is responsible, it is said, for cultural impoverishment. The history of European art, however, fully justifies the Islamic 'aniconism'. European art, as it has developed since the Middle Ages—in other words, since the naturalistic trend of the Renaissance—has strongly contributed to robbing religion of its credibility.

And let us not forget that the image of man is always the image that man conceives of himself. The image bears back upon its author, who thus never quite frees himself from the spell it casts upon him. The whole course of European art, with its increasingly accelerated phases of action and reaction, is mainly a dialogue between man and his image. Islam banished all this ambiguous play of psychological mirrors at an early stage, thus preserving the primordial dignity of man himself.

The European and Islamic conceptions of art are so different that one may wonder whether their common use of such words as 'art' and 'artistic' does not create more confusion than understanding. Almost everything in European art is image. Consequently the highest rank in the hierarchy of European art is held by figurative painting and sculpture. These are 'free arts', whereas architecture, as conditioned by technical necessities, occupies a lower rank. Even 'lower' are the 'decorative' arts. From the European point of view, the criterion of an artistic culture lies in its capacity to represent nature, and even more in its capacity to portray man. From the Islamic point of view, on the contrary, the main scope of art is not the imitation or description of nature—the work of man will never equal the art of God—but the shaping of the human ambience. Art has to endow all the objects with which man naturally surrounds himself—a house, a fountain, a drinking vessel, a garment, a carpet—with the perfection each object can possess according to its own nature. The perfection of a building, for instance, stems from three-dimensional geometry (following the perfection of matter in its crystalline state), whereas the art of the carpet involves two-dimensional geometry along with harmony of colours. Islamic art does not add something alien to the objects that it shapes; it merely brings out their essential qualities. It is essentially objective; in fact, neither the search for the most perfect profile for a cupola nor the rhythmical display of a linear ornament have much to do with the personal mood of the artist. The central theme not only of post-Renaissance European art but also of traditional Christian art is the image of man. In Islam too man is the centre to which all arts refer, but as a rule man is not the theme of visual art. If we fully consider the general Islamic resistance to figurative and anthropomorphic art, we discover a tremendous respect for the Divine origin of the human form. *Mutatis mutandis* the same is true for traditional Christian art, but the consequences are completely different in the two cases.

We should like here to outline the hierarchy of the visual arts in the world of Islam. The most noble of all its arts is calligraphy or the art of writing, for this has the privilege of translating into visual forms the divine speech of the Koran. Indeed, Arabic calligraphy not only attained the highest perfection, it also gave rise to a wide range of different styles from the purely rectangular *kûfî* to the most fluid and melodious forms of *naskhî*. Wherever Islam has reigned are to be found innumerable jewels of Arabic calligraphy.

Almost as important is the art of architecture. One can say that it occupies the central position among the arts shaping the human ambience and making it congenial to Islamic *baraka*. Most of the minor arts, such as woodcarving, mosaics, sculpture, and so on, are attached to architecture. We call them 'minor arts' according to the conventional terminology, but in fact they never occupied a lower rank in the Moslem world. This is true even of the so-called utilitarian arts, for they too share in the dignity of man as the 'representative of God on earth'.

Before the world of Islam was invaded by the products of modern industry, no object left the hands of a Moslem craftsman without being endowed with some beauty, whether it were a building or a domestic implement, whether it were for a rich customer or a poor one. The material used by the craftsman might be humble and his instruments very simple; his work was nonetheless noble. The reason for this remarkable fact is that beauty is inherent in Islam itself; it flows from its innermost reality, which is Unity (*at-tawhîd*) manifesting itself as justice (*'adl*) and generosity (*karam*). These three qualities of unity, justice and generosity are also the fundamental aspects of beauty and almost constitute its definition, as will be more apparent if we call them unity, equilibrium and plenitude. For, at the level of art, 'justice' becomes equilibrium and 'generosity' becomes plenitude, while unity is the common source of all perfections.

If we consider inward beauty and outward beauty, we find the latter has its origin in the former. To the extent that human activities are integrated into Islam, they become a support for beauty—a beauty which in fact transcends these activities because it is the beauty of Islam itself. This is particularly true of the fine arts, as it is their role to manifest the hidden qualities of things. The art of Islam receives its beauty not from any ethnic genius but from Islam itself.

The beauty of the arts of Islam—we might also say: the beauty that Islam normally conveys to its surroundings—is like a silent education which in an existential way renders plausible the doctrinal teaching of explicit religious education. It penetrates the soul without passing through rational thought, and for many believers is a more direct argument than pure doctrine. It is like the life and flesh of religion, whilst theology, law and ethics are its skeleton.

For this reason the existence of art is a vital necessity in the spiritual and social economy of Islam. Art, however, cannot exist without the artist or without the craftsman: no distinction is made between the two in the traditional Islamic world, where art without craftsmanship, and technical prowess without beauty, are equally inconceivable. This means that the progressive elimination of the crafts as a result of the inroads made by the machine entails the partial or total disappearance of the Islamic arts. At one stroke religious education is robbed of its two principal supports: the silent aid of an all-pervading beauty—there are still some traces left, but for how long?—and the more explicit aid of the professional artisanal activities themselves, which are normally oriented towards a spiritual end.

Education in the crafts converges with spiritual education whenever it strives towards that kind of perfection to which the Prophet referred in saying: 'God prescribes perfection in all things' (kataba 'Llâhu ihsâna 'alâ kulli shay). The word ihsân, translated here by 'perfection', also means 'beauty' and 'virtue'; more exactly, it means inward beauty, beauty of the soul or of the heart, which necessarily emanates outwards, transforming every human activity into an art and every art into the remembrance of God (dhikru 'Llâh).

There is no Moslem artist who has not inherited from his

predecessors. If he should disregard the models that tradition offers him, he would *ipso facto* prove his ignorance of their intrinsic meaning and spiritual worth; being ignorant of that, he could not put his heart into those forms. Instead of tradition, there would only be sterile repetition. This is precisely the phenomenon for which some European scholars reproach Islamic art; they argue that this art gradually died from lack of imagination. But in fact, the arts of Islam never lost their inward substance until modern industry dealt them a deadly blow. If the arts of Islam have now died, it is because their very foundations, the traditional crafts, have been destroyed.

But not all the traditional crafts and arts have disappeared; in some places they survive, and every effort should be made to protect them, for industrialization is not the real solution to social problems. We have considered the place that Islamic art occupies in modern academic teaching and also its relationship to the traditional crafts. And we have shown that Islamic art is not merely the art of Moslem peoples, but is deeply rooted in the spirit of Islam itself; not only do the various forms of Islamic art have common features, but its very variety is a manifestation of an essential unity, like variations on a single musical theme.

We can now return to our main subject, and ask the question whether a knowledge of Islamic art is vital to Moslem education. If we simplify the question, and put it in the following words: 'Is Islamic art vital to Islam itself?' every Moslem will, I presume, answer 'No'. Islam as a path to Divine Truth does not depend on any cultural circumstances; a Bedouin may be as perfect as a Moslem scholar, and a simple *musallâ* in the desert, surrounded by a line of stones with a bigger stone indicating the direction of the Kaaba, is as valid a place for prayer as the Pearl Mosque in Delhi. Cultural development is not necessarily identical with spiritual achievement. Let us then ask: 'Can a Moslem community live within a cultural framework alien to Islam?' Experience shows that it may survive, but that it does not prosper. But our question will probably elicit the remark that a cultural framework involves a variety of elements of greater or lesser importance, and that materialistic philosophy and sociology are a greater handicap to Moslem education than the presence of non-Islamic art or the absence of Islamic art; for art deals with appearances, whereas philosophy and psychology touch the heart of things.

This judgement, however, is one-sided; it forgets that art, while dealing in fact with the outward aspect of things, at the same time reveals an inward dimension of reality.

The essence of art is beauty, and beauty by its very nature is an outward as well as an inward reality. According to a well-known saying of the Prophet: 'God is beautiful and He loves beauty' (*Allâhu jamîlun yuhibbu 'l-jamâl*). Beauty is therefore a Divine Quality (*sifah ilâhiyyah*) reflected in whatever is beautiful on earth. Some scholars will perhaps object that the beauty referred to in the *hadîth* is of a purely moral character, but there is no reason why we should limit the import of the *hadîth* in this way, nor why the Divine Beauty should not shine forth at every level of existence. No doubt Divine Beauty is incomparably exalted above physical as well as moral beauty, but at the same time nothing beautiful can exist outside the dominion of this Divine Quality: that 'God is beautiful and He loves beauty' means that He loves His own reflection in the world.

According to a number of famous Moslem metaphysicians, Divine Beauty (*jamâl*) includes all the Divine Attributes expressing bounty and grace—in other words, the merciful radiance of God in the world—whereas Divine Majesty (*jalâl*) includes all the Divine Attributes expressing severity, which in a way manifest the transcendent nature of God with regard to His creation. In more general terms, each Divine Quality contains all the others, for they all refer to the one Essence. In this way, beauty implies truth (*haqq*) and truth implies beauty. There is no real beauty which does not have truth concealed in it, and there is no real truth from which beauty does not emanate. This reciprocity of the universal qualities has its reflection at the level of traditional education, and in this connection it has been said: 'In Islam every art is a science and every science is an art.' These words refer directly to the geometrical lore involved in Islamic art, a lore which allows the artist to develop harmonious forms from fundamental geometrical patterns. According to a higher level of meaning, however, art is a science because it opens up a way of contemplative knowledge whose ultimate objective is Divine Beauty, and science is an art insofar as it is oriented towards unity and therefore possesses a sense of equilibrium or harmony which cannot but lend it beauty.

Modern European art, whatever beauty it may offer incidentally, is generally enclosed within the particular psychic world of its author; it contains no wisdom, no spiritual grace. As for modern science, it neither possesses nor demands any beauty. Being purely analytic, it scarcely opens its eyes to a contemplative vision of things. When it studies man, for instance, it never contemplates his entire nature, which is at one and the same time body, soul and spirit. If we make modern science responsible for modern technology, it is at the very basis of a whole world of ugliness. The least we can say is that modern science, in spite of all its learning and experience, is an unwise science. Perhaps the greatest lesson traditional art can teach us is that beauty is a criterion of truth. If Islam were a false religion, if it were not a divine message but a system invented by man, could it have produced so many works of art endowed with everlasting beauty?

At this point we must ask the question: 'What ought to be the role of the fine arts in Moslem education today?' The study of Islamic art, if undertaken with an open mind and without the post-Medieval prejudices we have mentioned, is a way of approach to the spiritual background of all Islamic culture. The same is true for all traditional art. The main shortcoming that one has to avoid is the academic mentality that considers all works of art from earlier centuries as purely historical 'phenomena' which belong to the past and have very little to do with present-day life. We cannot even understand art, it seems, without knowing the historical circumstances of its birth. Against this relativistic point of view, we gladly affirm that for the Moslem, the great mosques of Kairawan, Córdoba, Cairo, Damascus, Isfahan, Herat and so on belong as much to the present as to the past, insofar as it is still possible to realize the state of mind of those who created them. Nor does it make sense to say: 'We are living in another time and therefore cannot take these famous buildings as models for contemporary mosque architecture.' Let us not run after time—it will always be faster than we are—but let us ask what is timeless in the art of our spiritual ancestors. If we recognize this, we shall also be able to make use of it within the inevitable framework of our own age.

Historical research has a certain use; it can give answers to questions like these: When was this mosque built? Who built it? Who paid for its construction? What were its nearest models? And so on. But Moslem education in the fine arts should not stop there; it should first and foremost point to the real values of Islamic art. Let students learn the technical procedures of the various arts, from pottery to the vaulting of a dome; let them discover the geometrical figures from which the proportions of a given building have been developed. In a word, let them experience, in their minds at least, the very genesis of a work of art. For the great artistic legacy—whether it be lost or only neglected; whether it can be rediscovered or not—is traditional art itself, not as an object but as a method, uniting technical skill with a spiritual vision of things, a vision which has its source in *tawhîd*.

# 22
# Perennial Values in
# Islamic Art

**M**UCH HAS BEEN written about the formation of Islamic art from pre-existing elements of Byzantine, Persian, Hindu and Mongolian origin. But very little has been said about the nature of the power that wrought all these various elements into a unique synthesis. No one will deny the unity of Islamic art, either in time or in space; it is much too evident: whether the work of art be the mosque at Córdoba, the great madrasa at Samarkand, a saint's tomb in the Maghrib, or a saint's tomb in Chinese Turkestan, it is as if the same light shone forth from all of them. What then is the nature of this unity? The religious law of Islam does not prescribe any particular forms of art; it merely restricts the field of their expression, and restrictions are not creative in themselves. On the other hand, it is highly misleading if, as is often done, one simply attributes this unity to 'religious feeling'. However intense an emotion may be, it is unable to fashion a whole world of forms into a harmony that is both rich and sober, both overwhelming and precise. It is not by chance that the unity and regularity of Islamic art remind us of the law that governs crystals: there is something here that transcends the mere power of emotion, which is necessarily vague and always fluctuating. We shall call it the 'intellectual vision' that is inherent in Islamic art, taking the word 'intellect' in its original sense, as a faculty more comprehensive by far than reason and thought, and involving the intuition of timeless realities. This is also the meaning of 'intellect' (*al-'aql*) in Islamic tradition: faith is not complete unless it be illumined by *al-'aql* which alone grasps the implications of *at-tawhîd*, the doctrine of Divine Unity. In a similar way, Islamic art derives its beauty from wisdom.

The history of art, being a modern science, inevitably approaches Islamic art in the purely analytical way of all modern sciences, by dissection and reduction to historical circumstances. Whatever is timeless in an art—and a sacred art like that of Islam always contains a timeless element—is left out by such a method. One may object that all art is composed of forms and, since form is limited, it is necessarily subject to time: like all historical phenomena, forms arise, develop, become corrupted, and die; therefore the science of art is of necessity a historical science. But this is only half of the truth: a form, though limited and consequently subject to time, is able to convey something timeless, and in this respect it escapes historical conditions, not only in its genesis—which in part belongs to a spiritual dimension—but also in its preservation, at least to a certain extent, for it is in respect of their timeless meaning that certain forms have been preserved despite and against all the material and psychic revolutions of an epoch; tradition means just that.

Moreover, the modern study of art derives most of its aesthetic criteria from classical Greek and post-medieval art. Whatever its latest developments may have been, it has always considered the individual as the real creator of art. From this point of view, a work is 'artistic' in so far as it shows the stamp of an individuality. Now, from an Islamic point of view, beauty is essentially the expression of universal Truth.

It is thus not surprising that modern science, when studying Islamic art, often stops short at a negative judgement. We find such negative judgements in many if not most of the learned works on Islamic art; they are all rather similar, though different in degree. One often reads that Islamic art was creative only in its first stage, in integrating and transforming earlier legacies, and that later it congealed more and more into sterile formulas. These formulas, we learn further, did not quite annul the ethnic differences of the peoples of Islam, but they unfortunately suffocated the individual initiative of the artist. This happened all the more easily—so it would seem—since Islamic art was deprived of a most vital and profound dimension by the religious prohibition of images. We have quoted all these judgements in their most extreme forms, knowing perfectly well that few European scholars would subscribe to all of them. But it is useful to confront these judgements head on, for they help us, by their very limitations, to indicate the point of view that truly corresponds to the nature of Islamic art.

Let us first consider the last of these reproaches, the one concerning the religious prohibition of images. This prohibition is twofold: firstly there is the Koranic condemnation of idolatry which, from the general Moslem point of view, involves the visual representation of God in any form, the nature of God being beyond all description, even in words. Secondly, there are the sayings of the Prophet according to which the wish to imitate the Creator's work by imitating the form of living beings, and particularly the form of man, is irreverent and even blasphemous. This last injunction has not always and everywhere been observed, since it concerns more the intention than the deed: in the Persian and Indian world especially, it was argued that an image which does not claim to imitate the real being, but is no more than an allusion to it, is allowed. This is one of the reasons for the non-illusive style of Persian miniatures, that is to say, the absence in them of shadows and perspective. No mosque, however, has ever been decorated with anthropomorphic images.

If we consider things superficially, we may be tempted to liken the Islamic point of view to that of Puritanism, which is ignorant of symbolism and consequently rejects all sacred art as an illusion. Symbolism is based on the analogy between the different degrees of Being: since Being is one (*al-wujûdu wâhid*), everything that is, or exists, must in some way reflect its eternal source. Islam by no means ignores this law, which the Koran proclaims in a thousand metaphors: *wa in min shay'in illâ yusabbi-hu bi-hamdi-hi* ('There is nothing which does not exalt His praise,' Koran, XVII, 44). It is not out of disregard for the sacred character of creation that Islam proscribes human images; on the contrary, it is because man is the viceregent (*khalîfah*) of God on earth, as the Koran teaches. The Prophet explained that God created Adam 'in His form' ('*alâ sûrati-hi*), 'form' in this case meaning qualitative likeness, for man is gifted with faculties which reflect the seven 'personal' qualities of God, namely Life, Knowledge, Will, Power, Hearing, Seeing, and Speech.

A comparison of the Islamic and Christian attitudes towards the human image will help to clarify matters. In response to Byzantine iconoclasm, which was influenced by the example of Islam, the Seventh Ecumenical Council justified the use of icons in the liturgy with the following argument: God is indescribable in Himself; but since the divine Logos assumed human nature, he reintegrated it into its original form and penetrated it with divine beauty. In representing the human form of Christ, art reminds us of the incarnation. There is a sharp distinction between this point of view and that of Islam, but nevertheless both refer to a common basis, namely the theomorphic nature of man.

It is worth mentioning that one of the profoundest explanations of the Christian attitude towards sacred art was given by the famous Sufi Muhyi 'd-Dîn ibn 'Arabî, *ash-shaikh al-akbar*, who, in his *Al-Futûhât al-Makkiyyah* ('Meccan Revelations'), writes as follows: 'The Byzantines developed the art of painting to its perfection, because for them the unique nature (*fardâniyyah*) of Jesus (*Sayyid-nâ 'Isa*), as expressed in his image, is the foremost support of concentration on Divine Unity'. As this witness proves, the symbolic role of an image is not in itself unintelligible to contemplative Moslems, although, in obedience to Koranic law, they reject the use of sacred images, thus giving precedence to 'incomparability' (*tanzih*) over 'analogy' (*tasbih*). In a way, the first of these two 'aspects'—that of divine incomparability or transcendence—even absorbs the theomorphic nature of man. Indeed, the seven universal qualities that constitute the divine 'form' of Adam, namely, life, knowledge, will, power, hearing, seeing, and speech, escape all visual representation; an image has neither life, knowledge, power, nor any other of these qualities; it reduces man to his corporeal limits. Although limited in man, the seven qualities are the potential bearers of a Divine Presence, according to the *hadîth qudsî*: '. . . I shall be the ear wherewith he heareth, the eye wherewith he seeth,' and so on. There is something in man that no natural means of expression can render. The Koran says: 'We offered the trust (*amânah*) unto the Heavens and the earth and the hills, but they shrank from bearing it and were afraid of it. And man assumed it.' (XXXIII, 72). This trust is merely potential in ordinary man. It is actual in perfect man: in Messengers (*rusul*), Prophets (*anbiyâ*), and Saints (*awliyâ*); in them it overflows, from the inward to the outward, shining forth even in their bodily appearance. Fearing to offend this divine trust within man, Islamic art shrinks from depicting the Messengers, Prophets, and Saints.

Instead of 'Islamic iconoclasm', we prefer to say 'Islamic aniconism', for the absence of icons in Islam has not merely a negative but a positive role. By excluding all anthropomorphic images, at least within the religious realm, Islamic art aids man to be entirely himself. Instead of projecting his soul outside himself, he can remain in his ontological centre where he is both the viceregent (*khalīfah*) and slave (*'abd*) of God. Islamic art as a whole aims at creating an ambience which helps man to realize his primordial dignity; it therefore avoids everything that could be an 'idol', even in a relative and provisional manner. Nothing must stand between man and the invisible presence of God.

Thus Islamic art creates a void; it eliminates in fact all the turmoil and passionate suggestions of the world, and in their stead creates an order that expresses equilibrium, serenity, and peace. From this it can clearly be seen how central the position of architecture is in Islam. Although the Prophet said that God favoured his community by giving it the whole surface of the earth as a place of prayer, it is architecture which, in populated regions, has to re-establish the conditions of purity and calm elsewhere granted by nature. As for the beauty of virgin nature, which is like the imprint of the Creator's hand, it is realized by architecture on another level, one nearer to human intelligence and therefore in a way more limited, but nonetheless free from the arbitrary rule of individual passions.

In a mosque, the believer is never a mere visitor. He is so to speak at home, but not in the ordinary sense of the expression. When he has purified himself by the ritual ablution—thus freeing himself from accidental alterations—and recites the revealed words of the Koran, he symbolically returns to the 'station' of Adam, which is at the centre of the world. In view of this, all Moslem architects have endeavored to create a space entirely resting in itself and showing everywhere, in each of its 'stations', the plenitude of spatial qualities. They achieved this end by means as different as the horizontal hall of pillars (as in the old mosque at Medina) and the concentric domes in Turkey. In none of these interiors do we feel drawn in any particular direction, either forwards or upwards; nor are we oppressed by their spatial limits. It has rightly been remarked that the architecture of a mosque excludes all tension between heaven and earth.

A Christian basilica is essentially a way leading from the outside world to the main altar. A Christian dome ascends to Heaven or descends to the altar. The whole architecture of a church reminds the believer that the Divine Presence emanates from the Eucharist on the altar like a light shining in the darkness. The mosque has no liturgical centre; its *mihrâb* merely indicates the direction of Mecca, while its whole order of space is made to suggest a Presence which encompasses the believer on all sides.

It is most revealing to see how the great Turkish architect Sinan, in adopting the constructive plan of Hagia Sophia, developed it according to an Islamic viewpoint until he achieved the perfect order of the Selimiye Mosque at Edirne. The huge cupola of Hagia Sophia is supported by two half cupolas and extended by several small apses. The whole interior space is elongated in the direction of the liturgical axis, its different parts melting into each other, in a kind of indefinite immensity. Sinan built the main cupola at Edirne on an octagon supported by straight walls on the cardinal sides and by vaulted apses on the four diagonal sides, creating a kind of clearly cut jewel, the contours of which are neither fluctuating nor narrow.

When Moslem architects took over and enlarged some Christian basilicas, they often changed the interior plan so that what had been its length became its breadth; frequently—even apart from such transformations—the arcades in a mosque run across the main space, they do not 'progress' in a longitudinal direction as do the arcades that run alongside the nave of a cathedral. They tend rather to stem the movement of the space, without however interrupting it, thus inviting one to rest.

Moslem architects lavished much attention and love on the form of arcades. It is no wonder that the Arabic word for arcade—*rawq*, plural *riwâq*—is almost synonymous with beautiful, graceful, and pure. European art knows two main forms of the arch: the Romanesque arch which is plain, rational, and static, and the so-called Gothic arch—indirectly derived from Islamic art—with its ascending movement. Islamic art developed a great variety of arch forms, of which two are most typical: the Persian arch in the shape of a ship's keel, and the Moorish arch in the shape of a horseshoe, with a more or less accentuated point. Both arches combine the two qualities mentioned above, namely static calm and lightness. The Persian arch is both generous and gracious; it ascends without effort like the calm flame of an oil lamp protected from the wind. As for the Moorish arch, its extreme width is balanced by its rectangular frame: a synthesis of stability and amplitude. There is in it a breathing without movement; it is the image of a space expanding inwardly by an overabundance of beatitude. In the words of the Koran: 'Did we not dilate thy breast?' (*a lam nashrah la-ka sadra-k*) (XCIV, 1).

A simple arcade, built according to the right measure, has the virtue of transforming space from a purely quantitative reality into one that is qualitative. Qualitative space is no longer mere extension; it is experienced as a state of being (*wajd*). Thus traditional architecture favours contemplation.

Between the architecture of a mosque and that of a private Moslem house, there is a difference in plan, but not in style, for every Moslem dwelling is a place of prayer: the same rites are performed there as in a mosque. In general, Islamic life is not divided into sacred and profane domains, and likewise the Islamic community is not divided into a consecrated clergy and a laity: every Moslem of sound mind and morality can act as *imâm*. This unity of life is manifested in the homogeneity of its framework: whether it be the interior of a mosque or that of a private house, its law is equilibrium, calm, and purity. Its decoration never contradicts the idea of poverty. Indeed ornament in Islamic architecture, by its rhythm and regularity, helps to create a void by dissolving the raw body of wall and pillars and thus enhancing the effect of the great white surfaces so characteristic of Moslem interiors.

The floor of a traditional Moslem dwelling, like the floor of a mosque, is never trodden on with shoes, nor are the rooms filled with furniture.

Much of the unity of Islamic life is lost when the clothes worn in everyday life are no longer adapted to the prescribed rites. Costume indeed is part of the framework that Islamic art has created for Islam, and the art of dress is not the least of the Islamic arts. As the Koran explicitly commands: 'O sons of Adam, look to your adornment when you approach a mosque' (VII, 31). The traditional masculine costume shows many variations, but it always expresses the role with which Islam endows man, that is, to be the viceregent and the slave of God. Therefore it is both dignified and sober; we might even say: majestic and poor. It veils the animal nature of man, enhances his features, dignifies his gestures, and makes easy the different postures of the ritual prayer. Modern European costume, on the contrary, while claiming to free man from his servitude (*'ubûdiyyah*), in fact denies his primordial dignity.

We have seen that the exclusion of images from Islamic art—more severe in Sunni that in Shiite countries—has a positive meaning, even on the level of art, as it restores to man the dignity which elsewhere is so to speak usurped by his image. The immobility with which Islamic art is reproached is in a certain sense connected with the absence of images, for it is by making images of himself that man changes. He projects his soul into the ideal he shapes, thus influencing himself until he is driven to change the image he has made of himself. This in its turn will awaken his reaction, and so on in an endless chain, as we can observe in European art since the Renaissance, that is, since the purely symbolical role of the image was forgotten. Sacred art is normally protected by its traditional rules from falling into such a torrent of change. Nevertheless the use of anthropomorphic images is always precarious, for man is always inclined to transfer his own psychic limitations to the image he shapes, in spite of all canonical prescriptions, and sooner or later he rebels against it—not only against the image, but also against what it stands for. Those epidemic outbursts of blasphemy which marked certain periods of European history would be inconceivable without the existence and the decay of anthropomorphic religious art. Islam deals with this whole problem at its root. In this respect as in others it shows itself as the last of the religions—one that takes full heed of the weakness of man as he is—and as a return to the primordial religion. The much criticized 'immobility' of Islamic art is simply the absence in it of all subjective motives; it is an art that is unconcerned with psychological problems and which retains only those elements that are valid for all time.

This is the reason for the extraordinary development of geometrical ornamentation in Islamic art. Attempts have been made to explain this development by the fact that the prohibition of images created a void that had to be filled by another kind of art. But this is not conclusive; the arabesque is not a compensation for images, it is rather their opposite and the very negation of figurative art. By transforming a surface into a tissue of colours or into a vibration of light and shadows, the ornament prevents the mind from fixing itself on any form that says 'I', as an image says 'I'. The centre of an arabesque is everywhere and nowhere, each 'affirmation' being followed by its 'negation', and vice versa.

There are two typical forms of the arabesque; one of them is geometrical interlacing made up of a multitude of geometrical stars, the rays of which join into an intricate and endless pattern. It is a most striking symbol of that contemplative state of mind which conceives of 'unity in multiplicity and multiplicity in unity' (*al-wahdatu fî 'l-kathrati wa 'l-kathratu fî 'l-wahdah*).

The second form, the arabesque commonly so-called is composed of vegetable motifs, stylized to the point of losing all resemblance with nature and obeying only the laws of rhythm. Indeed it is the science of rhythm transposed into graphic mode, each line undulating in complementary phases, and each surface having its inverse counterpart. The arabesque is both logical and rhythmical, both mathematical and melodious, and this is most significant for the spirit of Islam in its equilibrium of love and intellectual sobriety.

In such an art the individuality of the artist of necessity disappears, without for all that his creative joy being abated; it is simply less passional and more contemplative. Suppression of creative joy is the privilege of modern industry alone. As for traditional art, be it even at the level of mere handicraft, its beauty proves the profound pleasure involved in it.

Moreover, the universal character of geometrical ornament—the fundamental elements of which are essentially the same, whether they appear in a Bedouin rug or in a refined urban decoration—corresponds perfectly to the universal nature of Islam, which unites the nomads of the desert with the learned men of the city, and this latter-day epoch of ours with the time of Abraham.

In what we have said thus far we have implicitly answered the critics of Islamic art mentioned at the outset of this chapter. We have still to say what the notion of art means in Islamic thought. From this point of view, art can never be dissociated either from a craft (*san'ah*), as its material foundation, or from a science (*'ilm*), regularly transmitted. Art (*fann*), in its specific meaning, partakes of both craft and science. The latter moreover has to be not only a rational instruction, but also the expression of a wisdom (*hikmah*), which links things to their universal principles.

The Prophet said: 'God prescribed that every thing should be accomplished to perfection'—we might also translate: 'in beauty' (*inna 'Llâha kataba 'l-ihsâna 'alâ kulli shay*). The perfection or the beauty of a thing lies in its praising God; in other words, it is perfect or beautiful in so far as it reflects a divine quality. Now we cannot realize perfection in anything unless we know that a thing can be a mirror of God.

Taking architecture as an example, we see that its material foundation is the mason's craft, while the science involved in it is geometry. In traditional architecture, geometry is not limited to its more or less quantitative aspect, as in modern engineering, for instance; it also has a qualitative aspect, which is manifested in the laws of proportion through which a building acquires its quasi-inimitable unity. The laws of proportion are traditionally based on the division of the circle by inscribed regular figures. Thus all proportions in a building are ultimately derived from the circle, which is a clear symbol of the Unity of Being (*wahdat al-wujud*) that contains within itself all the possibilities of existence. How many cupolas with polygonal bases and how many vaults with alveolar squinches remind us of this symbolism!

When one considers the internal hierarchy of art—which comprises craft, science, and contemplative wisdom—it is easy to understand how a traditional art can be destroyed either from the top or from the bottom: Christian art was corrupted by the loss of its spiritual principles; Islamic art has gradually disappeared because of the destruction of the traditional crafts.

We have mainly spoken about architecture, given its central role in the Islamic world. Ibn Khaldun, indeed, relates to it most of the minor arts, such as carpentry, joinery, sculpture in wood and stucco, mosaic in earthenware, decorative painting, and even carpet-making, so characteristic of the Islamic world. Even calligraphy can be related to architecture in the form of decorative inscriptions; in itself, however, Arabic calligraphy is not a minor art; since it is used for the writing of the Koran, it occupies the highest rank amongst all Islamic arts.

It would take us too far to review the whole range of Islamic arts; let it suffice to consider the two extreme poles of visual art: architecture and calligraphy. The first of these is the art that is the most conditioned by material circumstances, whereas the second is the freest of all arts in this respect. It is nonetheless governed by strict rules with regard to the distinctive form of the letters, proportions, continuity of rhythm, and choice of style. On the other hand, the possible combinations of letters are well-nigh limitless, and styles vary from the rectilinear *kûfi* to the most flowing *naskhi*. It is the synthesis of utmost regularity and utmost liberty that lends Arabic calligraphy its royal character. In no other visual art does the spirit of Islam breathe more openly.

The frequency of Koranic inscriptions on the walls of mosques and other buildings reminds us of the fact that the whole of Islamic life is interwoven with quotations from the Koran, and spiritually supported by its recitation, as well as by prayers, litanics, and invocations derived from it. If one may call the influence emanating from the Koran a spiritual vibration—and we can find no better word for it, since the influence in question is of both a spiritual and an auditive nature—we may well say that all Islamic art must needs bear the imprint of this vibration. Thus, visual Islamic art is but the visual reflection of the Koranic word; it cannot be otherwise. However, there is a paradox here, for if we look for Koranic models of art, we cannot find them, either in the contents of the Koran or in its form. On the one hand, except in certain Persian miniatures, Islamic art does not reflect the stories and parables contained in the Koran, as Christian art for instance depicts episodes from both Testaments, nor is there any cosmology in the Koran which could be translated into architectural schemes, as Vedic cosmology finds its expression in Hindu architecture. On the other hand, it would be vain to look in the Koran for anything resembling a principle of composition that could be transposed into an art. The Koran is of a startling discontinuity; it shows no logical order nor any interior architecture; even its rhythm, powerful though it is, obeys no constant rule, whereas Islamic art is entirely made up of order, clarity, hierarchy, and crystalline form. The vital link between the Koranic word and visual Islamic art must not be sought on the level of formal expression. The Koran is not a work of art, but something entirely different, notwithstanding the overwhelming beauty of many of its passages, nor does Islamic art derive from its literal meaning or from its form, but from its *haqîqah*, its formless essence.

At its beginning, Islam had no need of art; no religion is concerned with art when it first enters the world. The need for a protective framework, composed of visual and auditive forms, comes later, just like the need for extensive commentaries on the revealed Book, although every genuine expression of a religion is already included as a latent possibility in its original manifestation.

Islamic art is fundamentally derived from *tawhîd*, that is, from an assent to or a contemplation of Divine Unity. The essence of *at-tawhîd* is beyond words; it reveals itself in the Koran by sudden and discontinuous flashes. Striking the plane of the visual imagination, these flashes congeal into crystalline forms, and it is these forms in their turn that constitute the essence of Islamic art.

# 23

# The Void in Islamic Art

WE SHOULD LIKE to elaborate further on certain of the characteristics of Islamic art to which we drew attention in the preceding chapter. Strictly speaking, the forbidding of images in Islam refers only to images of the Divinity; it is thus situated in the perspective of the Decalogue, or more exactly of Abrahamic monotheism, which Islam renews: in its last as in its first manifestation, this monotheism is directly opposed to idolatrous polytheism;[1] the plastic image of the Divinity—according to a 'dialectic' both historical and divine—is seen as the mark of the error of 'associating' (*shirk*) the relative with the absolute, or the created with the uncreated, the latter, in each case, being reduced to the former. The denial of idols, and even more so their destruction, is a translation into concrete terms of the fundamental testimony of Islam, the formula *lâ ilâha illâ 'Llâh* ('there is no divinity apart from God'), and just as this testimony in Islam dominates and consumes everything, after the fashion of a purifying fire, so the denial of the idols, be it effective or merely virtual, tends to become generalized: thus the portraying of divine envoys (*rusul*), prophets (*anbiyâ*), and saints (*awliyâ*) is avoided, not only because such images could become the object of an idolatrous cult, but also out of respect for what is inimitable in them; they are the vicegerents of God on earth; it is through them that the theomorphic nature of man becomes manifest; but this theomorphism is a secret whose appearance in the corporeal world remains ungraspable; the inanimate and congealed image of the man-god would be merely a shell, an error, an idol. In an Arab Sunni context, there is even a reluctance to represent

---

[1] It is not a pleonasm to speak of 'idolatrous polytheism', as is shown by the example of Hinduism which is polytheist but in no wise idolatrous, since it recognizes both the provisional and symbolic nature of the idols and the relativity of the 'gods' (*devas*) as 'aspects' of the Absolute. The Moslem esoterists, the Sufis, sometimes compare idols to Divine Names, whose meaning the pagans have forgotten.

any living being whatsoever, out of respect for the divine secret contained in creation.[2] And if the prohibition of the image is not quite so far-reaching in other ethnic environments, it is nonetheless observed in the case of anything that forms part of the liturgical framework of Islam.

This may seem paradoxical, for the normal basis of a sacred art is symbolism; in a religion which elsewhere expresses itself in anthropomorphic symbols, the rejection of images seems to undermine the roots of any visual art of a sacred character. But it is necessary to take account of a complex play of subtle compensations, and especially of the following: a sacred art is not necessarily composed of images, even in the widest sense of this term; it may simply be the exteriorization of a contemplative state, and in this case it will not reflect particular ideas, but will qualitatively transform the ambience with a view to its integration in a spiritual equilibrium whose centre of gravity is the invisible. It is easy to recognize that such is the nature of Islamic art: its object is above all the ambience of man—whence the dominant role of architecture—and its quality is essentially contemplative. Aniconism does not lessen this quality; on the contrary, by excluding every image that could invite man to fix his mind on something outside himself and to project his soul into an 'individualizing' form, it creates a void. In this respect, the function of Islamic art is analogous to that of virgin nature, especially the desert, which also favours contemplation, although, from another point of view, the order created by art is opposed to the chaos inherent in the nature of the desert.

Let it be said right away that ornamentation with abstract forms, so richly developed in the art of Islam, does not exist to fill this void, as some seem to think. In reality it corroborates it by its continuous rhythm and its resemblance to an endless piece of weaving: instead of ensnaring the mind and dragging it into some imaginary world, it dissolves mental 'coagulations', just as the contemplation of a stream

---

[2] According to a saying of the Prophet, artists who seek to imitate the work of the Creator will be condemned in the hereafter to give life to their works, and their inability to do so will throw them into the worst of torments. This saying can obviously be understood in various ways; in fact it has not prevented the flowering, in certain Moslem environments, of a figurative art entirely free from naturalistic pretensions.

of water, of a flame, or of leaves trembling in the wind can detach the consciousness from its inward 'idols'.

We have already mentioned the two principal modes of Islamic ornamentation: the arabesque in the strict sense of the term, made up of sinuous and spiral forms more or less related to vegetable motifs, and geometrical interlacing. The first is all rhythm and fluidity and continuous melody, whereas the second is crystalline in nature: the radiating of lines from multiple geometrical foci recalls snowflakes or ice; it gives the impression of calm and freshness. It is in Maghribi art in particular that these two ornamental modes appear in all their purity.

However rich it may be, ornamentation never destroys the simplicity, not to say the sobriety, of the architectural whole; such at least is the rule that is observed in all ages and places that are not decadent. In a general manner, the architectural whole manifests equilibrium, calmness and serenity.

Whereas the interior of a Romanesque basilica progresses towards the altar, and the apse of a Gothic church tends upwards, the interior of a mosque does not comprise any dynamic element; whatever be its type of construction, from the primitive mosques with a horizontal roof on pillars to mosques with cupolas, space is ordered in such a way that it reposes entirely in itself; it is not an expanse that waits to be traversed; its void is like the mould or womb of a motionless and undifferentiated plenitude.

Turkish architects such as Sinan, who adopted the construction plan of Hagia Sophia in order to develop it in an Islamic way, sought a perfectly static and fully intelligible synthesis of the two great complementary forms: the hemisphere of the cupola and the cube of the building itself. They achieved this in various ways which we have already referred to. It will suffice to mention here an architectural detail characteristic of their conception of space. It is known that Byzantine cupolas—like Roman cupolas—are supported on pendentives which vaguely prolong their curve and merge 'surreptitiously' with the four corners of the supporting walls. This somewhat irrational passage from the circular base of the cupola to the square of the supports is something that Turkish architecture seeks to avoid; it replaces the pendentives by a clearly articulated element, which is called *muqarnas* in Arabic and which is often compared to stalactites, although it is really more in the nature of an alveola composed of niches which overlap into one another; by means of their geometrical play, the passage from the continuous and 'fluid' form of the cupola to the rectangular and 'solid' form of the supporting walls appears as a gradual crystallization: the cube of the building 'coagulates' from out of the undifferentiated unity of the cupola, and since the latter always represents Heaven, it is the continuous movement of the heavenly sphere which is suddenly immobilized in the plenitude of the pure present.

This architectural conception is typical for Islam; at the same time, it is very far removed from that of Greco-Roman architecture, which is always more or less anthropomorphic, in the sense that it invites the spectator to participate subjectively in the drama of the forces of construction; one may mention especially the classical column, made to the measure of man—and also the architrave, corbels and cornices—which make one feel the weight and the force which they support; in Romanesque and Gothic architecture this drama is transposed to the spiritual plane: the clustered columns of a Gothic cathedral are as if animated by an irresistible impulse to ascend. There is nothing of all this in Moslem architecture, which remains objective.

This void which Islamic art creates by its static, impersonal and anonymous quality enables man to be entirely himself, to repose in his ontological centre. Certainly, the sacred image in its turn is a support for contemplation, wherever its use is called for by the nature of the doctrine,[3] and on condition that its symbolism and formal language remain guaranteed by the tradition. But the religious art whose forms are anthropomorphic is of an eminently precarious nature because of psychic tendencies, both individual and collective, which may all too easily gain access to it, and drag it into a naturalistic 'evolution', with reactions that are well known. Islam eradicates this problem by excluding from its liturgical framework any image of man. By this fact it maintains, in a certain fashion and on a higher and spiritual plane, the position of the nomad, who is not involved in the

---

[3] As it is in Christianity, in which 'God became man so that man might become God', according to the saying of St. Irenaeus.

turbulent evolution of a world that comprises the mental projections of man and his reaction towards them.

The aniconism of Islamic art comprises fundamentally two aspects: on the one hand, it preserves the primordial dignity of man, whose form, 'made in the image of God', is neither imitated nor usurped by a work of art that is inevitably limited and one-sided; on the other hand, nothing that could possibly be an idol, even in a relative and wholly provisional manner, may interpose itself between man and the invisible presence of God. What comes before all, is the witnessing that 'there is no divinity but God': this dissolves every objectivation of the Divine, even before it can occur.

# 24

# The Impact of the Arabic Language on the Visual Arts of Islam

THE EXPRESSION 'Arab art' is commonly employed to designate Islamic art; however the legitimacy of this term has often been contested with the aid of arguments which are seemingly plausible but which in reality are vitiated by a superficial or even prejudiced view of things. The question to be asked first of all is the following: what is it that characterizes the Arab genius, and how may this be discerned in art? The only arts possessed by the pre-Islamic Arabs, who were mostly nomads living at the crossroads of several civilizations, were a rectilinear architecture and the various kinds of crafts—which, incidentally, it would be wrong to underestimate, and whose influence was later to become very great; be that as it may, the predominant and most striking expression of the Arab genius is the language, including its script. The Arabs bequeathed their language to the whole civilization of Islam, and it was not only the means of preserving the heritage of the Arabs outside Arabia, but even caused this to bloom at a far remove from its own racial source. By the intermediary of this language, every essential of the Arab genius was effectively communicated to the whole of Islamic civilization.

The extraordinary normative power of the Arabic language derives both from its role as a sacred language and from its archaic character, these two things, moreover, being connected: it was its archaism that predestined Arabic to the role of a sacred language, and it was the Koranic revelation that in a sense actualized its primordial substance. In the linguistic realm, archaism is by no means synonymous with structural simplicity, quite the reverse: languages are generally impoverished with time, they lose both the hierarchical differentiation of meanings and the logical concision of forms, while becoming complicated on the plane of rhetoric in order to compensate this impoverishment. What surprises historians of language is that Arabic has been able to preserve a morphology already exemplified by Hammurabi's code in the nineteenth or eighteenth century B.C.[1] and a phonetic system which perpetuates, apart from one single sound, the very rich sound range borne witness to by the most ancient Semitic alphabets discovered,[2] and that it has done so despite the absence of any 'literary tradition' which might have acted as a bridge between this remote age of the Patriarchs and the time when the Koranic revelation was to fix the language forever. The explanation of this perenniality of Arabic resides precisely in the conservative role of nomadism: it is in the towns that language decays, by the very fact that it becomes attached to things and institutions and undergoes their fate; the well-nigh timeless life of the nomad, on the contrary, protects the language and permits it to bloom in all its fullness: the portion of primordial symbolism which fell to the lot of the nomads was the art of speech, which is not bound to place, and whose dynamic character corresponds to that of nomadic life itself, whereas the sedentary peoples developed the plastic arts, which require stability and which in their symbolism are connected, quite naturally, to the idea of a centre in space.[3] It can thus be stated, in general terms, that the Arabic language guarantees the survival, on the mental plane, of a primitive Semitism, nomadic in character.

To explain in a few words, and without the need of any special linguistic knowledge, what is the specific nature of this language, it should be recalled firstly that every language comprises two roots or poles, one or the other of which will predominate, and which may be designated by the terms 'auditive intuition' and 'imaginative in-

---

[1] Cf. Edouard Dhorme, *L'arabe littéral et la langue de Hammourabi* in 'Mélanges Louis Massignon' (Damascus, 1957).

[2] The most ancient Semitic alphabets comprise 29 sounds or letters, of which Arabic has preserved 28, the 'lost' sound being a variant of S. It may be that the reduction of the alphabet to 28 letters reflects a symbolic intention, since some Arab authors consider that the sounds correspond to the 28 lunar mansions: the phonetic cycle—ranging from the gutturals to the palatals, dentals and labials retraces the 'lunar' phases of the primordial sound emanating from the sun.

[3] As René Guénon has pointed out. See the chapter 'Cain and Abel' in *The Reign of Quantity*.

tuition'. The first is normally manifested by the fact that a given word is derived from a simple combination of sounds which, as such, express a typical event or, more exactly, a fundamental action; it does this in a more or less immediate manner, not by means of onomatopoeia, but because the sound itself is an event which unfolds in time, so that it corresponds *a priori*, and independently of all semantic conventions, to action; speech is essentially act and, according to this logic, the language fundamentally conceives everything that it names as an action or an object of action. Imaginative intuition, on the other hand, is manifested in language by means of the semantic association of analogous images: every word pronounced inwardly evokes a corresponding image, which calls forth others, general images dominating more particular images, according to a hierarchy which in turn is inherent in the structure of the language. The Latin languages belong mainly to this latter type, whereas Arabic displays an almost pure auditive intuition or phonetic logic, the identity of sound and act, as well as the primacy of action, being affirmed throughout the rich tissue of this language: in principle, every Arabic word is derived from a verb whose root, consisting of three invariable sounds, is like the sonorous ideogram of a fundamental act such as 'gathering-together', 'dividing', 'including', 'penetrating', with the full physical, psychical and spiritual polyvalence of the idea in question; from one single root up to twelve different verbal modes are developed— simple, causative, intensive, reciprocal, and so on—and each of these modes produces, by the polarization of the active and the passive, of the subject and the object, a whole pleiad of substantives and adjectives, whose meaning is always connected, in a more or less direct manner, with the fundamental act represented by the triliteral[4] root of the whole verbal 'tree'.

It is obvious that this semantic transparency of the language—the fact that, in its symbolism, it derives entirely from the phonetic nature of the verb—is a proof of its relative primordiality. In the origin, and in the very depth of our consciousness, things are spontaneously conceived as determinations of the primordial sound which resounds in the heart, this sound being none other than the first and

---

[4] There are in fact verbs composed or four or five root sounds, but in these cases groups of consonants such as TS or BR play the role of simple sounds.

non-individualized act of consciousness; at this level or in this state, to 'name' a thing is to identify oneself with the act or the sound which produces it;[5] the symbolism inherent in language—more or less veiled or deformed by acquired habits—grasps the nature of a thing not in a static manner, as one grasps an image, but so to speak *in statu nascendi*, in the act of becoming. This aspect of language in general and of the Arabic language in particular is, in the Moslem world, the object of a whole group of sciences, some philosophical, others esoteric. It may be said that Moslem scholars have not only preserved this structure of Arabic, but that they have even contributed to rendering it explicit.

In order to understand how Arabic, which is of Bedouin origin, could become, with almost no borrowings, the language of a civilization that was intellectually very rich and differentiated, it is necessary to know that its verbal roots are capable of expressing, in a so to speak active manner, determinations which the Indo-European languages generally express by an adjective associated with the verb 'to be': the root BTN, for example, comprises the meaning of 'being inside', and the root ZHR that of 'being outside'; the root RHM summarizes all the modes of 'being merciful' or 'having compassion', etc. The fundamental act which is at the root of a 'tree' of expressions is thus not necessarily an action in the ordinary sense of the term; it may be an existential act, like that of light which shines, or even a purely logical act, such as 'being big' or 'being small', and it is in this possibility of gathering every manner of being of a thing into a principial act, that the great power of abstraction of the Arabic language resides. What we must grasp here, as far as art is concerned, is the implicitly auditive character of this abstraction: the passage from the particular to the general is *a priori* indicated by the presence, in a given expression, of root sounds which recall a given prototypal act.

The relationship between prototypal acts and their verbal derivations is however not always easy to grasp, because of the sometimes very particular and conventionally fixed meaning of such and such a derived term, and also, above all, because the fundamental ideas

---

[5] According to the Koran, it was Adam who knew how to 'name' all beings, whereas the angels could not do so.

expressed by the roots are of an eminently complex nature. An orientalist went so far as to say that 'the structure of the Arabic language would be of an incomparable transparency if the meaning of the verbal roots was not arbitrary'; it is however scarcely possible that the basis of a language should be arbitrary. In fact, the verbal roots mark the threshold between discursive thought and a kind of synthetic perception which has its models in both mind and body; the Arabic language is as though suspended from auditive intuition.[6]

If these data are transposed into the realm of art, with all the reservations which generalizations of this nature presuppose, it can be said that the Arab is *a priori* an auditive rather than a visual type, in other words, he is the former before he is the latter;[7] in fact, his need for artistic exteriorization is largely absorbed by the culture of his language, with its fascinating phonetism and its almost limitless faculty of producing new verbal derivations. Nor is the Arab a contemplative in the ordinary sense of the word, if one means by this the type of man who looks or contemplates rather than acts, and who spontaneously reduces perceived forms to prototypal forms that are in principle immutable; the Arab loves to analyze things with a view to their intrinsic functions and the activities reflected in them; this

---

[6] The phonetic symbolism which underlies the Arabic language shows itself more particularly in the permutation of the root sounds. In fact, according to *al-jafr* ('the science of letters'), the words which are formed from the same letters arranged in different orders all spring from the same 'Pythagorean number' and therefore from the same idea. This is not easy to grasp, however, owing to the often too particularized use of the words, but it can be sensed in certain cases: the root RHM, for example, means 'being merciful', 'having pity', whereas its permutation HRM has the meaning of 'forbidding', 'making inaccessible', *sacrum facere*; the underlying complementarism is to be seen more clearly in the most simple nouns derived from these two roots: RaaHM means 'womb' and by extension 'bond of relationship', whereas HaRaM means 'sacred place'; we can divine here the idea of maternity both in its inclusive and exclusive character. Another example is offered us by the root RFQ which has the meaning of 'accompanying', 'binding', and its permutation FRQ which means 'separating', 'dividing' (the Latin *furca* seems to be derived from an analogous root), whereas the group FQR means 'being poor, needy' (whence the expression *al-faqîru ilâ 'Llâh*, 'the needy unto God', 'the poor in Spirit); these give us three variants of the theme 'polarity': joining (RFQ), separation (FRQ), and dependence (FQR).

[7] Which obviously does not exclude the existence of pure visual types in the Arab race.

means that his mentality is not static, but essentially dynamic. However, since he is nevertheless a contemplative—Islam proves it, and the Arabic language includes this possibility—he finds access to unity by means of rhythm, which is like the refraction of the eternal present in the current of time.

The plastic examples that illustrate these tendencies spring to mind: the arabesque in particular, with its deployment at once regular and indefinite, is indeed the most direct expression of rhythm in the visual order. It is true that its most perfect forms are not conceivable without the artistic contribution of the nomads of Central Asia; nevertheless it was in Arab surroundings that it had its fullest development. Another typical element in Moslem art, one whose development goes hand in hand with Arab domination, is the interlacing motif; it appears in all its perfection from the time of the Omayyads, in the form of sculpted lattices in the windows of mosques and palaces.[8] To enjoy the geometrical interplay that constitutes the interlacing motif, it is not enough to look at it directly, it is necessary to 'read' it by following the course of the forces that cross one another and compensate one another. Interlacing already exists in the pavement mosaics of lower Antiquity, but in a rudimentary state and deriving from a naturalistic conception devoid of the complexity and the rhythmic precision of the Arabo-Moslem interlacing. These examples belong to abstract, not figurative, art, and this also characterizes the Arab genius: contrarily to what is usually believed, the average Arab scarcely possesses a 'luxuriant imagination'. In so far as this appears in Arab literature, for example in the tales from the 'Thousand and One Nights', it is non-Arab in origin, being in this case Persian and Indian; only the art of story-telling is Arab. The creative spirit of the Arabs is *a priori* logical and rhetorical, then rhythmical and incantatory; the richness is in the mental arabesque and not in the profusion of images evoked.

The more or less categorical rejection of images in the art of Islam obviously has its explanation in reasons of a theological order. But it is a fact that the Semitic nomads did not possess a figurative tradition—the pre-Islamic Arabs imported most of their idols—and

---

[8] In the Omayyad mosque at Damascus, for example, or in the palace of Khirbet al-Mafjar.

that for the Arabs images never become a transparent and spontaneous means of expression,[9] as they are for Iranians and Mongols who are Moslems by religion. The reality of the verb eclipsed that of static vision: compared with the word which is always in act, and whose root plunges into the primordiality of sound, a painted or sculpted image appears as an alarming coagulation of the mind. For the pagan Arabs, it smacked of magic.

But the Arabic language is not entirely dominated by the idea of the verb-act; it also comprises a static, or more exactly, a timeless pole, which shows itself in particular in what is called the 'nominal sentence', in which the 'noun' (subject) and the 'predicates' are juxtaposed without a copula. This permits the formulation of a thought in a lapidary fashion and outside any consideration of time. A sentence of this sort is like an equation; but the use of certain prepositions can impress on it an internal logical movement. The most striking example of this kind is the formula constituting the fundamental 'testimony' of Islam: *lâ ilâha illâ 'Llâh*— ('there is no divinity apart from God'), a phrase that would be translated literally as: 'no divinity if not The Divinity'; in Arabic, the symmetry of the negations—*lâ* and *illâ*, 'not' and 'if not'—is even more apparent. In this formula, the static character of the nominal phrase disappears as a result of a purely intellectual action, which corresponds to an integration: 'There is no autonomous being apart from the only Being.' It is the distinction between the relative and the absolute and the reduction of the first to the second. The Arabic language thus comprises the possibility of condensing a whole doctrine in a brief and concise formula that has the appearance of a diamond with sharp edges and reverberating facets. It is true that this possibility of expression is only fully actualized by revelation; it belongs above all to the Koran; but it is nonetheless inherent in the genius of Arabic and reflected in its fashion in Arabo-Islamic art, for this is not only rhythmical, it is also crystalline.

The concision of the Arabic sentence, while it obviously does not

---

[9] It is not absolutely certain that the miniatures of the 'Baghdad school' are attributable to the Arabs; in any case, their style is crude, and owes its few positive elements to Byzantine and Asiatic influences.

limit the profundity of the meaning, nevertheless does not favour a synthesis at the level of description: Arabic rarely accumulates several conditions or circumstances in a single sentence; it prefers to link together a whole series of short sentences. In this connection, an agglutinating language like Turkish, which is related to the Mongol languages, is less dry and more supple than Arabic; it is clearly superior when it comes to describing a situation or a landscape, which is also true of Persian, which is an Indo-European language close to Gothic; nevertheless both of these languages have borrowed not only their theological terminology but almost all their philosophical and scientific terminology from Arabic.

The extreme opposite of Arabic is a language like Chinese, which is dominated by a static vision of things and which groups the elements of a thought around typical 'pictures', as the ideographic character of the Chinese script itself indicates.

The Turks are of nomadic origin like the Arabs, but their language connects them to a very different mental type; the Arab is incisive and dynamic in his way of thinking; the Turk, on the other hand, is enveloping and prudent. Within the general framework of Islamic art, the Turkish genius is revealed in a powerful capacity for synthesis, one might almost say, by its totalitarian spirit. The Turk possesses a plastic or sculptural gift which the Arab does not have; his works always derive from an inclusive conception; they are as though chiselled out of a single block. The interior of the most ancient Turkish mosques with a cupola recalls the closed space of the yurt, and Turco-Arabic calligraphy reveals a Mongol influence.

As for Persian art, it is distinguished by its sense of hierarchical differentiations; Persian architecture is perfectly articulated, without ever being 'functional' in the modern sense of the term. For the Persian, Unity is manifested above all by harmony. The Persians, moreover, are 'visuals' by nature and by culture—but lyrical visuals, so to speak, their artistic activity being as it were animated by an inward melody. It is commonly said in the East that 'Arabic is the language of God, and Persian the language of Paradise', which sums up very well the difference that exists, for example, between a typically Arab architecture, like that of the Maghrib, where the crystalline geometry of the forms proclaims the unitary principle, and Persian architecture, with its blue cupolas and floral ornaments.

The Arab architect is not afraid of monotony; he will add pillar after pillar and arcade after arcade and will dominate this repetition only by rhythmical alternation and by the qualitative perfection of each element.

The language of the Koran is everywhere present in the world of Islam; the whole life of the Moslem is constellated with Koranic formulas, as well as prayers, litanies and invocations in Arabic, whose elements are derived from the sacred Book; innumerable inscriptions bear witness to this. One might say that this ubiquity of the Koran acts as a spiritual vibration—there is no better term to designate an influence that is both spiritual and sonorous in nature—and that this vibration necessarily determines the modes and measures of Moslem art; the plastic art of Islam is thus in a certain manner the reflection of the Koranic Word. It is nonetheless very difficult to grasp the principle that unites this art to the Koranic text, not on the narrative plane, which plays no part in the normal plastic art of Islam, but on the plane of formal structures, for the Koran obeys no law of composition, either in the internal relationships of its contents, which are strangely discontinuous, or in its verbal style, which eludes all metrical rules. Its rhythm, although so powerful and so penetrating, follows no fixed measures; it is composed entirely of the unforeseen, sometimes employing a striking rhyme, then suddenly changing its breadth and pace, and upsetting cadences in a manner that is as unexpected as it is remarkable. To assert that the Koran is Arabic poetry because it comprises passages in monotonous rhyme, similar to the Bedouin *rajaz*, would be an error; but to allege that its monotonies and abrupt discontinuities do not correspond profoundly to the Arab soul would also be an error. In reality, the state of inward harmony which the Koran engenders, and to which both its consonances and dissonances, both its beauty and its harshness, contribute, is situated on a completely different plane from that reached by art. Perfect poetry—like every perfect work of art—plunges the soul into a certain state of plenitude; the Koran on the other hand engenders, in whoever hears its words and experiences its sonorous magic, both plenitude and poverty. It gives and it takes; it enlarges the soul by lending it wings, then lays it low and strips it bare; it is comforting and purifying at one and the same time, like a storm; human art can scarcely be said to have this virtue. This amounts to saying that there is no Koranic 'style' which can without more ado be transposed into art; but there exists a state of soul which the recitation of the Koran supports, and which predisposes to certain formal manifestations while excluding others. The diapason of the Koran always unites intoxicating nostalgia with the greatest sobriety: it is a shining of the Divine sun on the human desert. To a certain extent, the flowing and flamboyant rhythm of the arabesque and the abstract and crystalline character of architecture correspond to these two poles; they are two elements which constantly recur.

The most profound link, however, between Islamic art and the Koran is of a completely different kind: it resides, not in the form of the Koran, but in its *haqîqah*, its supra-formal essence, and more particularly in the idea of *tawhîd* (unity or union), with its contemplative implications; Islamic art—in the sense of all the plastic arts of Islam—is essentially the projection, in the visual order, of certain aspects or dimensions of Divine Unity.

Let us not forget, nevertheless, that sacred calligraphy reflects in its fashion the majestic style of the Koranic *suras*, without it being possible to define the nature of this analogy in detail. By the very fact that writing serves to fix the word of God, it is the noblest art of Islam;[10] and it is also, almost by definition, the most typically Arab art.

In this latter connection, it is significant that the abstract nature of the signs—the Arabic script being purely phonetic—gives rise to an extraordinary development of graphic rhythms, without the essential forms of the letters being thereby diminished. The general and to some extent natural development of Arabic writing tends towards a fluidity of forms; very different styles not only follow one another, they exist side by side, especially in monumental epigraphy. Arabic calligraphy is at the antipodes of Far-Eastern calligraphy, which should be mentioned here because it too represents a peak in the art of writing: the Chinese or Japanese calligrapher isolates the signs, each one of which corresponds to a distinct idea; using a brush, he

---

[10] In a certain sense its role is analogous to that of the icon in Christianity, since it represents, like the icon, the visible form of the Divine Word.

evokes in a few more or less broad strokes a key-picture or a visual
nucleus of related ideas. The Arab calligrapher, on the other hand,
uses a pen—a reed trimmed to a double point—and with this he
traces out precise and often interlacing lines; as far as possible he
joins the letters to each other, while stressing their contrasts: the
writing runs from right to left, and it is in this horizontal direction that
the forms interlink and marry with one another, whereas in the
vertical direction the uprights of the letters stand out in isolation and
in a sense punctuate the continuous melody of the lines. From the
point of view of the symbolism of the spatial axes, which is
appropriate here, and which moreover is also inherent in the art of
weaving, the vertical elements of the letters, which 'transcend' the
flow of the writing, correspond to their essences, while the horizontal
movement represents the 'material' continuity of their forms; the
upright is like a ray from the one Essence, which distinguishes by its
very unity, just as the present instant distinguishes between past and
future; the horizontal movement, on the other hand, which proceeds
in continuous waves, is the image of becoming or of life. In certain
calligraphic styles, such as *thulûth*, for example, this polarity is
carried to its limit; in the direction of the horizontal current, the
melody of the ample and varied curves corresponds to the rhythm of
the incisive uprights, formed especially by the vertical lines of the *alif*
and the *lam*: it is like a tireless attestation (*shahâdah*) of Unity
accompanied by a joyous and serene expansion of the soul.

The classical poetry of the Moslem Arabs is linked by its form—its
monotonous rhyme and complex metre—to the pre-Islamic Bedouin
poetry. It thus shows the influence of the Koran only through the
ideas that it may vehicle. But there exists a semi-poetic literature
whose very forms reflect the Koran, namely that of the prayers,
litanies, and incantations composed by the holy masters. One
example of this sort is the *dalâil al-khairat* of Shaikh al-Jazûli, a
collection of praises of the Prophet, or more exactly 'prayers upon the
Prophet': the Moslem addresses his prayers to God alone, in
conformity with his unitary perspective, but in asking God to bless
the Prophet, he is so to speak in communion with him. One after the
other, these prayers evoke the human and cosmic perfections present
in the nature of Mohammed, the synthesis of all the Divine

reverberations within creation. Sometimes the form of the prayers or incantations remains the same, while their terms of comparison vary, going from the virtues to the beauties of the visible and invisible universe; and sometimes the subject of the prayers is constant, while their forms vary; and this alternating repetition describes a spiral movement, whose aim is the integration of all the positive aspects of the world in the Spirit, in the inward prophet, who is 'nearer to men than their own souls', according to a verse in the Koran.

The inversion of perspective in relation to Christianity will be evident; whereas the latter views God from the starting-point of man, Islam views man from the starting-point of God, which excludes any fixation of an anthropomorphic image; the image of the Divine man is as it were dissolved in its elements; it disappears in the universal theophanies, whence its absence from plastic art, which becomes an impersonal incantation like the waves of the sea or the twinkling of the stars.

The predominance of the auditive over the visual in the Arab soul cannot but show itself even in plastic art; and it is the same for a certain form of spiritual intuition or ecstasy, which finds its support more especially in rhythm and sound: it is like a sudden cessation of time, an immobilization of all movement in the lightning flash of the pure present. The world may henceforth be compared to a water-fall, which flows without changing form, or to a flame which, although being consumed, appears motionless. Arabo-Moslem ornamentation essentially expresses this suspension in the instant.

# V
# ENVOI

# 25

# A Letter on Spiritual Method

THERE IS NO spiritual method without these two basic elements: discernment between the real and the unreal, and concentration on the real. The first of these two elements, discernment or discrimination (*vijñâna* in Sanskrit), does not depend on any special religious form; it only presupposes metaphysical understanding. The second element, however, requires a support of a sacred character, and this means that it can only be achieved within the framework of a normal tradition. The aim of method is perpetual concentration on the Real, and this cannot be achieved by purely human means or on the basis of individual initiative; it presupposes a regular transmission such as exists only within a normal tradition. For what is man? What is his puny will? How can he possibly adhere to the Absolute without first integrating his whole being into a non-individual (i.e. a supra-individual) form? To be precise: there is no spiritual path outside the following traditions or religions: Judaism, Christianity, Islam, Buddhism, Hinduism and Taoism; but Hinduism is closed for those who have not been born into a Hindu caste, and Taoism is inaccessible.

The guarantee of a spiritual method is that it be received from a spiritual master; the guarantee of spiritual mastership, besides doctrinal orthodoxy, is the initiatic chain going back to one of the great founders of religion—or *avâtaras*, as the Hindus would say. It is the duty of the disciple to obey his master; it is the duty of the master to prove his attachment to the initiatic chain. A master has the right not to accept a disciple; he has the right to conceal his teaching from outsiders, but he does not have the right to conceal from his disciples the spiritual chain he represents or his spiritual predecessors.

The master transmits: (1) the spiritual influence which derives from the founder of the tradition and through him from God; (2) the keys for the understanding of the method or the keys to meditation; (3) the sacred supports for perpetual concentration on the Real.

The distinctive sign of a spiritual master is his awareness of the relativity of forms—as well as of their necessity. Only a man whose knowledge transcends forms knows what forms involve. A master whose spiritual outlook is limited by a particular formal or traditional framework is not a complete master (although a true master may in practice be unfamiliar with traditions other than his own); and a master who rejects all forms is a false master (although a true master may reduce traditional form to its essential elements, and he surely will). No true master puts himself outside a given tradition (or religion), for he knows its meaning and sees its divine origin.

In the spiritual life there is no place for individual experiments; they are too ruinous.

# APPENDIX

# Bibliography of Titus Burckhardt

## BOOKS IN GERMAN

*Land am Rande der Zeit*, Basel, Urs Graf Verlag, 1941.

*Schweizer Volkskunst/Art Populaire Suisse*, Basel, Urs Graf Verlag, 1941.

*Tessin* (Das Volkserbe der Schweiz, Band 1), Basel, Urs Graf Verlag, 1943.

*Vom Sufitum—Einführung in die Mystik des Islams*, Munich, Otto Wilhelm Barth-Verlag, 1953.

*Vom Wessen heiliger Kunst in den Weltreligionen*, Zürich, Origo-Verlag, 1958.

*Siena, Stadt der Jungfrau*, Olten (Switzerland) and Freiburg-im-Breisgau (Germany), Urs Graf Verlag, 1958.

*Tessin* (Das Volkserbe der Schweiz, Band 1), Basel, Urs Graf Verlag, 1959, [Greatly enlarged edition.]

*Alchemie, Sinn- und Weltbild*, Olten and Freiburg-im-Breisgau, Walter-Verlag, 1960.

*Fes, Stadt des Islam*, Olten and Freiburg-im-Breisgau, Urs Graf Verlag, 1960.

*Chartres und die Geburt der Kathedrale*, Lausanne, Urs Graf Verlag, 1962.

*Von wunderbaren Büchern*, Olten and Freiburg, Urs Graf Verlag, 1963.

*Lachen und Weinen*, Olten and Freiburg, Urs Graf Verlag, 1964.

*Die Jagd*, Olten and Frieburg, Urs Graf Verlag, 1964.

*Der wilde Westen*, Olten and Freiburg, Urs Graf Verlag, 1966.

*Die maurische Kultur in Spanien*, Munich, Callwey, 1970.

*Marokko, Westlicher Orient: ein Reiseführer*, Olten and Freiburg, Walter-Verlag, 1972.

*Wissenschaft und Weisheit* (collected articles), in preparation.

*Scipio und Hannibal: Kampf um das Mittelmeer* by Friedrich Donauer. Cover design and six illustrations by Titus Burckhardt. Olten and Freiburg, Walter-Verlag, 1939.

*Wallis* (Das Volkserbe der Schweiz, Band 2) by Charles Ferdinand Ramuz. Translated and edited by Titus Burckhardt. Basel, Urs Graf Verlag, 1956.

*Zeus und Eros: Briefe und Aufzeichnungen des Bildhauers Carl Burckhardt* (1878–1923), edited by Titus Burckhardt. Basel, Urs Graf Verlag, 1956.

*Das Ewige im Vergänglichen* by Frithjof Schuon. Translation from the French

by Titus Burckhardt of *Regards sur les Mondes anciens*. Weilheim, Oberbayern, Otto Wilhelm Barth-Verlag, 1970.
*Athos, der Berg des Schweigens* by Philip Sherrard. Translation from the English by Titus Burckhardt of *Athos, the Mountain of Silence*. Lausanne and Freiberg, Urs Graf Verlag, 1959.

### ARTICLES IN GERMAN

Foreword to *Der Sinn der Ikonen* by Leonid Ouspensky and Wladimir Lossky, Olten (Switzerland) and Freiburg-im-Breisgau (Germany), Urs Graf Verlag, 1952.
'Die Symbolik des Spiegels in der islamischen Mystik', *Symbolon*, 1960.
'Symbolik des Islams', *Kairos* (Salzburg), 1961.
'Von der Heiligkeit des Wassers', *CIBA-Blätter* (Hauszeitschrift der CIBA Aktiengesellschaft, Basel) Sondernummer: Wasser; Vol. 18, No. 174, July–August 1961.
'Die Lehre vom Symbol in den Grossen Ueberlieferungen des Ostens und des Westens', *Symbolon*, 1962.
'Cosmologia Perennis', *Kairos* (Salzburg), No. 1, 1964.
Letter to the Editor, *Kairos* (Salzburg), No. 2, 1964.
'Moderne Psychologie und überlieferte Weisheit', *Kairos* (Salzburg), Nos. 3 & 4, 1964.
'Weil Dante Recht hat', *Antaios* (Stuttgart), May 1965.
'Abstrake kunst im alten Fes', *Du* (Zürich), March 1972.
'Die überlieferten Handwerke in Marokko: ihr Wesen und ihr Schicksal', *Zeitschrift für Ganzheitsforschung* (Vienna), No. 2, 1974.
'Betrachtungen zur Alchemie' (translated from the French by Margreth Pietsch), in *Initiative 42: Wissende, Verschwiegene, Eingeweihte* (Freiburg-im-Breisgau, Herder, 1981).
'Die heilige Maske' (translated from the French), in *Initiative 48: Die Macht der Masken* (Freiburg-im-Breisgau, Herder, 1982).
(All of the above-listed articles are in the original German of the author, except for the two translations indicated.)

### BOOKS IN FRENCH

*Clef spiritualle de l'Astrologie musulmane*, Paris, Les Editions Traditionnelles, 1950; Milan, Archè, 1964.
*Du Soufisme*, Lyons, Derain, 1951.
*Principes et Méthodes de l'Art sacré*, Lyons, Derain, 1958.
*Introduction aux Doctrines ésotériques de l'Islam*, Paris, Dervy-Livres, 1969.
*Alchimie* (translated from the English edition by Madame J. P. Gervy), Basle, Fondation Keimer, 1974; Milan, Archè, 1979.

*Symboles: Recueil d'essais*, Milan, Archè, 1980; Paris, Dervy-Livres, 1980.

*Science moderne et Sagesse traditionnelle*, Milan, Archè, 1985; Paris, Dervy-Livres, 1985.

*L'Art de l'Islam*, Sindbad, Paris, 1985.

*Fès, Ville de l'Islam* (translated from the German by Armand Jacoubovitch), in preparation.

(All of the above-listed books are in the original French of the author, except for the two translations indicated.)

## ARTICLES IN FRENCH

'Du *Barzakh*', *Etudes Traditionnelles* (Paris), December 1937.

'De la Thora, de l'Evangile, et du Coran', *Etudes Traditionnelles*, August–September 1938.

'Le Prototype Unique', *Etudes Traditionnelles*, August–September 1938.

"Folklore et Art ornemental', *Etudes Traditionnelles*, August–September–October 1939.

'Une Clef spirituelle de l'Astrologie musulmane', *Etudes Traditionnelles*, June 1947, July–August 1947, December 1947, January–February 1948.

'Généralités sur l'Art musulman', *Etudes traditionnelles*, March 1947.

'Principes et Méthodes de l'Art traditionnel', *Etudes Traditionnelles*, January–February 1947.

'Nature de la Perspective cosmologique', *Etudes Traditionnelles*, July–August 1948.

'Considérations sur l'Alchimie (I)', *Etudes Traditionnelles*, October–November 1948, April–May 1949.

' "Nature sait surmonter Nature" ', *Etudes Traditionnelles*, January–February 1950.

'Le Temple, Corps de l'Homme Divin', *Etudes Traditionnelles*, June 1951.

'Extraits du Commentaire des Noms Divins par l'Imâm Ghazâlî' (Translation and notes by Titus Burckhardt), *Etudes Traditionnelles*, October–November 1952, December 1954.

' "Je suis la Porte" ', *Etudes Traditionnelles*, June 1953, July–August 1953.

'La Genèse du Temple hindou', *Etudes Traditionnelles*, October–November 1953, December 1953.

'Les Fondements de l'Art chrétien', *Etudes Traditionnelles*, April–May 1954.

'Les Fondements de l'Art musulman', *Etudes Traditionnelles*, June 1954.

'Le symbolisme du jeu des échecs', *Etudes Traditionnelles*, October–November 1954.

'Le Paysage dans l'Art extrême-oriental', *Etudes Traditionnelles*, April–May 1955.

'Commentaire succinct de la Table d'Emeraude', *Etudes Traditionnelles*, November–December 1960.

'Considérations sur l'Alchimie (II), *Etudes Traditionnelles*, November–December 1961.

' "Chevaucher le Tigre" ', *Etudes Traditionnelles*, July–October 1962.

'Le Masque Sacré', *Etudes Traditionnelles*, November–December 1963.

'Cosmologie et Science moderne', *Etudes Traditionnelles*, May–June 1964, July–October 1964, January–February 1965, March–April 1965, May–August 1965.

'La Prière d'Ibn Mashîsh', *Etudes Traditionelles*, January–February 1967.

'Mise au point en ce qui concerne l'édition française du livre *Alchemie: Sinn-und Weltbild*', *Etudes Traditionnelles*, January–February 1967.

'Le Vide dans l'Art Islamique', *Hermès*, 1970.

'Caractères perennes de l'art arabe', *Journal of World History*, 1972.

'Fès, une ville humaine' (causerie faite le 21 avril 1973 dans le palais du Pacha devant les membres de l'Association pour la sauvegarde de Fès), *Etudes Traditionnelles*, July–September 1984.

'Note sur le Prophète Mohammed', in *Formes et Substance dans les Religions* by Frithjof Schuon, pp. 86–87 (Paris, Dervy-Livres, 1975).

Préface à *Islam, Perspectives et Réalités* by Seyyed Hossein Nasr (Paris, Buchet-Chastel, 1975).

'Les Sciences traditionnelles à Fès', *Etudes Traditionnelles*, October–December 1977.

'Le Retour d'Ulysse', *Etudes Traditionnelles*, January–March 1979.

'Fès et l'Art de l'Islam', in *Actes du Séminaire expérimental d'Animation culturelle*, 7 mars-28 avril 1978, Fonds international pour la Promotion de la Culture, UNESCO, *Conférences*, volume 1, pp. 109–119, 1980.

'La Danse du Soleil', *Connaissance des Religions* (Nancy, France), 1985.

TRANSLATIONS FROM ARABIC INTO FRENCH

*De l'Homme Universel* (Traduction partielle de 'Al-Insân al-Kâmil' de 'Abd al-Karîm al-Jîlî). With an introduction by the translator. Lyons, Derain. 1953; Paris, Dervy-Livres, 1975.

*La Sagesse des Prophètes* (Traduction partielle des 'Fusûs al-Hikam' de Ibn 'Arabî). With an Introduction by the translator. Paris, Albin Michel, 1955 and 1974.

*Lettres d'un Maitre Soufi* (Traduction partielle des 'Rasâ'il' de Moulay al-'Arabî ad-Darqâwî). With an Introduction by the translator. Milan, Archè, 1978; Paris, Dervy-Livres, 1978.

BOOKS IN ENGLISH

*An Introduction to Sufi Doctrine* (translated from the French by D. M. Matheson), Lahore, Ashraf, 1959; Wellingborough, England, Thorsons, 1976.

*Siena, City of the Virgin* (translated from the German by Margaret Brown), Oxford University Press, 1960.

*Famous Illuminated Manuscripts* (partial translation of *Von wunderbaren Büchern*), Olten and Lausanne, Urs Graf Verlag, 1964.

*Sacred Art in East and West* (translated from the French by Lord Northbourne), Bedfont, Middlesex, England, Perennial Books, 1967,

*Alchemy: Science of the Cosmos, Science of the Soul* (translated from the German by William Stoddart), London, Stuart and Watkins, 1967; Baltimore, Maryland, Penguin Books, 1972.

*Moorish Culture in Spain* (translated from the German by Alisa Jaffa), London, Allen and Unwin, 1972; New York, McGraw-Hill, 1972.

*Art of Islam: Language and Meaning* (translated from the French by Peter Hobson), London, Islamic Festival Trust Ltd, 1976.

*Mystical Astrology according to Ibn 'Arabî* (translated from the French by Bulent Rauf), Sherbourne, England, Beshara, 1977.

*Fez, City of Islam* (translated from the German by William Stoddart), Cambridge, England, Islamic Texts Society, in preparation.

*Mirror of the Intellect*: Essays on Traditional Science and Sacred Art (translated by William Stoddart), Cambridge, England, Quinta Essentia, 1987.

*Chartres and the Genesis of the Gothic Cathedral* (translated by Peter Hobson), in preparation.

ARTICLES IN ENGLISH

'Principles and Methods of Traditional Art', in *Art and Thought* (Coomaraswamy Festschrift), London, Luzac, 1947.

'The Spirit of Islamic Art', *Islamic Quarterly* (London), December 1954.

Foreword to *The Meaning of Icons* by Leonid Ouspensky and Vladimir Lossky (translated by E. Kadloubovsky and G. E. H. Palmer), Boston, The Boston Book and Art Shop, 1956; Crestwood, New York, St. Vladimir's Seminary Press, 1983.

'Insight into Alchemy', *Tomorrow*, Winter 1964; *Studies in Comparative Religion*, Summer–Autumn 1979.

'Cosmology and Modern Science', *Tomorrow*, Summer 1964, Autumn 1964, Winter 1965. Also included in *Sword of Gnosis* (edited by Jacob Needleman), Baltimore, Maryland, Penguin Books, 1974.

'Because Dante is Right', *Tomorrow*, Summer 1966.

'Perennial Values in Islamic Art', *Al-Abhath*, March 1967; *Studies in Comparative Religion*, Summer 1967; in *God and Man in Contemporary Islamic Thought*, Beirut, Centennial, 1972; in *Sword of Gnosis* (edited by Jacob Needleman), Baltimore, Penguin Books, 1974.

'Islamic Surveys: Four Works by Seyyed Hossein Nasr', *Studies in Comparative Religion*, Winter 1968.

'The Symbolism of Chess', *Studies in Comparative Religion*, Spring 1969.

'Teilhard de Chardin (I), *Studies in Comparative Religion*, Spring 1969.

'The Seven Liberal Arts and the West Door of Chartres Cathedral', *Studies in Comparative Religion*, Summer 1969; also Winter–Spring 1985.

'The Heavenly Jerusalem and the Paradise of Vaikuntha', *Studies in Comparative Religion*, Winter 1970.

'The Void in Islamic Art', *Studies in Comparative Religion*, Spring 1970; also Winter–Spring 1985.

Note on the Prophet Mohammed, in *Dimensions of Islam* by Frithjof Schuon, pp. 69–70 (London, Allen and Unwin, 1970).

'Arab or Islamic Art?', *Studies in Comparative Religion*, Winter 1971; also in *Sword of Gnosis* (edited by Jacob Needleman), Baltimore, Penguin Books, 1974.

'Abstract Art in Ancient Fez', *Du* (Zürich), March 1972.

Foreword to *Geometric Concepts in Islamic Art* by Issam El-Said and Ayse Parman, London, Islamic Festival Trust Ltd, 1976.

'Introduction to Islamic Art' in *The Arts of Islam*, catalogue to the special exhibition in the Hayward Gallery, London, The Arts Council of Great Britain, 1976.

'The Prayer of Ibn Mashîsh', *Studies in Comparative Religion*, Winter–Spring 1978; *Islamic Quarterly*, September 1978.

'The Return of Ulysses', *Parabola*, November 1978.

'Concerning the "Barzakh" ', *Studies in Comparative Religion*, Winter–Spring 1979.

'Fez', in *The Islamic City*, UNESCO, Paris, 1980, pp. 166–176.

Preface to R. W. J. Austin's translation of Ibn 'Arabî's *The Bezels of Wisdom* (Fusûs al-Hikam), London, S.P.C.K., 1980; Ramsey, New Jersey, The Paulist Press, 1980.

'The Sacred Mask', *Studies in Comparative Religion*, Winter–Spring 1980.

'Teilhard de Chardin (II)', in *The Destruction of the Christian Tradition* by Rama Coomaraswamy, pp. 211–212. Bedfont, Middlesex, England, Perennial Books, 1981.

'The Role of Fine Arts in Muslim Education', in *Philosophy, Literature and Fine Arts* (edited by Seyyed Hossein Nasr), Sevenoaks, Kent, England, Islamic Education Series, 1982.

'Traditional Science', *Studies in Comparative Religion*, Winter–Spring 1985.
Two short extracts from *Schweizer Volkskunst, Studies in Comparative Religion*, Winter–Spring 1985.
'The Spirituality of Islamic Art', in *The Encyclopedia of World Spirituality*, vol. 20 (edited by Seyyed Hossein Nasr), London, Routledge and Kegan Paul, 1987.
'The Universality of Sacred Art', in *The Unanimous Tradition* (edited by Ranjit Fernando), The Institute of Traditional Studies, Colombo, Sri Lanka, in preparation.

### TRANSLATIONS FROM ARABIC
### INTO FRENCH AND THEN INTO ENGLISH

*Letters of a Sufi Master* (partial translation of the 'Rasâ'il' of Mulay al-'Arabî ad-Darqâwî), Bedfont, Middlesex, Perennial Books, 1973.
*The Wisdom of the Prophets* (partial translation of 'Fusûs al-Hikam' by Ibn 'Arabî), Sherbourne, Beshara, 1975.
*Universal Man* (partial translation of 'Al-Insân al-Kâmil' by 'Abd al-Karîm al-Jîlî), Sherbourne, Beshara, 1983.

### BOOKS IN ITALIAN

*L'Alchimia* (translated from the German by Angela Terzani Staude), Turin, Boringhieri, 1961; (translated from the French by Ferdinando Bruno), Milan, Guanda, 1981.
*Scienza moderna e Sagzzu tradizionale* (translated from the German by Angela Terzani Staude), Turin, Borla, 1968.
*Siena, Città della Vergine* (translated from the German by Gisella Burgisser), Milan, Archè, 1978.
*L'Arte sacra in Oriente e Occidente* (translated from the French by Elena Bono), Milan, Rusconi, 1976.
*Introduzione alle Dottrine esoteriche dell'Islam* (translated from the French by Barbara Turco), Rome, Edizioni Mediterranee, 1979.
*Simboli* (translated from the French by Elisabetta Bonfanti Mutti), Parma, All'Insegna del Veltro, 1983.
*Chiave spirituale dell'Astrologia musulmana* (translated from the French), Genoa, Basilisco, 1985.

### ARTICLES IN ITALIAN

'Una Chiave spirituale dell'Astrologia secondo Muhyiddin ibn 'Arabî', *Rivista di Studii Iniziatici*, Naples, August–October 1947.

Nota sul Profeta Mohamed in *Forma e Sostanza nelle Religioni* di Frithjof Schuon (Roma, Edizioni Mediterranee, 1984).

## TRANSLATIONS FROM ARABIC INTO FRENCH AND THEN INTO ITALIAN

*L'Uomo Universale* (translated from the French by Giorgio Jannaccone), Rome, Edizioni Mediterranee, 1981.

*La Sapienza dei Profeti* (translated from the French by Giorgio Jannaccone), Rome, Edizioni Mediterranee, 1987.

*Lettere d'un Maestro Sufi* (translated from the French by Giorgio Jannaccone), Milan, La Queste, 1987.

## BOOKS IN SPANISH

*Alquimía* (translated by Ana María de la Fuente), Barcelona, Plaza y Janés, 1971.

*La Civilización Hispano-Arabe* (translated by Rosa Kuhne Braban), Madrid, Alianza Editorial, 1977.

*Esoterismo Islámico* (translated by Jesús García Varela), Madrid, Taurus Ediciones, 1980.

*Sabiduría Tradicional y Ciencia Moderna* (translated by Jordí Quingles and Alejandro Corniero), Madrid, Taurus Ediciones, 1980.

*Símbolos* (translated by Francesc Gutiérrez), Mallorca, José J. de Olañeta, 1982.

*Principios y Métodos del Arte sagrado*, Buenos Aires, 1984.

## ARTICLES IN SPANISH

Nota sobre el Profeta Mohámed en *Forma e Sustancia en las Religiones* por Frithjof Schuon, capítulo sobre Mohámed (Madrid, Taurus Ediciones, 1981).

'El Simbolismo del Ajedrez', *Cielo y Tierra* (Barcelona), No. 1, 1982.

'El Arte sagrado', *Cielo y Tierra* (Barcelona), No. 6, 1983/1984.

# Index